Beyond Knowledge Management

We work with leading authors to develop the strongest educational materials in human resource management, bringing cutting-edge thinking and best learning practice to a global market.

Under a range of well-known imprints, including Financial Times Prentice Hall, we craft high quality print and electronic publications which help readers to understand and apply their content, whether studying or at work.

To find out more about the complete range of our publishing please visit us on the World Wide Web at: www.pearsoned.co.uk

Beyond Knowledge Management

Dialogue, creativity and the corporate curriculum

Bob Garvey
Bill Williamson

An imprint of **Pearson Education**

Harlow, England · London · New York · Reading, Massachusetts · San Francisco · Toronto · Don Mills, Ontario · Sydney
Tokyo · Singapore · Hong Kong · Seoul · Taipei · Cape Town · Madrid · Mexico City · Amsterdam · Munich · Paris · Milan

Pearson Education Limited
Edinburgh Gate
Harlow
Essex CM20 2JE
England
and Associated Companies throughout the world

Visit us on the World Wide Web at:
www.pearsoned.co.uk

First published 2002

ISBN-13: 978-0-273-65517-6

British Library Cataloguing-in-Publication Data
A catalogue record for this book is available from the British Library.

10 9 8 7
12 11 10

Typeset in 9.5/13pt Stone Serif by 30.
Printed in Great Britain by Henry Ling Limited., at the Dorset Press, Dorchester, DT1 1HD

Contents

Contents

Foreword by Rosemary Harrison

This engaging and demanding book is a response to the implications of turbulent competitive conditions and of a knowledge economy for workplace learning. Its main focus is knowledge productivity – the management of such learning in ways that generate and disseminate organisationally valuable knowledge (Kessels, 1996). Garvey and Williamson are particularly concerned with the expertise and culture needed to facilitate knowledge-productive organizations, and with the competencies and ethical issues involved in working in a continuous learning environment.

The book is timely and unique. There is now great interest in ways in which learning and knowledge processes may link to the progress of an organization. This interest is due to a variety of factors, including the decline of some well-established firms, the diminishing competitive power of many, the impact of new information technologies and a globalized economy, and the consequent need for organizational renewal (Nevis *et al.*, 1995). Despite this interest, it is rare to find books that deal convincingly with learning as part of the knowledge process rather than as an end in itself; rarer to find any that then explore implications for the strategic capability of organizations. I have been involved with many of this book's contributors in discussions about strategic capability, knowledge productivity and the corporate curriculum, and have written elsewhere about the outcomes of my own research (Harrison, 2000a). This book therefore has a special meaning for me. However, it is of relevance for anyone who is interested in the survival and progress of organizations in increasingly knowledge-based environments.

The theoretical underpinning for any attempt to relate learning to the development and management of an organization's knowledge base is complex, emerging as it does from the literatures of organizational science, business strategy, knowledge management and human resource management and development (Harrison, 2000b). Although a comprehensive literature review is not one of the book's aims, Garvey and Williamson usefully explore a number of themes that, in the literature, are nebulous or rest on untried assumptions. It has been claimed that there is a disturbing divergence in the focus, assumptions and epistemology of 'learning organization' writers and of writers on 'knowledge management' (Scarbrough, 1998:222). Garvey and Williamson bring an appropriately holistic and integrative approach to their enquiry, and this yields important insights. Their use of Kessels' 'corporate curriculum' framework in Part 1 is particularly enlightening. It suggests a promising new methodology for those who are working across the fields of learning, knowledge and organizational renewal.

One of the book's major themes concerns the building of a climate of trust and collaboration in order to achieve knowledge-productive organizations. Nonaka (1991:103) saw co-operative learning as vital to the process of questioning and challenge that is 'especially essential during times of crisis or breakdown when a company's traditional categories of knowledge no longer work'. It is frequently asserted that an organization's top management must formulate and communicate a vision and sense of purpose that will encourage stakeholders to co-operate in seeking and using new knowledge to drive the organization forward (see, for example, many of the contributors in Starkey, 1996). However, the organizational restructuring and devolution of power that are often needed if those stakeholders are to work fruitfully together must be informed by a sophisticated understanding of the knowledge process and of the dynamics of human relationships in the workplace. Such understanding is not apparent on a wide scale. The book's contributors avoid taking a prescriptive stance on these difficult matters. Instead, they capture interest by engaging the reader in an ongoing dialogue, offering provocative but thoughtful reflections, metaphors and case material.

Attempts to 'manage' learning for strategic ends raise issues of power, politics and ethics (Coopey, 1995; Harrison and Smith, 2001). Reassurances that 'more safeguards are needed to prevent the learning organisation from being misused as a cover for harsh and non-developmental regimes' and that 'companies have to become more aware of internal politics they must tackle if they are to become learning organisations' (Burgoyne, 1999:41–4) merely scrape the surface here. It is good to see Garvey and Williamson's text identifying various dilemmas that have no easy answers, and offering analysis and ideas that move the debate forward productively.

Another theme in the book is the extent to which 'knowing' is about relational and emotional as well as rational processes, social as well as psychological factors. Both practical and social competencies are crucial in helping to explain 'contextually appropriate behaviour' (Ginsberg, 1994:155) and social context is seen by many to be significantly shaped by the employment system of the firm. It has been claimed that failure to address the social relations and institutional contexts in which organizational knowledge is embedded is a fundamental weakness in the literature of the resource-based view of the firm, dominated as it is by 'the outmoded command and control model of management' (Scarbrough, 1998:230). In Part 3 of this book many of the contextual factors affecting workplace learning are explored, and chapter 6 on 'Creative Environments' challenges much traditional thinking in its discussion of learning and change.

Themes of change are also examined in Part 4, with close attention paid to structural and human resource dimensions and strategies. There is a special resonance to the critiques on the sections that have been written by Dutch and US contributors. As more organizations enter and compete in fast-moving global markets there is an increasing need to devise and implement internationally collaborative learning strategies, and to build inter-organizational learning networks that encompass not only local but also global partners.

The book is imbued with a belief that a fresh approach is needed to the knowledge process – one that places people squarely at its heart. This is welcome. In the literature and in the field no operationally transparent linkages between individual and collective learning, the development of knowledge and the strategic progress of the organization seem yet to have emerged (Harrison, 2000a:397–418). There is much rhetoric and conceptualization, but scant progress in theory building or in practice. The knowledge process remains opaque, and human resource problems continue to throw up obstacles in its path. There is certainly a growing interest by employers, managers, human resource professionals and information technology experts in what is loosely called 'knowledge management'. However, there is also a worrying failure to identify or deal effectively with human issues involved in developing, sharing and using knowledge that flows from workplace learning. This raises the possibility of a narrowly conceived knowledge management approach that produces an 'obsession with tools and techniques' and overlooks the centrality of people throughout the knowledge process (Scarbrough *et al.*, 1999; Harrison, 2000b). In this book people's centrality to that process is a major theme, and the contributors provide much to challenge and stimulate on a range of demanding questions, including the following:

- In what ways can top management's 'vision' stimulate and give collective purpose to organizational learning and knowledge development processes?
- How can an organizational philosophy based on mutuality of endeavour, interest and benefit be generated, and how then can it become embedded in organizational context?
- What roles, actions and practices can stimulate, identify and connect strategically relevant learning at every organizational level in order to enhance the organization's knowledge base?
- What learning networks, routines and processes can stimulate the continuous development of that base?
- What kind of organizational context, structure and management actions can promote and sustain the knowledge-productive organization?

Garvey and Williamson's book does not have a specific focus on the organizational process of human resource development (HRD). Nonetheless it contains vital messages for those who are involved in that field. In my own recent work (Harrison and Miller, 1999; Harrison 2000a, 2000b) I have tried to make links between HRD, organizational learning and knowledge productivity. Whatever links I have proposed have only been tentative, but I remain convinced that in a knowledge economy HRD professionals must take on leading roles in the development and management of knowledge as well as of learning. HRD involves the integration of many learning and development processes, operations and relationships. Its most powerful strategic outcomes are to do with enhanced organizational effectiveness, adaptability and sustainability. Yet that said, its rhetoric is often remote from its organizational reality, and the connections that should be forged between HRD practice and the knowledge process in organizations remain frustratingly weak. Some progress is being made at the macro level in the United Kingdom, where since 1997 there has been a strong policy focus on 'lifelong learning' in a knowledge economy and on the mechanisms to achieve that. Still, though, the exact nature of the relationship between learning and knowledge productivity remains poorly articulated. The Chartered Institute of Personnel and Development (CIPD) emphasized that relationship in its new (2001) Learning and Development professional standards. Since the Institute is probably the largest professional body in Europe this marked a significant step forward in drawing the attention of human resource practitioners to their role in the 'knowledge' field.[1] However, no similar emphasis has far appeared in drafts of the revised national occupational standards. It is to be hoped that by the time those standards have been finalized it will have emerged.

An intriguing theme of metaphors surfaces from time to time in Garvey and Williamson's book, and it is fascinating to realize how far the book itself gradually becomes, for the reader, a metaphor for learning and knowledge productivity. The 'feel' is of an ongoing dialogue interspersed with periods of reflection, analysis and creative breakthroughs. The style is direct, with contributors actively involving the reader in their discussions, avoiding didactic monologue around fixed points, systems or processes. Notions of evaluation, reflection and creativity permeate the text, linking the concept of knowledge productivity in illuminating ways to learning, to strategy, to dialogue and to narrative. Case studies provide signposts through the territory, and the independent critiques that conclude the main parts of the book provide an appropriate counter-point to the more subjective observations that those parts contain.

This unusual and stimulating book is to be welcomed for its insightful coverage of workplace learning and the knowledge process. It offers real value to those who are directly involved in tasks of organizational renewal and transformation. It has an equal importance, however, for all who are striving to become more knowledge productive in complex organizational worlds.

Note

[1] A copy of the CIPD's 2001 Professional Qualification Scheme Standards can be obtained from the Institute, telephone 0208 2633 293 or email j.whittaker @cipd.co.uk

References

Burgoyne, J. (1999) 'Design of the times', *People Management*, vol. 5, no. 11, pp. 39–44.

Coopey, J. (1995) 'The learning organization, power: politics and ideology', *Management Learning*, vol. 26, no. 2, pp. 193–213.

Ginsberg, A. (1994) 'Minding the competition: from mapping to mastery', *Strategic Management Journal, Winter Special Issue*, vol. 15, pp. 153–74.

Harrison, R. (2000a) *People and Organizations: Employee Development*, (2nd edn.) London: Chartered Institute of Personnel and Development.

Harrison, R. (2000b) 'Learning, knowledge productivity and strategic progress', *International Journal of Training and Development*, vol. 4, no. 4, pp. 244–58.

Harrison, R. and Miller, S. (1999) 'The contribution of clinical directors to the strategic capability of the organization', *British Journal of Management*, vol. 10, no. 1, pp. 23–39.

Harrison, R. and Smith, R. (2001) 'Practical judgement: its implications for knowledge development and strategic capability', In Hellgren, B. and Lowstedt, J. (eds) *Management in the Thought-Full Enterprise: A Socio-cognitive Approach to the Organization of Human Resources*, Norway: Fagbokforlaget in association with Copenhagen Business School Press, pp. 195–213.

Kessels, J.W.M. (1996) 'Knowledge productivity and the corporate curriculum', in Schreinemakers J.F. (ed.) *Knowledge Management: Organization, Competence and Methodology*, Proceedings of the Fourth International ISMICK Symposium, 21–2 October, Rotterdam, the Netherlands, Wurzburg: ERGON-Verl, pp. 168–74.

Nevis, E.C., DiBella, A.J. and Gould, J.M. (1995) 'Understanding organizations as learning systems', *Sloan Management Review*, vol. 36, no. 2, pp. 73–85.

Nonaka, I. (1991) 'The knowledge-creating company', *Harvard Business Review*, November–December, pp. 96–104.

Scarbrough, H. (1998) 'Path(ological) dependency? Core competencies from an organizational perspective', *British Journal of Management*, vol. 9, pp. 219–32.

Scarbrough, H., Swan, J. and Preston, J. (1999) *Knowledge Management: A Literature Review*, London: Institute of Personnel and Development.

Starkey, K. (ed.) (1996) *How Organizations Learn*, London: International Thomson Business Press.

The authors and contributors

Bill Williamson

Bill Williamson is Professor of Continuing Education at the University of Durham. He is a sociologist with long-standing research interests in education, lifelong learning and in social and contemporary history. His publications cover each of these fields. His work in the field of work-based learning has grown from an interest in professional development, team-based work systems, creativity and in the development of a theory of learning that embraces all the contexts of learning in adulthood. He has worked in universities in Germany and the Middle East. He is married with grown-up children and amusing grandchildren.

Bob Garvey

Bob Garvey is the subject leader for the HR/OB subject groups at Sheffield Hallam University. He holds a PhD from the University of Durham in Social Science – his special interest being mentoring in the workplace. Bob has published widely on the topic of mentoring including the best-selling *Mentoring Pocket Book* and he is a director of the European Mentoring Centre (a not-for-profit organization). Bob is interested in workplace learning and is a founding member of the Vanwoodman Institute (an international group of academics and practitioners interested in Knowledge Productivity). Bob is married with two teenage daughters, three cats and two dogs.

Rosemary Harrison

Rosemary Harrison is a human resource academic and professional, and an established writer in the human resource development field. She is Chief Examiner in Employee Development for the UK's Chartered Institute of Personnel and Development. She is also an associate faculty member of the University of Durham Business School, where she was formerly Director of the Human Resource Development Research Centre and Lecturer in Human Resource Management. Her texts have an international readership, and include *Human Resource Management: issues and strategy* (1993, Addison-Wesley), *The Training and Development Audit* (1999, Cambridge Strategy Press) and *People and Organisations: Employee Development* (2000, London, CIPD).

Joseph Kessels

Dr. Joseph W.M. Kessels is professor of Human Resource Development at the University of Twente, in the Netherlands. He held a similar chair at the Leiden University until 2001. He is partner in Kessels & Smit, a consultancy firm that specializes in promoting powerful learning environments in organizations. He is director of the Foundation for Corporate Education and was awarded the prestigious 'Training & Development Prize' of the Dutch Training and Development Association. As a consultant he conducted projects for national government bodies, health care, banking, transport, telecom and industry. He has consulted with international firms such as DSM Chemicals, Shell, Philips, Sara Lee-DE, Heineken and KLM.

Jussi Koski

Jussi T. Koski's Ed.D. (Doctor of Education) speciality is creativity at individual, group and organizational levels, on which subject he gives lectures and consultation, especially in his native Finland. He is currently acting Professor of Education at Helsinki University. Previously he has worked, for example, as Director of Research at the Center for Knowledge and Innovation Research, Helsinki School of Economics and Business Administration, and as secretary general for the Council for the Promotion of Information Society through Education, Research and Culture, Ministry of Education, Finland. His latest book called *Luova hierre (Creative abrasion)* was published in Finland in September, 2001. The book is in Finnish only.

Harm Tillema

Harm Tillema's (senior lecturer, Leiden University) field of interest is performance assessment and appraisal as it might be related to competence development of employees. Providing insight into performance by means of assessment is a powerful way to improve competence levels. In his research, he studies assessment intervention techniques like portfolio and development centres. In his consultancy work in several organizations he is involved in establishing powerful learning environments which make use of assessment-provided feedback.

Olav Sorenson

Olav Sorenson is a professor at UCLA's Anderson Graduate School of Management, where he teaches courses on business strategy and organizational design. He holds an undergraduate degree from Harvard University and a doctorate from Stanford University. His research – which has been published in the *American Journal of Sociology*, the *Harvard Business Review, Research Policy*, and the *Strategic Management Journal*, as well as several other academic and managerial periodicals – focuses on what influences the rate at which organizations can acquire knowledge and the effectiveness with which they use that information. He also researches the dynamics of industrial districts to determine who benefits from these concentrated clustering of firms within an industry.

List of abbreviations

BA	British Airways
CIPD	Chartered Institute of Personnel and Development
EAZ	Educational Action Zone
EDB	Economic Development Board
GE	General Electric
GM	general manager
HRD	human resource development
ICT	information and communication technology
KP	knowledge productive
KPL	knowledge-productive learning
MD	managing director
NASA	National Aeronautics and Space Administration
OECD	Organization for Economic Cooperation and Development
R&D	research and development
SHRD	strategic human resource development

Acknowledgements

Authors' Acknowledgements

We would like to thank our friends and colleagues at the Universities of Durham, Sheffield Hallam, Leider, Helsinki, UCLA and managers and students with whom we have worked for their interest and support in writing this book. Special thanks are needed for colleagues in the Vanwoodman Global Institute who share our enthusiasms for learning and talking.

Without the support of our families this book would still have been written but it wouldn't have been so much fun.

Publisher's acknowledgements

We are grateful to the following for permission to reproduce copyright material:

Chapter 5 based on 'Learning to be Knowledge Productive – the contribution of mentoring' in *Mentoring and Tutoring*, Vol. 8, No. 3, December, pp. 262–272 (Alred, G. and Garvey, B. 2000) and 'Mentoring and the tolerance of complexity' reprinted from *Futures*, Vol. 33, 6, July, pp. 519–530 (Garvey, B. and Alred, G. 2001) with permission from Elsevier Science.

In some instances we have been unable to trace the owners of copyright material, and we would appreciate any information that would enable us to do so.

Introduction

We shall not cease from exploration
And the end of all our exploring
Will be to arrive where we started
And know the place for the first time.

T.S. Eliot, Little Gidding

Aims

The aim of this introductory chapter is to set out the following:

➤ **why this book has been written;**

➤ **the key ideas that have shaped it;**

➤ **the organization of the book and how it can be used.**

The key ideas of this book are creativity, dialogue and the corporate curriculum. The book seeks to engage its readers in a discussion about how they can become knowledge productive (KP) in their work. The key to KP is new learning and learning is shown to be a process that generates new knowledge and understanding. The term 'knowledge management' is not commonly used in this book. This is because we believe it to be a rather sterile term associated with past conceptualizations of management control. Recent developments in knowledge management seem to suggest that 'it is in danger of being hijacked by the IT community and turned into a vehicle for the marketing of new IT systems' (Scarbrough *et al.*, 1999:2). This, we believe, is a mistake. We believe 'knowledge productivity' as a concept offers a different perspective on knowledge. This takes us beyond knowledge management and into the realms once inhabited by the ideas associated with learning organizations. We recognize that in many ways these are just names; however, names are important in the way that meaning is attached to them and these terms 'symbolise somewhat different views of the world and different visions of what an organisation does or should do' (Scarbrough *et al.*, 1999:2).

Experience, theory and practice

This book arises from two kinds of experience. First, our own experience of trying to understand the implications for management practice of social science theory. The process of reading, reflection and research leads us to the conviction that the social sciences provide a resource of powerful ideas that enable those who engage with them to think about their world in fresh and innovative ways. Secondly, the experience of teaching, consultancy and research in a wide range of work organizations – both private and public – that have enabled us to test out theoretical ideas in practice.

We experience these two worlds – the world of theory and that of practice – as a landscape of ideas with boundaries that can be crossed and new territories to explore. The journeys we make in these new territories help us appreciate a very important point that runs throughout this book: management is not a codified body of knowledge. It is not an orthodoxy of belief anchored in sacred texts – though it sometimes has that appearance. It is much more a journey of discovery in which intelligent human beings ask questions about ordinary practices and arrive at astonishingly new conclusions about how their organizations work.

Over time ideas about how to manage and achieve the objectives of an organization build up to constitute a body of knowledge and of 'know-how' that constitutes a form of intellectual capital. In the most knowledge-productive, innovative organizations that capital is continually enriched. Unfortunately in many organizations knowledge is not replenished or put to productive use. We hope our book will address this by providing a different understanding of how to achieve high rates of return on the intellectual capital of the work organization.

Our conviction about the need for this book has been strengthened through reflection on our work with practising managers. We work with many people who are keenly interested in ideas and well able to reflect on their experiences. We have also met others who are not like this. Some managers we meet are so incapable of appreciating the strengths of the people they manage that they actively suppress the creative potential of the people and the organizations they work for. Some people we meet are so indifferent to new ideas that we are astonished they survive in the modern world at all.

A premise of this book is that there are ways of changing work organizations that enable creativity to be released. This premise leads us to our key proposition that there are two basic ways to organize working life. One enables organizations to capitalize on employees' ideas and the other seeks to suppress, curtail and control. To build on this we further propose that the more managers are aware of the complexities in the two options the better their chances of progress and survival in a complex global economy.

This book develops accounts of learning in the workplace, of strategic human resource development (SHRD) and creativity that enables managers to work with colleagues in ways that promote knowledge productivity, innovation and successful organizational development, survival and progress.

Management orthodoxies

Through engaging in dialogue with practising managers we have become suspicious of the claims made about the nature of knowledge, creativity and learning that are found in the general management literature. Many of these ideas are too 'pat', too neat and simplistic to offer any credibility – we find that they do not sit well within managers' own experiences.

Management is an essential function in all work organizations. Management literature is itself an important element of modern management. It provides managers with a justification for their actions and a research base from which to know what to do. It is a field of writing and discourse heavily dominated by the work of university business schools throughout the world and shaped considerably by a number of leading theorists whose work has become part of that tradition of thinking. Key ideas within this tradition, for example such as ideas empowerment, learning organizations, work-based learning, experiential learning, organizational development, human resource development, add up to a framework of ideas that take on the characteristics of a canon. Repetition of many of the ideas within this canon create a form of liturgy. The ability to use this language fluently – if not always intelligently – has become one of the defining characteristics of a modern managerial identity. For example:

'People are our most important asset.'

'We're in it for the long haul.'

'We respect and value our employees.'

'We seek to delight our customers.'

'Our mission will be achieved by the willing efforts of our people.'

'Empowerment.'

'Personal autonomy.'

'Entrepreneurial.'

'Fostering commitment.'

Students of management encounter this tradition of writing as a body of knowledge they have to assimilate. In our experience many developing managers find it a daunting prospect to see this literature and to negotiate their way through it. In the face of what global armies of experts say they feel themselves inadequate, that their own experience and understanding of management has little value. They are encouraged to think that the solution to their companies' problems lies somewhere outside both their own experience and that of the organization. *Problem*

Our concern is that many managers are either too accepting or reject out of hand this literature. As they struggle to see the relevance of theoretical ideas in the complexity of their workplaces their confidence to doubt what the theorists are saying is diminished. Their ability to think analytically and reflectively about their own work experience is inhibited. As a result many managers in many organizations are not as knowledge productive as they might be. Many organizations do not therefore achieve development based on the growing understanding of new modes of practice of their own personnel.

The power of talk

Our aim in this book is to encourage our readers to take their own experience very seriously and to engage in a critical dialogue with the dominant discourse of management theory itself. The idea of critical dialogue is central to this book. Our commitment is to the view that it is through creative dialogue between practitioners and theorists that new knowledge can be generated.

We work with many people who respond with real interest and enthusiasm to some complex philosophical ideas about knowledge, learning, relationships and values. They see immediately the relevance of these ideas to the issues they themselves are struggling with at work. Our hope is that readers of this book will become more confident with some of these ideas and therefore more knowledge productive in their own working environments.

Learning as a social process

Learning is central to the nature of this book. Building on some very potent ideas in contemporary social science we develop a way of thinking about learning that shows it to be a process with the following characteristics.

First, learning is a social activity. It takes place through interaction with other people. Learning is either helped or hindered by the framework of social relationships within which it occurs. Learning is simultaneously a social and cultural activity made possible through the ability of human beings to communicate with one another through a common language.

Language enables us to codify our experience into bodies of knowledge that can be passed from one generation to another. It gives us the ability to build up ideas and to confer meaning, significance and purpose to what we do.

Secondly, learning is a situated activity. What people learn, the pace at which they do so, the quality and depth of their understanding, are very much related to the circumstances in which they have to live and work. When little is required or demanded of people at work it is not surprising they will not display the qualities of curiosity and innovative thinking. It is our general experience that, if given the opportunity, people do rise to the challenges of innovation and creativity and open their minds to new ideas and influences.

Thirdly, all learning involves personal transformation. Learning therefore opens up new possibilities within human social relationships. Through learning people transform their sense of who they are and of the possibilities in their lives. It provides them with a deeply personal measure of how they themselves have changed. New learning inevitably asks new questions about the world and new possibilities in human lives. Learning generates a new sense of openness in human identities and nurtures new hopes. In addition, because learning is so tied up with change, an organization that wishes or needs to change will have to be constantly encouraging its people to learn in order to achieve and progress that change. Learning and change are inextricably linked. Some organizations and settings will nurture this and some will not.

Finally, at least for the purposes of this introduction, learning is continuous throughout life. It takes place in all domains of human experience, and learning in one domain is potentially transferable to others.

Learning is part of human experience – hence the importance of experiential learning in contemporary management theory – but it is not only an individual experience. Only individuals, of course, can learn, but there is a very real sense in which organizations can nurture new learning. The implications of these propositions are profound. They help us to see that for too long most people who have worked in modern economies have been prevented from developing their human potential to the full. Not only have the individuals lost out on the opportunities potentially open to them, but organizations and society at large have lost the benefit of the further development of their most precious asset: their people.

Past, present and future

Defenders of the conventional management faith could point out here that none of these propositions are new. We would have to agree. On the other hand, their full implications have never been fully tested. Despite being well known they are not that well understood or widely acted upon.

There is no easy slide from theory into good practice. We meet hundreds of innovative managers who are baulked and frustrated by the unwillingness of their organizations to respond to new ideas. There are certainly many work organizations where there is no real commitment to training and development or indeed to change. Despite the importance attached to education and training in the workplace by most governments within the developed economies of the world too much of the training that does take place is narrow, competency based and instrumental. If theory did translate easily into practice and if practice, always achieved its intended outcomes, we would all be living in Shangri-La. As it is, there is a great chasm between the thought and the deed.

We believe that one clue as to why this is so lies in the realization that all organizations exist in three tenses as follows:

1 They exist in the flow of time and therefore carry much of their history into their contemporary working methods and practices.
2 They function in the present tense, meeting the needs of clients and customers and solving all of the operational problems of their daily work.
3 They live in the future, anticipating new developments, planning forward investments and developing strategies for long-term survival.

In some organizations the past is the strongest time frame of the three; in others the pressures of the present are decisive. In all organizations the future is important but is interpreted in different ways: some see it as a framework of opportunity, others as a series of threats. Each time frame provides a way of thinking about the human resources of the organization. Organizations that live in the past can rely complacently on their existing skills and competencies. Those that live too much in the present often ignore their future skill requirements. Some organizations that hope for a successful future do so in the belief that it is people in the future who will help them out rather than those members who work for them in the present.

Our belief is that the successful organizations are those which take these three tenses seriously and draw important conclusions about them for the development of the people they work with. We show in this book the ways in which past skills, ideas and accumulated knowledge can be reformulated to meet the challenges of an uncertain future. We also show that the knowledge and skills of members of organizations are the most precious asset they have and that there are ways to nurture those assets to become knowledge productive.

Management and values

Our contact with managers leads us to see another dimension of their work that is not well represented in the standard discourse of modern management. This concerns the nature of the modern economy and the patterns of working relationships it generates.

Capitalism is a ruthless economic system. It delivers high standards of living for a few, affluence for millions of others, but unsustainable global inequalities and unacceptable patterns of social exclusion. The following facts highlight this tension of inequality and exclusion.

If we could shrink the earth's population to a village of precisely 100 people, with all the existing human ratios remaining the same, it would look something like the following. There would be:

57 Asians, 21 Europeans, 14 from the western hemisphere (both north and south), 8 Africans; 52 would be female, 48 would be male; 70 would be non-white, 30 would be white; 70 would be non-Christian, 30 would be Christian; 89 would be heterosexual, 11 would be homosexual.

6 people would possess 59 per cent of the entire world's wealth and all 6 would be from the United States.

80 would live in sub-standard housing; 70 would be unable to read; 50 would suffer from malnutrition, 1 would be near death; 1 would be near birth; 1 (yes, only 1) would have a college education; 1 would own a computer.

The above list of statistics indicates that millions of people experience the pressures of capitalism as relentless claims to work harder, to be more narrowly specialized, to be more vulnerable economically and to experience work as if it were emptied of all moral significance. Millions of workers experience the future as an uncertain threat.

Individual employees, however, cannot see themselves merely as units of labour in an economic mechanism. They are people with families, with obligations and with commitments to particular communities in particular countries at particular points in time. The tension between the ruthless pressures of the market and the personal commitments of human beings are the stuff of human resource management.

Every modern manager lives within the framework of a legal order – stronger in some societies than in others – in which their decisions have to be legitimate, public and within the law. More than that, all of the complex decisions they make take on meaning within a moral framework that is inescapable. Managers have to judge their actions not only in terms of their efficiency but also by whether or not they are morally correct.

Most of the managers we work with take these issues seriously. The moral and critical thread running through the analysis we develop in this book is therefore not an alien import drawn from another discourse. It is crucial to our understanding of how managers work, and how they arrive at decisions. It is particularly crucial to the ways in which organizations can innovate and develop.

The twentieth century has provided us with too many examples of moral indifference among managers and of organizations devoid of any moral purpose that were nonetheless successful in achieving their goals. The Mafia and the Nazis, Stalin's KGB and many business organizations that have asset stripped their way to fortune and fame fall into this category. This reminds us that there is an obligation on all of us to question the moral value of the ends that organizations seek to achieve.

In so far as organizational development and change requires new learning, there is an inescapable moral dimension to it. The reason is simple. People learn most effectively when they have good reasons to do so and when their learning is valued.

New learning brings with it new ways of thinking and new abilities. If people are not allowed to act on the basis of new knowledge they will become demotivated and cynical. A part, therefore, of any credible idea of the learning organization (at least in open, democratic societies) is a moral commitment to nurture human beings and live with the consequences of their development. Organizations have to become open to new ideas that are based on new learning. Those that deny people the opportunity to develop are in effect confirming in their practice a moral judgement that some people are inferior and have neither needs nor rights to develop as people. People who are undervalued in this way too often take on as part of their own self-evaluation the negative view others have of them. Devaluing people then becomes a self-fulfilling prophecy. It results in an unwillingness to seek out new learning or ideas. It devalues the human capital of an organization.

Theory and practice

A key proposition in this book is that organizations which take a strategic view of their future and seek to anticipate the knowledge demands of the future will be the ones that are successful. The task involved here is much more than that of knowledge management. It is much more than keeping up to date with key technologies or current practices or management theory. The challenge is to release ideas and creativity and to respond to those in positive ways.

The arguments developed in this book are meant to be practical. In academia we have enjoyed the experience of playing with ideas for the sake of doing so. In our work with organizations we are acutely aware of the problems of turning ideas into action. Managers want action. They need solutions to problems. As consultants we daily live with the tension of being asked to supply specific advice to solve particular problems while realizing that the problems dissolve away into something else if they are approached from a different perspective. We hope this book will enable practical managers and students of management to reframe the way in which they approach what they think of as practical problems.

We have no simple recipes. There are none. Unfortunately too many business organizations waste fortunes purchasing the latest managerial fashion, the latest 'quick fix' to help them change. Our aim in pointing this out is to help people develop a language of ideas and concepts that will enable them to diagnose present-day practical problems in an entirely new light.

The arguments, case studies, illustrations and data upon which the chapters of this book are based provide ample justification of the view that the process of engineering change and development in organizations is itself a process of learning and of becoming knowledge productive. So the thrust of this book is different, for it starts with the assumption that most organizations already possess the resources they need to help them change. To really understand the implications of this is the key challenge.

Organization of the book

Part 1 sets its arguments against the broad backcloth of changes in the global economy, with the aim of highlighting the importance of knowledge in the new information economy. The main purpose of this part is to clarify the observation that the challenge of knowledge productivity goes well beyond that of good knowledge management, and to explore the ways in which all groups of people in organizations can be helped to develop new ways of thinking and interaction with one another.

Part 2 develops ideas and propositions about the nature of expertise and the way in which skills and understanding in work-based settings can be developed further. A critical thread running through these is that of reflection and dialogue. Building on propositions about the nature of human learning these chapters demonstrate that knowledge-productive organizations are the ones which build into their routine practices ways to stimulate, nurture and value further learning among employees.

Part 3 is about organizations changing to become knowledge-productive. We show that all organizations teach and that all organizations, whether they realize it or not, operate a curriculum. There are ways to analyse these corporate curricula that result in innovative forms of training and development and new learning.

Part 4, the final one of the book, discusses change. Theory translates into action when managers understand change. In case studies of successful change in organizations we highlight the key themes of change management for knowledge productivity. These are not recipes for successful change. Each organization must find its own way forward. Since all organizations are unique and manage the time frames of the past, present and future in very different ways the only generalizations we could make about them would surely be empty ones.

And finally...

None of us can afford to be naive about the size of the task of change. There are many complex interdependencies of different organizations and institutions that in a modern economy influence individual organizations. The social and political complexity of the modern economy has to be understood and appreciated.

A new world has emerged based on global trade and transfers of capital and labour and many attempts have been made to capture its essence. It has been characterized as the 'weightless economy' (Leadbetter, 2000), as the 'network society' (Castells, 1996), as the 'knowledge economy' (Stehr, 1994). Many more such descriptors will emerge to capture the historical transition, at least in the post-industrial economies of the modern world, of economic activity based on industry to that based on information and expertise. In this new economy the nation states play a decisive regulatory role. They do so through dense networks of political alliances and through international bodies to regulate finance, trade and political relationships. Through the complex interactions of all this there arises a new kind of unstable complexity that is a challenge to all management.

Knowledge-productive organizations are those that can reframe the circumstances of their operation to discover new solutions to the problems they face. By locating the knowledge-productive organization against the complex background of the global, information economy, we hope to enable managers and employees at every level in all work organizations to think about themselves in new ways. We aim to nurture new forms of dialogue at work that will help people escape the constraints of their past and the pressures of the present and build ideas to create a new future.

Our aim is to engage you, our reader, in discussion. We invite you to pause, to reflect, to question and to debate the propositions you encounter. We aim for this book to itself become a catalyst for knowledge productivity, a means to other ends rather than an end in itself. We intend that it encourages discussion – dialogue and reflection – among groups of readers who will assess its implications for themselves and the people they work with.

The book is not written as a recipe book or, indeed, a map. Maps indicate what a journey may entail but can never reproduce the experience of the journey. We hope the experience of working with this book is a voyage of discovery in which you discover more about your own world than ours. Have a good journey!

Part I

The big picture

1 The knowledge economy

People know what is happening now.
The gods know things of the future,
the entire and sole possessors of all the lights.
Of things of the future, wise men perceive
approaching events.

C.P. Cavafy, *But Wise Men Perceive Approaching Things*

Aims

This chapter introduces some key themes of the book. These are:
- ➤ the nature of the knowledge-based economy;
- ➤ the changing climate of management within it;
- ➤ the role of governments in a knowledge economy;
- ➤ the nature of learning as a social activity;
- ➤ the moral dimension of knowledge productivity.

The essential idea developed is this: in the global knowledge economy the survival and development of organizations demands of managers a disciplined and effective approach to discover, understand and apply new knowledge and ideas. To do this they must develop a climate of enquiry that builds a capacity to help people think both rationally and critically about 'approaching events'. The cliché that captures the force of this point is well known: chance favours the prepared mind. The prepared mind requires a clear understanding of the changing ways in which knowledge is created in the global economy.

The knowledge economy

All economies are knowledge economies. It is not possible to conceive of a form of human economic life that is not based on specialized knowledge of some kind. Pre-industrial economies relied on what is, from our point of view, simple, human or animal-powered technology and the craft skills and understanding associated with its use. From the fifteenth and sixteenth centuries onwards global trade and, later, industrialism, brought new skills, science and technology and profound changes to the fabric of commercial, financial, legal and political life. Indeed it fashioned an entirely new order of human society and experience.

Two ideas that capture this are those of modernity and complexity. Modernity highlights the driving force of ideas such as progress, the rational organization of society, democracy and ever higher living standards. It encodes within itself the belief that human beings can achieve rational control of their lives and the future development of their societies. Complexity captures a key feature of both: the growth of new ideas, knowledge and understanding, driven forward by science and scholarship.

Ours is a world whose complexity is ultimately unmanageable. Not only are social and economic changes always one step ahead of our knowledge, but new knowledge reflects back into the ways in which human societies are organized and change. This phenomenon has been characterized as reflexivity (Soros, 2000).

In the age of science, technology and mass communications, economic life is driven by a competitive search for advantage and profit based on the exploitation of new knowledge. All sectors of the modern economy depend for their survival and growth on maintaining and developing ideas, skills and products that increasingly require advanced scientific, technological and social scientific research. The results of such research are applied in all domains of social, economic and political life, acting as catalysts of social change. The unintended consequences of such change can never be fully mapped out but they require new ways of thinking and understanding. This is the essence of reflexivity and one of the most decisive features of modernity.

Our knowledge of the world is both an imperfect and ordered analytical picture of the realities of our lives. It is also more powerful than that; it constitutes those realities. Our world becomes what we know it and want it to be and in so doing challenges all our previous assumptions about how it actually works, requiring from us further efforts of understanding.

In the advanced sectors of this economy in the most advanced industrial societies of the world change and innovation are programmed into the routine operations of organizational life. The expectation of change – conceived still by many as progress – is pervasive. Change is the norm. The future is open; no one knows what it will be, but everywhere it is anticipated, planned for and predicted.

'Keeping ahead of the game' has become a sine qua non of commercial survival. It requires high levels of investment in research and development (R&D) and long-term plans of human resource development to keep abreast of the pace of change and developments in knowledge.

The frameworks within which new knowledge is generated and disseminated are complex in themselves and they interact with one another to produce new orders of complexity in economic and political life. The knowledge system of the world, still dominated by the developed industrial societies, is an almost unimaginably successful mechanism to generate information and new ideas in all domains of human enquiry. It is a global system with complex political, economic and scientific interactions made possible with new global networks of communication. Our human powers to see and to listen and talk to one another have been extended far beyond biological limitations. Our communications compress both space and time and enable us to see into the distant reaches of our universe.

Complexity within our systems of knowledge is confronted, at least in the developed industrial societies, with a new phenomenon: super-complexity. Ronald Barnett (2000a) has traced out this phenomenon in its implications for the future development of the university, one of the most potent institutions of the knowledge economy. Complexity exists, he claims, as 'a surfeit of data, knowledge or theoretical frames within one's immediate situation' (2000a:6). It is for this reason that no specialist can ever hope to keep abreast of developments within a given field of knowledge. In addition, however, we live in a world where all the frameworks of thinking and understanding that shape our actions and institutions are themselves being contested and challenged. Barnett characterizes this postmodern condition as super- complexity. It defines an intellectual universe devoid of certainty and one that is essentially open to new ideas and ways of thinking.

As will be seen in subsequent chapters, super-complexity and reflexivity present entirely new challenges to those responsible for managing the institutions of the global economy. Unless they are themselves tuned to the super-complexity of their circumstances and actively pursue novel ideas and ways to solve current problems they will be left behind in the economy of ideas.

Within the complex circumstances alluded to there is both tragedy and hope. It is tragic that the political and economic contours of the global economy map out a social world of great inequalities between nations. It is a ruthlessly competitive order that generates both success and failure for countries, organizations, communities and individuals. It is a world dominated by a relatively few, global corporations with wealth beyond the dreams of many nation states and ruthless in controlling world markets. That control is not just of trade and raw materials; it extends to intellectual capital, to knowledge and ideas and the means to control their dissemination.

Words such as success and failure do not, however, grasp the social and cultural realities of global modernity. War, poverty, despair, environmental degradation, inter-communal violence and the insatiable anxieties of ever higher levels of consumerism are ubiquitous. The horsemen of the Apocalypse maraud their way through many regions of our globe. Global fashions and media dilute local cultures and identities. They nurture new kinds of dependencies and close off possibilities of development of a different kind. Within such circumstances hope has to rest in the knowledge and the belief that it is through new knowledge, made widely accessible, that new responses to problems can develop.

Much of this has now the status of a cliché. Less understood is that this knowledge system sustains a uniquely modern attitude and outlook that is arguably its most precious characteristic: the ability to stand back, to consider what we know and do not know, to identify areas where our knowledge is inadequate. This ability to conjecture and to criticize, to go beyond the constraints of our current patterns of thinking and knowledge and to question all that we know, is both a defining feature of postmodernity and the source of our creativity. That capacity, however, is not uniformly developed either throughout nations or among the organizations of economic life.

A central tenet of this book is that this meta-cognitive capacity is a quality of individual human minds and something that can be nurtured to become a feature of the ways in which organizations of many different kinds can function. The managers of those organizations – nation states, corporations, public services, voluntary groups – that nurture in their colleagues this critical awareness are the ones most likely to become successful and, in our terms, knowledge productive. They will be the organizations best able to handle knowledge and information, to act on the basis of it and to be geared up to keep abreast of the changes taking place around them.

A precondition of this is a clear understanding of the role of knowledge in the global economy and a determination to develop the means to keep abreast of it, translate it into new possibilities and be open to change.

The knowledge system

Consider the work of the following selection of organizations and individuals. Each is structured to undertake or commission research, to review policies, develop programmes that bring together many different groups of specialists, to understand and interpret and report on the complex changes of an increasingly complex world.

International bodies

- the World Bank;
- the United Nations;
- the International Monetary Fund;
- the International Court of Human Rights;
- the North Atlantic Treaty Organization;
- the World Council of Churches;
- the European Union;
- the Organization for Economic Cooperation and Development.

The list is not exhaustive. But these are among the institutions through whose work we come to understand much of the social, economic and political conditions of the world. They are, as the principle of reflexivity reveals, among some of the global institutions whose actions change the global economy itself and through that challenge our understanding of how that economy works.

Nation states

National states organize the search for new knowledge. They do this in several domains. Consider the following:

- science policies;
- military R&D programmes;
- higher education policies and institutions;
- intelligence services;
- policy evaluation programmes;
- think tanks.

Each area of state action listed is organized to generate intelligence, knowledge and understanding and of course not all is in the public domain.

Private commercial organizations

Commercial organizations in the knowledge economy play an increasingly important role in developing new ideas, technologies and products. They do so through R&D, market research, product development technology, through information sharing in trade associations and through training. Companies work closely with governments and higher education. This working relationship has been characterized recently as 'the triple helix' (Leydersdorff *et al.* 1994) to highlight, through the analogy of the double helix, the knowledge-generating capacity within the modern economy.

Universities and research institutes

These institutions generate new knowledge through research and scholarship and make it available through publications. They work in partnership with government and industry and with international research programmes. They are connected to knowledge networks that know no international boundaries.

Professional bodies

Knowledge has been thoroughly professionalized. Professional organizations designed to protect the needs and interests of their members have become guardians of particular knowledge domains. This is clearly true of law, medicine, engineering, architecture, and is becoming increasingly true for a range of new professions. Through their associations they legitimate particular ways of thinking and license practitioners. In the marketplace of ideas the professions seek monopoly positions. In that same marketplace, however, their monopoly is fragile and open to challenge as information once unique to them becomes widely available.

Civil society

Churches, pressure groups, trades unions, local authorities, community groups, leisure clubs, amenity societies and voluntary associations constitute the dense network of social relationships being increasingly characterized as civil society. They, too, generate knowledge and understanding in their own field of action and enquiry. Through the actions of their members society itself changes, challenging all our previous frameworks for comprehending it.

Individuals

Knowledge must be thought of as a collective human achievement. On the other hand, it is inconceivably apart from individual human minds. It is through the work of inventors, scholars, researchers and of millions of unsung, unrecognized individuals who daily solve intricate problems in the workplace or in the community that new ideas emerge. Under the conditions of the global information economy more people can become more aware of the ideas of more people than anyone in the past was able to imagine. This is both a source of almost infinite creativity among human beings and of real instability in the institutions that organize their lives. Expanding horizons of communication are the catalysts of super-complexity.

Such a list of contributors to knowledge is inevitably both incomplete and static. The knowledge-generating capability of modern societies is beyond our capability fully to describe or control. Furthermore, our descriptions can only begin to hint at the complex ways in which the frameworks listed above interact with one another. Governments commission research from universities and private commercial organizations. Government military expenditure funds commercial research and production. The work of international bodies – in law, economics, environmental management and many other areas of global, collective life – feeds into the work of governments, companies and universities.

It all amounts to a dense network of interrelated activities that constitute a knowledge system (Altbach, 1987) in the global framework of a 'knowledge society' (Stehr, 1994). The lives of millions of citizens are caught up in this framework. Their lifeworlds (Williamson, 1998) – the ways in which they comprehend themselves and their way of life – are patterned and shaped – some say colonized (Habermas, 1989) – by the prevailing frameworks of knowledge and understanding of this global, knowledge-based and fast-changing culture.

Knowledge productive organizations

Powerful political and economic interests dominate this knowledge system in some areas, and some areas of knowledge are highly secret. Global methods of communication mean, however, that knowledge cannot be kept hidden for long. New knowledge quickly becomes part of everyday life because it is translated into products – technology, pharmaceuticals, new materials, transport systems and so on – that become part of the requirements and routines of daily life itself.

Private companies and public organizations have found ways to adapt to this changing climate of knowledge. Successful organizations anticipate change and act upon it; those destined to fail are the ones that remain complacent about their own knowledge productivity and their place in the knowledge networks of the global marketplace. Successful organizations are the ones structured to learn new ways of doing things and to be creative in the way they solve problems and develop business.

Three further dimensions of the knowledge system come into view at this point. The self-critical, knowledge-productive organization is one possessed of arrangements to identify, articulate, consolidate and refine what its members know about their work. It is an organization well placed to build on the knowledge of its members and arrive at new solutions to problems. Of even greater importance is the ability of key managers to identify where their knowledge base is weak and to take action to correct that. Knowledge-productive organizations know what they do not know.

Secondly, the knowledge base of an organization is not simply formal and capable of description in terms of the skills and qualifications of its members. It is also informal, tacit and taken for granted. It includes what its members have come to know to do their jobs, what they have come to appreciate and understand about each other's strengths and weaknesses. It covers their attitudes towards their work and their willingness to work with and for one another. In this sense it embraces those dimensions of organizational life that can only be described using terms such as trust, commitment, respect and loyalty.

When these conditions exist people share ideas and information informally. They help each other solve problems. They think and learn outside the requirements of their own jobs. Without these elements organizations find it difficult to nurture enthusiasm, creative thinking, hard work and the willingness to change that is at the heart of all successful learning and communication.

Finally, it stands out clearly that all questions about the knowledge economy are embedded in frameworks of morality and law. Manuel Castells (1996) has noted that one of the great beneficiaries and growth industries within the network society is global crime. Crime flourishes in the chaos and disorder of the global economy. The Mafia is a successful, knowledge-productive organization and a global economic player finely attuned to new commercial possibilities. It works well with a range of other organizations and secures its own supply lines of trained expertise. The commitment of its members is absolute and loyalty is a high moral imperative among its members. Yet it is beyond any moral constraint.

These issues are taken up in more detail in subsequent chapters of this book. For the moment it is important only to recall the key elements of the knowledge economy and the knowledge productive organization within it. The knowledge economy is all of the following:

- global in its reach and fast changing;
- driven forward by competition;
- a system for exploiting the commercial possibilities of new knowledge and information;
- organized through international networks of production, management, communication and control;
- dependent on global mechanisms of R&D;
- an economic order that thrives or falters on the quality of the learning which takes place in the organizations that make up its most important networks;
- vulnerable to policy failures, crime and unmanageable risks;
- a morally fragile order of economic and political transactions dependent ultimately on the moral dispositions of people at work, their values, commitments and loyalties.

Work organizations – public and private – in this global economic network can be characterized in many different ways. Crucial to the future of all of them, however, are the relationships they strike up between themselves and the wider framework of knowledge-based economic change. Some organizations will be able to characterize themselves as *knowledge productive*. Others will be trapped in various states of *knowledge dependency* in which their future is uncertain and dependent on the skills and expertise of others. Some organizations are structured internally to be flexible in response to challenges; others are not. Some organizations nurture in their members a capacity and a willingness to step outside the frames of their conventional ways of thinking and doing things. Others do not. Some organizations look outwards and build strong knowledge-productive networks. Others fail in this. The future lies with those who find the means to adapt quickly to changing circumstances and reframe what they know by being open to new ideas and ways of thinking.

The future is not what it used to be!

The changing managerial climate

As a result of the changing economic condition there is a changing managerial climate in Europe and the United States. Ideas about management are changing as business leaders and their academic collaborators seek better models of practice to face the changing business environment. Some employers are recognizing the need for co-operation at work rather than conflict. A firm's survival is now linked to the idea of co-operation between all parties and the notion of 'stakeholderism' (Hutton, 1995) is taking a grip of people's thinking. Thorn Lighting, Joshua Tetley, Ilford Films, The Halifax plc, NatWest, Myson Radiators, Pizza Hut, the Health Service (the list goes on), are all examples of UK work organizations attempting to shift their thoughts towards a more 'humane' way of working.

The move towards this approach has both moral and economic considerations. The economic argument is gaining momentum; 'people mean business' as a slogan has gained much credence. As Kessels (1996a:5) puts it: 'Perceptions of the role of human intervention in economic transactions have changed. Appreciation of an individual's physical labour and ability to regulate and co-ordinate has made way for an emphasis on potential contribution to knowledge productivity'.

Clawson (1996:8) contrasts the 'shift' as a move away from the 'bureaucratic way' towards a 'process way'. The contrast between the bureaucratic way and the process way is shown in Table 1.1. Clawson suggests that in the 'bureaucratic' way the basic assumption is that 'the boss knows best'. In the 'process way' the basic assumption is that the 'process owner knows best'. In other words the person who holds the know-how.

Table 1.1 The contrast between the bureaucratic and process ways

Bureaucratic	Process
Planning	Scanning
Focus on the structure	Focus on the work
Focus on title	Focus on skills
Controlling	Empowering
Enacting	Harmonizing
Excluding	Including
Focus on organization	Focus on customer
Meeting set goals	Continuous improvement
Hierarchy oriented	Team oriented
Results oriented	Relationship and results oriented

Clawson, (1996: 8–9) goes further by suggesting that human activity occurs at three levels, as shown in Table 1.2.

Table 1.2 Three levels of human activity

Level	Activity
1	Observable behaviour
2	Conscious thought
3	Pre-conscious thought – values and beliefs

(Source: Clawson, 1996, pp. 8–9.)

He suggests that Level 1 is the 'bureaucratic paradigm': 'We do not care what you are thinking or feeling, just do what the job description demands of you and do it well.' In other words, treating people as a 'means' to an 'end'. He argues that this underpinning logic led to industrial unrest and social division in the past. Levels 2 and 3 are part of the 'Process Age', where we realize 'that to do anything collectively really well, especially in a service-based economy, we need to engage employees as a whole people and to invite their minds and their hearts as well as their bodies to come to work' (1996:8–9). In other words, treating people as 'ends' in themselves.

There is increasing evidence (Garvey, 1999) to suggest that Clawson's position is becoming a reality. However, it is also clear that moving towards such a position often challenges the whole foundation of management thinking. Traditional perspectives on organizational structure, hierarchies, working environments, policies, training and development need to be rethought to accommodate the notion of knowledge productivity. British Airways (BA) has taken this very seriously and invested £200 million in a new building that attempts to create a different type of physical environment aimed at facilitating good communication, networking and ideas flow.

Niels Torp, the designer of the BA Business Centre and his colleagues in 'Space Syntax' (www.bartlett.ucl.ac.uk/spacesyntax/offices/offices.html), studied the movements of people in a number of office buildings. They discovered that the best work is often done as a result of 'chance' encounters with colleagues working in different parts of the organization. They observed that the pattern of movement inside buildings is key to the way these encounters occur. Space Syntax's investigation suggests that the work environment can impact directly on both the working atmosphere of an organization and the effectiveness with which its people interact.

It is therefore important for organizations to capitalize on the 'usefulness' of what people seem to do naturally at work – interact. The research suggests that in a well-managed organization management will bring together those individuals and groups that can see a 'need' to interact to tackle a particular problem or project. Buildings could contribute by creating the physical environment that brings people together to interact in ways in which nobody could have predicted. This, Space Syntax believes, may play a central role in innovation within an organization. It seems to be a question of 'management sorts, buildings shuffle', and you need both in equal measure for new, innovative forms to emerge.

The new process paradigm places learning, innovation and creativity as central features of the workplace. And, in this new, fast-moving and complex environment, those who learn are those who offer the greatest potential to the organization. However, it is also the case that in such environments it is rarely possible to predict from where the latest innovation will come. This means that the work organization needs to build potential or strategic capability within its people so that they are ready to adapt, react, respond and innovate. Chance favours the prepared mind and the preparation comes through people being open to rich learning opportunities so readily available in the workplace (this is discussed in later chapters).

The role of government

Knowledge-productive organizations do not function in a vacuum. They are part of a network of relationships – both public and private – that influence the ways in which they develop and change. Adam Smith knew at the end of the eighteenth century that there was much to be gained from competitors in a marketplace co-operating with one another. He had in mind the Sheffield steel industry, in which competing manufacturers benefited from close geographical proximity and could share information on markets, trade conditions, workers and new technologies.

Modern European governments promote regional policies for similar reasons. Some of the most successful regions in the European Union – Baden-Wurtemberg, Paris-Sud, Emiglia-Romana, the Thames Valley corridor – and elsewhere in the world, in Silicon Valley in the United States or in the science parks of Japan and Taiwan, all depend for their economic vitality on the synergies derived from co-operation among competitors. This co-operation is promoted through government regional policies.

Policies to promote competitiveness throughout the modern industrial economies of the world work at several levels. There are inter-governmental policies that operate through institutions such as the European Union and its programmes. Individual nation states have their own macro-economic programmes touching on taxation, investment, interest rates and supply side factors such as training and education. Public policies with respect to health, welfare and education are crucial to the long-term viability of commercial organizations for they affect such factors as labour supply and quality. The interactions can be pictured as shown in Figure 1.1.

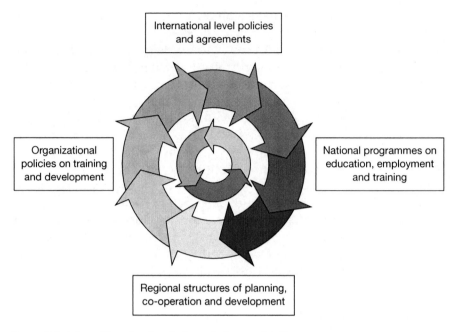

Figure 1.1 Interactions leading to knowledge production

It is widely acknowledged that the political and commercial leadership of countries strike different attitudes towards public policies in the realm of human resource development. For much of the 1980s the British government left such matters to the marketplace, and well into the 1990s took a limited, competency-based view of education and training needs. In contrast, governments in France and in the Netherlands were much more determined to promote effective long-term training and development.

The relative achievements of these different policies in the context of modern Europe can be debated. What is striking about recent discussions about them in Europe is that they are inseparable from discussions about wider dimensions of social inequality and of social exclusion. Policies to promote competitiveness and employability are linked inextricably to those that promote social inclusion and enhanced models of citizenship. For it is now clear that no economy can succeed in the long term if whole groups of people are excluded and marginalized from mainstream society. Social inequality exacerbates poor heath conditions, it limits educational opportunities and deepens unemployment. Social exclusion wastes ability and potential and is a terrible cost to the public purse.

Commercial organizations thrive best in conditions of relative economic stability and in countries where the social infrastructure of society is in good shape. There are no guarantees, here, of course. Much depends on how well companies themselves respond to the policy environments in which they operate and the climate they create. These environments and climates may either value innovation, learning and development or stifle it.

Knowledge-productive organizations are those finely tuned into the possibilities of public support for their commercial effort. They are the ones that seek partnerships with government, local government and development agencies; they value further education and training; and they participate in the public domain to promote their work, acknowledge their links with the professions on whose expertise they depend and build strong links with their local communities. They are the work organizations which recognize that society does exist and it does matter.

Learning is a social activity

The implications of the previous section become clear if we accept that learning is something that all people do and it tends to happen as a social activity. There can be little doubt, as will be shown in subsequent chapters, that learning happens in social contexts through social discourse and dialogue. Therefore, productive learning happens in certain social environments (Polanyi, 1958; Argyris and Schon, 1981; Nonaka, 1991; Boisot *et al.*, 1996). The reverse is also true. Some environments may hinder productive learning processes and may foster learning that is unproductive or unhelpful to the progression of the organization. This is an aspect of what Egan (1993) calls the 'shadowside' of an organization. The implications of this are serious, for it is well understood that people in the workplace have as much capacity to sabotage the organization as to contribute to it. As discussed earlier in this chapter, the assertion that learning is a social activity and has the power to add or take away value may present a huge challenge to the structure, management and physical environments of organizations.

In a knowledge economy managerial concern for control, power and authority are inappropriate conditions for learning. On the other hand, the 'core conditions' (Rogers, 1961) of an effective learning environment include the following:

- self-organization and genuine flexibility;
- creativity and open dialogue;
- individual responsibility, control and authority;
- security, empathy;
- extensive and open information exchange;
- a climate of trust based on mutual respect and genuineness;
- unconditional positive regard for other people;
- an ability to communicate all these to others (Rogers, 1961:281).

Learning to be knowledge productive – the moral dimension

Implicit in the 'core conditions' are a number of moral considerations.

Fredrick Taylor and Henry Ford, the grandfathers of 'scientific management', would have recognized that the idea of learning in the workplace to achieve economic prosperity was an obvious one. It is not a new concept. However, Taylor and Ford ignored the moral dimension and simply focused their attention on financial reward for 'trained' people or, in other words, treating people as a 'means' to an 'end'. They did not want their staff to 'think' – just to do what they were trained to do, like human machines.

In the context of a modern capitalist community the issues of manipulation, control and the abuse or use of power within a learning environment cannot be ignored. This is because, as Jarvis (1992:7) put it, 'learning, and perhaps knowledge itself, has significant moral connotations'. Jarvis argues that the moral dimension is inescapable in learning and knowledge acquisition. He traces his argument to the myth of Adam and Eve. Before eating from the tree of knowledge both were innocent, but afterwards they had acquired the knowledge of good and evil. Some theologians describe this event as 'the fall' but:

> Archbishop William Temple once commented that if this was a fall, it was a fall upwards! Perhaps this is the greatest paradox of all human learning – the fact that something generally regarded as good has been intimately associated with a myth of the origin of evil in the world ... learning, and perhaps knowledge itself, has significant moral connotations' (Jarvis, 1992:7).

Given the now pervading view that management is about 'achieving results through people' the implications of this are considerable, for the moral dimension is implicit in the statement. Organizations that ignore this may find problems in implementing such a statement.

There are always two imperatives in business – effectiveness and efficiency. Both are important and yet there is an inherent conflict between the two. Effectiveness is related to the quality of an activity and efficiency is linked to time. There are human tensions between these two business imperatives 'to do things *effectively* is not the same as to do them *well*' (Harrison and Smith, 2001:199). It is interesting to speculate 'whether one would prefer to be managed by the good manager or the effective manager, let alone the efficient one' (2001:199). These natural tensions may be resolved through flexibility, innovation and creativity. But these things require new ways of thinking and changes in the organizational narrative in areas such as power, status and control. It is very difficult for a manager to empower. The conflict here is similar to the tensions that naturally occur in learning.

Kolb (1984) clearly argued that learning from experience is a process and not a product or outcome. The process is viewed as cyclic but within the cycle are tensions. Kolb's model offers two aspects of learning: gaining experience through action and gaining experience through reflection. Action-based experience leads to 'apprehension' whereas reflective experience leads to 'comprehension'.

Kolb (1984) suggested that experience gained during action or testing is 'concrete experience'. Experience that is gained through apprehension may involve feelings of the 'heat' of the situation, the mood and the ambience; while the concrete experience will include a whole range of events, some of which will be tangible and others intangible. The resultant knowledge is 'accommodative knowledge'.

Inherent in Kolb's model of learning are paradoxes and conflicts and it is these very tensions that create the conditions for learning. A task may be performed identically by two separate individuals and the resultant concrete experience may be completely different but just as relevant. The implication here is that the 'one best way' philosophy has no place in a true learning environment and the resultant management approach of scientific method is also redundant.

Activities at work that involve learning have been linked with faster achievement and 'fast tracking' (Clutterbuck, 1992; Garvey, 1995a). There is a danger here that organizations wishing to accelerate learning may be looking for a quick return on investment. Quick return learning tends to involve knowledge or skills transfer where there are clearly defined inputs from the 'teacher' and clearly expected and demonstrable outputs shown by the learner. The emphasis is on efficiency at the expense of effectiveness. The argument is very strong. As Kessels (1996a:4) puts it:

> organisations have a direct stake in the personal enrichment of employees because excellence on the job requires employees who are comfortable with their work and who have strong and stable personalities. Personal enrichment is thus less an employee privilege than a condition for good performance.

Kessels is throwing down a big challenge to managers.

There are many challenges in taking knowledge and learning 'beyond management'. Specialization needs what some Dutch colleagues call 'lummel' time. Lummel time is an acknowledgement of the need to be 'seriously playful' at work and to be 'playfully serious'. Creative energy comes from this recognition of the need for space. An organization that is alert to learning will invest in anything which enables its people to see themselves as learners. People need security to 'get on with it' and support to use their time wisely.

Clearly, the implications for human resource management and human resource development are considerable and Pfeffer (1998:65) suggests that for an organization to achieve economic prosperity in the knowledge economy it needs to pay attention to seven factors:

1 Employment security.
2 Selective hiring of new people.
3 Self-managed teams and decentralisation of decision making as the basic principles of organisational design.
4 Comparatively high compensation contingent on organisational performance.
5 Extensive training.
6 Reduced status distinctions and barriers, including dress, language, office arrangements, and wage differences across levels.
7 Extensive sharing of financial and performance information throughout the organisation.

Human resource specialists need to stress these points for each one will directly influence an individual's ability to deliver efficiently and effectively.

Further, the term 'human resources' is (in a learning climate) a misconceived expression because this implies that people are resources just like plant and machinery and as such need controlling and managing. While in some industries this may be the case we argue in this book that if people are treated with disrespect they will respond in kind. Management can no longer talk 'loyalty', 'commitment' and 'trust' on the one hand and repay them with redundancy and job insecurity on the other. Such behaviour is immoral and has no place in a knowledge-productive environment. (In March 2001, the steel company Corus announced the closure of its plant in Wales. This decision followed years of employee co-operation and participation to secure their future.)

In conclusion we offer four aspects for consideration in a learning climate that is effective, efficient and moral. The organization needs to build:

■ confidence;
■ competence;
■ collaboration;
■ communication.

These will help to create a climate that includes the core conditions for learning and in turn the product of learning, knowledge, may be exploited for economic prosperity.

It is essential to consider the moral dimension because, at the risk of being painfully obvious, if an organization 'treats people well, they behave well; if it treats people badly, they behave badly'. This was understood at the time of Mayo's Hawthorne experiments in the 1930s, which offered a moral challenge to business. How much progress have we made since then?

2 Strategy, capabilities, knowledge productivity and the corporate curriculum

There is a tide in the affairs of men
Which, taken at the flood leads on to fortune;
Omitted, all the voyage of their life
Is bound in shallows and miseries:

Shakespeare, *Julius Caesar*, Act 4 Scene 2: 265

This chapter extends our account of the broad social and economic frameworks of knowledge productivity. Our aim is to develop a way to understand the contexts and the environments in which organizations function. We believe that for knowledge productivity to 'work' in organizations managers themselves need to work out the implications of these ideas for the specific circumstances of their own organizations. The chapter looks at the links between strategy, capability, knowledge productivity and learning.

Aims

The main themes are:
➤ social science assumptions;
➤ the relationship between the past, the present and the future;
➤ the competitive context, strategy and capability;
➤ introducing the corporate curriculum and linking it to knowledge productivity and strategic capability;
➤ becoming knowledge-productive and building capability.

Social science assumptions

Throughout this book there is a constant cross-referencing between theory and practice, ideas and interpretation. We see social science as a collection of ideas from which we all draw selectively. The challenge is to understand them and use them wisely and critically and with clear intention, and never merely by default or simply because they are fashionable.

Subjectivist vs objectivist paradigms

The first assumption in this chapter is that all work organizations, large and small, public, private and not-for-profit, are complex social systems. Because of this they operate by complex social 'rules' that are often ill-defined, vague, emotional and 'messy'. The following may help to explain this.

Theories of social science have evolved and changed over many years. The way we come to understand our society is often as a result of a complex interaction between such ideas and the societies in which they are embedded. There is a natural dynamic between the creation of theory and the lived experience of individuals and groups in what we often refer to as the 'real world'. This dynamic helps to establish beliefs and values and influences the ways in which people think and behave. For example one perspective, as put forward by Burrell and Morgan (1979) could be to view communities through the 'subjectivist' paradigm. If this is the case the basic, core knowledge (ontology) of the 'subjectivist' is that of 'nominalism'. Societies are observed and described through a naming process and one name is perhaps as good as another. The fundamental approach or epistemology of the 'subjectivist' is the notion of 'anti-positivism'. This is where human affairs are seen as indeterminate, highly situational and only understandable within specific social and cultural contexts. The 'subjectivist' believes that human social organization is based on negotiation and choices. Finally, the 'subjectivist' believes that the best approach to understanding human activities is through a multi-layered description that simultaneously interprets the world being described.

To counterbalance this, there is the 'objectivist's' perspective. Here the ontology is rooted in 'realism' and the epistemology is 'positivism'. The assumptions made by the 'objectivist' are that human nature is deterministic and predictable, and therefore the approach to investigating human affairs is about scientific method aimed at conclusive proof and the finality of naming the condition under examination.

The links to the concepts of 'modernity' and 'complexity' as outlined in Chapter 1 are evident here. The 'modernity' concept is more about 'objectivism', whereas the 'subjectivist' is more closely allied to the 'complexity' perspective. One sees the world as a framework of facts and things; the other as a realm of meanings and particular ways of understanding that vary between cultures, and that all changes through time.

Conflict vs order

Another perspective on human affairs may be characterized by positions taken on 'conflict' or 'order' within society. Table 2.1 expresses these paradoxes.

Table 2.1 The paradoxes of 'conflict' and 'order'

Conflict	Order
Coercion	Commitment
Division	Cohesion
Hostility	Consensus
Dissension	Agreement
Conflict	Co-operation
Malintegration	Integration
Change	Stability

In the 'sense of order' domain, the fundamental assumptions are as follows:

- All societies are relatively persistent and stable.
- All societies are well-integrated structures.
- All aspects of a society have a function and contribute to the maintenance of the structure.
- Every functional element of a social structure is based on a consensus of values among its members.

In the 'conflict' domain the fundamental assumptions are the following:

- All societies are subject to processes of continual and constant change.
- All societies display dissensus and social conflict constantly. Conflict is a continuous state.
- Each element in a society contributes to its disintegration and change.
- All societies are rooted on the coercion of some of its members by others.

Regulation vs Radical

A further layer to add to this background are the views taken by social scientists on change. Some see change in social settings as a 'regulated' process, others see it as a 'radical' process, often with unintended and unanticipated outcomes (Table 2.2). In the first perspective change is thought to be predictable; in the latter, all futures and all planning are uncertain and open.

Table 2.2 The paradoxes of change

Regulation	Radical change
Status quo	Radical change
Social order	Structural conflict
Consensus	Modes of domination
Social integration and cohesion	Contradiction
Solidarity	Emancipation
Need satisfaction	Deprivation
Actuality	Potentiality

Conclusions

The main point illustrated by these opposing perspectives is that individuals and groups may adopt such beliefs and positions on how society works and then make decisions and enact behaviours based on their particular set of beliefs. Such perspectives are part of society. They may not have been 'taught' but they circulate through social interactions and create a 'dominant narrative' that is passed on from group to group, individual to individual.

For example, the 'objectivist' perspective will value rationality in the structures and systems in the organization and will therefore seek to develop a detailed, planned strategy for the organization. (This is discussed later in this chapter.) As to the model of 'conflict' and 'order', arguably, for example, the concept of human resources management is based on the 'order' paradigm or 'unitarist' agenda, while the 'conflict' model is part of the 'pluralist' agenda. With regard to change, some believe that change is only achieved through radical means and others believe it to be incremental and regulated. Some believe that in management now there is a neo-unitarist or neo-pluralist agenda as we move towards an appreciation of teamworking and diversity. The concept of 'super-complexity' as outlined in Chapter 1 applies here. 'Super-complexity' is perhaps related to the 'neo-pluralist' perspective.

These assumptions form a backdrop for decision making, strategy formulation and policy creation. They also help to account for the complexities of human response in the changing circumstances of the workplace.

We believe (and there is much evidence to support this) that western management is dominated by the concept of the 'pragmatic, rational manager', and when this is overlaid on the complex social system of the work organization as outlined above unpredictability results. The pragmatic manager attempts to control and manage the system using rational and pragmatic approaches, which sometimes work and sometimes fail. Predictability is fast becoming a redundant concept in the knowledge economy.

Another assumption is the pace of change in organizational life, which is influenced by technological change and that political initiatives has accelerated. The implications of this fast-changing and competitive climate on individuals are considerable. The need for people who are able to adapt to change rapidly, be innovative and creative, be flexible and adaptive, learn quickly and apply their knowledge to a range of situations has increased. The whole nature of work appears to be changing and the notion of having a career for life is transformed.

One response to this situation has been a growing tendency, in both the public and private sectors, towards 'objectivity' and 'rationality' in all work activities. Scientific method applied to organizational life has become a dominant preoccupation of managers. The exponential growth in performance league tables for organizations and performance objectives for individuals provides evidence of this. This mode of thinking aims to establish systematic bodies of generalized knowledge or explicit rules and procedures. It sets out to specify objectives and learning outcomes. It then becomes possible to judge success in learning if these outcomes or objectives are met.

The merits of this approach include the possibilities of accountability and quality control. The emphasis on outcomes should not preclude attention to 'process' and the relational aspects of learning, but it often does. The result is that the 'hegemony of technique' (Habermas, 1974) can only engineer that which has been prespecified (Bernstein, 1971). This 'outcome' approach is effective in getting us to where we want to go but it cannot develop our awareness of the different sorts of destination available, nor does it promise that travelling to them will enrich us despite the destination. The following extracts from Cavafy's poem *Ithaca* (1911) illustrate this point very well.

> When you set out on your journey to Ithaca,
> pray that the road is long,
> full of adventure, full of knowledge ...
>
> Always keep Ithaca in your mind.
> To arrive there is your ultimate goal.
> But do not hurry the voyage at all ...
>
> Ithaca has given you the beautiful voyage.
> Without her you would have never set out on the road.
> She has nothing more to give you.
>
> And if you find her poor, Ithaca has not deceived you.
> Wise as you have become, with so much experience,
> you must already have understood what Ithacas mean.

The 'outcome' approach cannot be adequate to guide the learners in an organization if they are to be capable of flexibility, innovation, creativity and improvisation – the widely agreed qualities required of the learners of the future. It has been maintained that 'genuinely interactive and collaborative forms of reasoning' (Barnett, 1994:37) are in danger of being driven out by technical or 'strategic' reasoning.

Past, present and future

Time is an inescapable dimension of human experience. Any satisfactory account of how an organization (and the people within it) works must attend to the ways in which lives are constructed in time and are changing constantly.

Our 'pasts' are in our 'presents' but we are not often aware of this – we simply 'get on' with our lives. There are times when the 'past' confronts our 'present' and this tends to happen in 'moments' of awareness or significance. These points can be clarified in three propositions about how people relate to their past.

Proposition 1

We may choose to live in the past and function on the basis of traditionalism, using expressions such as 'We have always done it this way ...' This has the effect of making people resistant to change as their basic reference point for action in the present is their traditionalism and perspectives on how actions are taken and decisions are made from their particular perspective on their history. However, it is often the case that the tacit assumptions that frame everything people do in an uncritical celebration of the past act as a guide to everything that is done in the present and the future. This is despite a strongly held perception that the organization may feel itself 'modern' – the tried and trusted paths dominate.

Proposition 2

We may choose to reject our past or rewrite our history. This has the potential effect of devaluing our past and making it worthless, or we may apportion blame, attach guilt or have a 'rose-tinted' perspective on our history. This attitude often prevents people in organizations from learning from the past or encourages them to suppress its continuing influence on their present-day actions.

Proposition 3

A third option attempts to build on our past by understanding it profoundly. We do this through adequate reflection on our past and through critical awareness of it. This requires openness, a willingness to be critical, to learn and to change. It invites people to take risks – with their reputations, status and careers. For some it will be a painful realization that cherished beliefs were misplaced, that attitudes were unhelpful. It is not easy, though, we suggest, it is necessary to confront the past in this way. Otherwise it becomes our prison.

One way of thinking about this is to consider the idea of the significant moments of change in our lives. Of course, these can often be understood only in retrospect. And, as time changes, perceptions of moments and significant turning points may alter. How people talk about and analyse critical moments in organizational history is often a real clue about the defining character of an organization's culture.

Moments

Defining 'moments' happen in the workplace. We cannot control the 'moments', only our response to them. In an increasingly complex working environment the opportunities that present themselves are unknowable, complex and often happen quickly. People respond to these 'moments' by referencing their past. As we cannot predict from where or when these 'moments' happen we can only prepare for our response by understanding our past. This is another example of 'chance favouring the prepared mind'.

We speculate that proposition 3 offers the most potential for organizations to realize a positive future that does not repeat the failings of the past. Proposition 3 contains profound implications for SHRD. For organizations to realize their futures they need to understand their 'pasts' because the past is the backdrop of actions and decision making. An organization's past is remembered through the dominant narratives within its culture. The writer Salman Rushdie expresses this point as follows:

> Those who do not have the power of the story that dominates their lives – power to retell it, rethink it, deconstruct it, joke about it, and change it as times change – truly are powerless because they cannot think new thoughts. (Quoted in Williamson, 1998)

According to the psychologist Jerome Bruner (1985), people shape meaning from the past through narrative, metaphor and stories. Often, in an organizational setting, the perspective we have on the past is created by the holders of the power and those who dominate the narrative. Karl Marx gives us an insight into this with the following:

> Men make their own history, but not of their own free will; not under circumstances they themselves have chosen but under the given and inherited circumstances with which they are directly confronted. The tradition of the dead generations weighs like a nightmare on the minds of the living. (Quoted in McLellan, D, 1971: 207)

A legitimate question to ask at this point is 'So what? Enough of the theory and more of the real world.' Thus says the pragmatic, rational voice within.

There are many answers to the 'so what' question here. The core of these points about the 'past', the 'present' and the 'future' is that if organizations are to be prepared for an uncertain future they need to be completely open to learning 'as' experience as much as learning 'from' experience. The challenges of the competitive context in the modern world, dominated by the capitalist doctrine, are the reality. These are the 'real world' and they impact on all of us. How we respond to the 'real world' will depend on the dominant narrative within our organization. If, for example, the narrative is dominated by the pragmatic manager or by the 'technical' perspective decisions will be made against the pragmatic and technical backdrop and any alternative perspective may not even be considered. This is not to denigrate the pragmatic perspective, which can often be very helpful but may not offer the best opportunity for creativity, flexibility and innovation – the essentials of the fast-moving knowledge economy.

The competitive context

The competitive environment of modern economic life is a challenge to all work organizations in all sectors of the economy and civil society. The notion of 'strategy' is important here, but there are many varying views taken on strategy.

One approach, as outlined by Stacey (1995), suggests that strategy is a rational process in which organizations can make choices in relation to their operating environment. The assumption is that environmental changes are largely identifiable and consequently the organization rearranges itself to adapt to changes in the environment. Linked to this is the idea of the 'ecology school'. Here, organizations adapt and survive on the basis of competitive forces and, as there are a limited number of adaptations possible, those who get there first will survive and those who don't will fade away.

Both these perspectives are of the 'objectivist' school. Stacey (1995:476) suggests:

> In both cases irregular behaviour occurs because the environment bombards organisations with events that agents within them have not foreseen (random shocks) or cannot deal with. Any disorder is therefore viewed and interpreted as the consequence of ignorance, inertia or incompetence.

These perspectives naturally raise the issues of 'intention' or 'emergence' in strategy. It is our contention that the dominant narrative or, put another way, the construction of the organizational history determines the strategic perspective adopted. This also means that it will be the dominant actors who determine how successful the strategy has been *post hoc*. This is not necessarily a rational evaluation but one that is influenced by the social politics of the organization – therefore we strongly challenge the notion of 'objectivism' and 'intention' in strategy.

A further perspective is linked to the ideas of 'choice' and 'determinism'. The ecology perspective states that the survival and progress of an organization is determined by its

> initial institutional and resource choices, its inertia and the subsequent changes in the environment. According to strategic choice theory, organisations are not so constrained by inertia but success still requires that an organisation be adapted to its environment – this implies a deterministic relationship. Stacey (1995:477)

Another perspective on strategy is the 'resource-based view' as expressed by C.K. Prahalad: 'If you are committed to continuity and change, then you need to focus on resources' (1997:64).

In short, it is about examining all resources and maximizing their use and contribution to the organization. With, for example, plant, machinery and finance it is often easier to find ways to exploit their use, but with people as a resource exploitation is morally wrong and, from a competitive perspective, not sensible. We have already raised the idea that if we treat people well they behave well and that if we treat people badly they behave badly. Yet managers continue to forget this simple fact as organizations downsize, rightsize, cut and chop – basically, the folly of focusing on one resource at the expense of another. David Skyrme highlights this with his comment that: 'Human capital – competencies – are a key component of value in a knowledge-based company, yet few companies report competency levels in annual reports. In contrast, downsizing is often seen as a positive 'cost-cutting' measure.' (www.ionet.net/~jburch/c9612ke.html)

Another risk is that the pragmatic manager could spend too much time in the analysis and planning phase of strategy formulation at the expense of implementation. This is a natural way of behaving as the pragmatic manager sees analysis and planning as 'real work'. This concept is reinforced by the well-known time management slogan 'Failing to plan is planning to fail.'

However, analysis and planning do not in themselves generate new ideas. Experimentation, alertness and awareness – the knowledge-productive way – do. In the dynamics of the knowledge economy it is new ideas, implemented and brought to market quickly, that count.

These couple of pitfalls alone mean that the resource-based strategy must take a holistic perspective. This takes into account all resources and considers how they may interact. A resource-based view includes both tangible and intangible resources alike, for example brand name, location, proximity of raw materials and people (Hall, 1994).

Any resource-based strategy in a fast-changing environment must be subject to constant change and review driven by the interactions and variable dynamics of the internal and external environment, and tangible and intangible resources. These interactions create opportunities and it is only people who are capable of spotting, creating and exploiting opportunities in the dynamic environment of a knowledge economy. As Campbell and Alexander. (1997:44) point out 'the basic ingredient of a good strategy [is] insight into how to create value'.

Organizations are complex social systems and are full of paradoxes and contradictions. It is likely that in some cases and in certain situations managers may be able to control environments and be able to exercise choice and therefore be capable of managing towards a prespecified end point. It is also likely (more so in a knowledge economy) that the social system of the work organization located within 'super-complex' networks and interactions will spontaneously self-organize. The 'actors' involved in this situation will not be able to predict and control towards a specific end. In such an environment the behaviour of the actors is determined by the dominant narrative. However, 'irregularities and disorder can occur … individuals are free to disrupt institutions' (Stacey, 1995:480). Success, however understood, in this environment is therefore the process of creativity, innovation, flexibility and emergence.

These different perspectives on strategy within the framework of 'super-complexity' clarify the question: 'What does it mean for people in work organizations?'

We believe that it is vital to build capability (or insight) within an organization through learning. However, the conventional view of training and development is that it should be closely allied to the organizational strategy. In the knowledge economy strategies have to be dynamic, changeable and, to an extent, opportunistic. They need to be rooted in learning that develops alertness for 'scanning', interpreting and understanding the environment (see Chapter 1). So what does this mean for training and development? This too must be dynamic, changeable and opportunistic. It must recognize both tacit and explicit knowledge and be aimed at developing learning, thinking people, alert to their environment and willing to contribute and participate in the activities of the organization as whole people who can be 'themselves' at work (Garvey and Alred, 2001).

The corporate curriculum framework

One way to take these ideas further is to consider the notion that an organization can be conceived as having a curriculum, a framework of order and values within which learning takes place. The idea of curriculum is central to all debates about education and training. It is actually central to any credible account of culture in organizations. A curriculum is a programme or course of study. We believe that this is an appropriate term to use in the context of workplaces.

According to educational curriculum theory, put forward by Bernstein as long ago as 1971, it is important to decide on the following:

- valid knowledge;
- valid pedagogy;
- valid evaluation;
- valid realization.

For any curriculum this is, by its nature, specific to certain contexts and situations. According to Bernstein there are two main elements to a curriculum – the 'formal' or 'closed' curriculum and the 'open' or 'informal'.

The 'formal' or 'closed' curriculum contains the following elements:

- 'closed' content;
- content boundaries (specific subjects with no overlaps);
- strong classification (categories of content – technical, arts etc.);
- criteria, objective and outcome driven;
- evaluation against the prespecified outcomes or objectives is dominant.

In contrast, the 'informal' or 'open' curriculum may be characterized as follows:

- 'open' content;
- content boundaries loose (subject overlaps and relationships);
- loose classification (integrated and complex view of content);
- circumstance and need driven;
- evaluation uncertain but related to circumstance and need.

The type of learning embedded by the 'formal' or 'closed' curriculum is associated with high 'teacher' control of the knowledge and it socializes a sense of order and rationality. This type of curriculum is part of the 'objectivist's' paradigm and therefore it creates in the minds of the recipients a dominant narrative of power in the hands of the knowledge holders and lack of power in the minds of the 'learners'. It can also have its roots in the 'past', and to an extent the 'present'. As the 'formal' curriculum is driven so strongly by assessment and evaluation it offers a greater opportunity for managerial control and direction. Indeed, the UK governments of recent times have been preoccupied with educational measurement or, as discussed earlier,

'technicism' in education. As a consequence of the above the 'closed' curriculum tends to socialize a narrative of low initiative, low innovation and
creativity for the 'learner'.

In contrast, the 'open' curriculum places the 'learner' in control and consequently encourages challenge, questioning, high initiative, innovation
and creativity. The 'open' curriculum socializes a sense of 'disorder' as the
dominant narrative is more a part of the 'subjectivist's' paradigm. It has its
roots in the 'past', the 'present' and the 'future'.

This is deeply significant and has implications for both organizations that
take learning seriously and for educationalists in schools. We argue that the
dominant narrative currently held in education is the 'objectivist' agenda
and that this will not generate the innovation, flexibility and creativity
needed for the knowledge economy. We also recognize that the 'subjectivist'
agenda is higher risk, less certain and hard to evaluate (using objective
means at least) but it does offer the opportunity of developing the kind of
people who are so necessary in the turmoil of the knowledge economy.

We argue that most development in the workplace is of the formal,
instructor-led or 'closed' (Bernstein, 1971) curriculum kind. We are all very
familiar with this approach – it is regarded as normal in the workplace. Also,
this is the approach advocated in many textbooks on the subject of training
and development. The dominant narrative here suggests the need for strategic alignment of training and development.

These processes, we suggest, are becoming increasingly redundant in
modern organizational contexts. Many managers observe that this type of
development simply does not deliver the results expected of it (Broad and
Newstom, 1992). The challenge here is for managers to recognize that the
workplace itself is potentially a rich learning environment that can provide
the necessary stimulus and support for learning and knowledge generation.
Further, there is much evidence that this 'situated approach' (Lave and
Wenger, 1991) offers a greater depth, understanding and participation in
learning to be knowledge productive.

This is not to suggest that 'formal' or 'closed' education or training programmes are poor. In some situations they are particularly useful for
knowledge and skill development. But the real issue is that if effective learning is inextricably linked to specific social contexts (as outlined in Chapter
1) and behaviours, the things people are taught in 'formal' or 'closed' programmes are not always relevant to the specific work settings. Perhaps more
importantly the opportunities to even engage in a meaningful dialogue
about application, development and transfer into the specific work setting
may not occur within such programmes.

Another, more complex metaphor is that of a 'rich landscape' (Kessels,
1996) in which learning takes place. Kessels proposes the idea of a 'corporate

curriculum' as an inclusive framework of learning at work, in all its manifestations and, in particular, its social dynamic. According to Kessels (1996:173), the 'corporate curriculum' consists of seven elements or 'learning functions', as follows:

1 expertise related to the core competence;
2 problem solving;
3 reflection and generation of new knowledge;
4 communication;
5 self-knowledge, meta-cognitions;
6 peace and stability;
7 creative turmoil.

(There are close links here to the conditions for learning presented earlier in Chapter 1.)

The seven elements in the 'rich landscape' contain both 'formal' and 'closed' elements in which learning is holistic and relatively boundary free. In the 'rich landscape' learning occurs through an active engagement and participation that encourages creativity, lateral thinking and flexibility – the much-needed abilities of an employee of the future.

Case study 2.1, on the 'corporate curriculum', illustrates both the 'corporate curriculum' in action and the effect of a dominant 'rational' view of learning.

Case study 2.1

Company A, United Kingdom

Company A, working to the highest quality levels in Continental Europe, specializes in the design, development and manufacture of automotive components. It is part of a global network of companies. The parent organization, Company A Corporation, has 30 companies in 12 countries that together employ over 10,000 people.

Company A is highly successful. Its success has been built on the philosophy of continuous incremental improvement, just in time and total quality management systems. However, its future is not so certain. The industry is changing rapidly. There are technological, legal and environmental considerations ahead for Company A. The systems of the past may not be sufficient to help the business realize a secure future. The assumption is that the 'rich landscape' of learning offers the people in the business both a challenge and a real opportunity to progress and innovate towards securing a strong future.

▶

The research team spent three months with the Manufacturing Department of the business. We used interview, focus group and questionnaire techniques to probe the nature and form of the 'corporate curriculum' in Company A.

The findings

Expertise related to the core competence

There is clear understanding of the 'formal curriculum' and little appreciation of an 'open curriculum'. All people have a good appreciation of the element 'expertise related to the core competencies' although there is evidence that this is under strain. Due to the pressures of 'lean' production they are beginning to develop a 'lean' approach to training and development.

Problem solving

Being a manufacturing site it is not surprising that there is clear evidence of problem-solving activities. The main, perhaps only, vehicle for this is Kaizen (see case study 4.1). This activity also seems under strain.

Reflection and generation of new knowledge

There seem few opportunities for reflection and the generation of new knowledge. The dominant approach to learning is based on people 'showing each other' how to do something rather than a combination of 'show and discuss'. People do not know how to conduct 'learning conversations'.

Communication

Despite the above point there are well-defined lines of formal communication that do not always work.

Self-regulation and meta-cognitions

This organization has tight control of its production methods. Training activities are strongly focused on the technical aspects of the job. Leanness in production has led to leanness in training. This results in a reluctance to give the time to training activities that are not 'technical' in nature. Opportunities to develop the more emotional side and motivation of individuals are absent. Consequently there is much tension among those interviewed and, in some cases, anger and frustration at the pace of work.

Peace and stability

The business is relatively stable (not peaceful) but this is also under strain. The strain manifests itself in an emerging 'blame culture', often driven by the demands of 'lean' production.

Creative turmoil

We were unable to find any sign of creative turmoil; only a climate of high pressure.

Comment

The pressure of competition, measured in Company A using cost efficiency, time control and product productivity, biases management towards technical development and training. Personal and interpersonal development is a low priority.

Company A's training and development programmes are mainly short term and just in time – purely outcome driven. These are generally evaluated through technical measures. Attributes of co-operation with others, learning about emotional interaction and adaptation are mainly ignored. These behavioural elements feature in the appraisal system as measures to be assessed but are not developed or exploited.

The central issue here is that teamwork is regarded as essential in Company A but the 'technicist' approach to learning mainly ignores the social context. Therefore the seven core conditions for a rich landscape of learning within teams become unbalanced. The consequence of this is employees' needs and perceptions tend to be neglected and the social context largely ignored. The organization's philosophy is at odds with its current practice.

Becoming knowledge productive

Old knowledge and practices have to give way to innovative ways of solving problems, improving efficiency and sustaining organizational development. The hypothesis at the core of the above points is that successful organizations of the future will be those that find the best ways to become knowledge productive (OECD, 1996; Seltzer and Bentley, 1999).

Knowledge-productive organizations are those that have the means to generate new ideas and ways of thinking which enable them to sustain competitiveness and continuously improve their products or services. Typically they are organizations in which there is a high level of HRD activity as reflected by a balanced corporate curriculum and high levels of team working. Additionally they are organizations that have a culture of creativity and support risk taking. A further necessary feature of such organizations is that they have well-developed means to monitor and evaluate their performance. (Huselid, 1995; Patterson *et al.*, 1998; Pfeffer, 1998)

Necessary as these characteristics are, they are still not sufficient to guarantee knowledge productivity, innovation and change. Two key elements that need to be brought into view to specify the range of sufficient conditions for knowledge productivity are the nature of an organization's commitment to learning from the past and the ways in which organizations evaluate the different futures open to them.

Recent work in the field of organizational histories (Gold *et al.*, 1998) has demonstrated that the process of undertaking a systematic analysis of the history and experience of individual work organizations – through methods of oral history and narrative analysis – can often be catalytic of change and innovation. In short, it is a process that enables people to learn from success and failure and build on what they know in ways that enable them to reframe what they know. Therefore, engaging in a facilitated dialogue about the organization influences and changes the behaviours of participants in that dialogue. The future itself cannot be known. But the process of exploring it reveals new perspectives on the present and opens up new options for development.

An organization will have many capabilities, but arguably the most important is strategic capability (Harrison, 2000). Strategic capability is related to profound knowledge of the environment and reflects the organization's ability to be strategically aware of change and opportunity. We suggest that strategic capability is strongly allied to knowledge productivity and that this in turn is influenced by the quality of learning within an organization. Figure 2.1 illustrates this relationship.

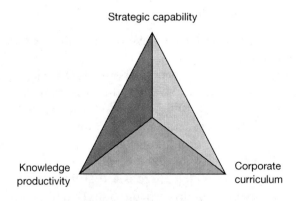

Figure 2.1 The relationship between strategic capability, knowledge productivity and the corporate curriculum

The quality of the corporate curriculum, as discussed in Chapter 1, influences an organization's ability to be knowledge productive and, in turn, the more knowledge productive the organization, the more strategically capable it becomes. The greater the strategic capability the more able an organization is to progress and survive in the dynamics of a fast-changing environment.

Case study 2.2, based on research work conducted by Garvey in 1999/2000, illustrates this point.

Case study 2.2

An investigation into the Corporate Curriculum at Oil Company Co.

In discussing the first element of the corporate curriculum – domain-specific knowledge – with a group of managers at Oil Company Co. it became clear that we had reached a pivotal moment.

I asked the question: 'What is the core domain knowledge of Oil Company Co.?' 'That's easy,' replied one of the managers in the group. 'It's all here' and he handed me a very large training manual. I flicked through the manual and it was full of training course details and outlines. In the main these were technical courses to do with the use and applications of lubricants in mechanical engineering, chemical engineering, production, refrigeration and the food industry. There were a few courses on presentation skills, negotiating skills and selling skills. There was silence as I thumbed through the manual. Then Andy, another manager in the group, broke the silence. 'Hang on a minute,' he said, 'I'm doing an MSc. course in Environmental Science, I think that could be domain-specific knowledge.'

'How do you mean?' the others asked.

'Well,' began Andy, 'I went to a factory by a canal recently and when I was shown around I noticed an oil slick on the water. The slick could only have come from the factory's storage tanks. I asked the Plant Manager if he had had a visit from the Environment Agency. The Plant Manager asked how I knew and I pointed to the oil. The Plant Manager then went on to say that the factory was due for closure if they couldn't solve the pollution problem. I said, Oil Company Co. can sort it for you – with our storage system. The Plant Manager was delighted and we got a new customer!'

'What are you saying?' asked one of the group. 'That we all have to do an MSc. in Environmental Science?'

'No,' said Andy. 'It means a lot of things – if I hadn't been doing the course I wouldn't have noticed or recognized the problem and opportunity, my specific knowledge became a commercial asset but I had to be alert to apply it. We don't need everyone doing the course but we do need people learning

▶

other things, being aware of how to exploit and apply the knowledge. We also need to know who knows what and where and how they have applied it so that we can learn form each other.'

Comments on the case

Learning on a formal education programme had enhanced Andy's capability but he had to have the ability to realize this and apply it in order to fulfil the requirements of Oil Company Co.'s strategy. As he said himself, he had to be alert. Andy spotted the 'moment' and his past experience informed his present so that a new commercial future could unfold. So, where does alertness, for example, come from? It is part of our holistic capability as people and not something that can necessarily be learned on a course. Andy is motivated, committed and enthusiastic about his work. Oil Company Co. recognized this, nurtured it and provided an environment where he could be himself at work. Of course there are the pressures of sales targets on Andy and his colleagues, but the management system in Oil Company Co. rewards financially both 'target' performance and development activity. It is sensible to do so, as Andy is developing a niche as an 'expert' for himself and Oil Company Co. is benefiting from it. He is being knowledge productive as a result of a combination of an aspect of Oil Company Co.'s corporate curriculum and his own personal capabilities, developed in an environment that is encouraging and rewarding.

One challenge for both Oil Company Co. and Andy is to continue learning, applying and being alert. Another is to make sure that others know about this type of success and, as discussed in Chapter 1, translate the learning into other areas of work.

Summary and conclusion

This section has covered two main elements of the 'big picture'. In Chapter 1 we explored the nature of the knowledge economy and the changing managerial climate within it.

In Chapter 2 we have offered a backdrop of social science theory that will act as a reference point throughout the book. We have also raised the issue of our pasts, our presents and our futures as further reference points for decision making in organizations. We have introduced the concepts of the corporate curriculum, knowledge productivity and strategic capability.

Part 1 has explored the role of governments within a knowledge economy and the notion that learning is essentially a social activity and as such has various moral implications.

The knowledge economy is influenced by a complex web of competing concepts. Each organization needs to find its way through the complexity in the knowledge that there is no arrival, only the journey.

Critique of Part 1

Joseph Kessels, *University of Twente, the Netherlands*

You cannot be smart against your will

Knowledge productivity

An important assertion in Chapters 1 and 2 is that the economy is transforming into a knowledge economy. Therefore individuals, teams and companies need to develop the necessary competencies to be able to participate in a working life that is mainly based on knowledge productivity. The dramatically increased interest in knowledge over the past decade has given rise to the concepts knowledge-intensive organizations, knowledge workers, knowledge systems, knowledge centres, knowledge creation, knowledge management and citizens in a knowledge society. At the same time it is questionable whether the traditional approaches to management, training and development will provide the learning environment that is required for knowledge work.

When I first developed the concept of knowledge productivity (Kessels, 1995) I stated that knowledge productivity involves signalling, absorbing and processing of relevant information, developing new competencies on the basis of this information, and applying these competencies to the improvement and innovation of work processes, products and services. It chiefly concerns the way that teams of people achieve knowledge-based improvements and innovations. In fact, the driving force of knowledge productivity is a complex learning experience. It also expresses that the knowledge we value in an economic context should be perceived as competencies, as capabilities, as the skills to bring about gradual improvement and radical innovation. The knowledge-productivity concept is based on the view that knowledge is an individual competence: it involves a subjective skill that is inextricably linked with the individuals concerned. We first explored the concept of knowledge as a competence in studies of successful educational programmes (Kessels, 1993, Kessel and Harrison, 1998; Kessels and Plomp, 1999). Malhotra supports the view of knowledge as a competence:

> Even procedural knowledge, when translated into symbols that are later processed by another human, does not ensure that the outcome of his knowledge will rival that of the original *carrier*. Knowledge needs to be understood as the *potential for action* that doesn't only depend upon the stored information but also on the individual interacting with it. (Malholtra, 2000: 249)

Therefore companies, government agencies and institutions should consciously develop a corporate curriculum, an 'open' plan for learning that offers a rich landscape of development, that turns the day-to-day work environment into a powerful learning environment. The corporate curriculum's various learning functions help individuals, irrespective of their formal education, to develop their talents and take part in various forms of knowledge work. As knowledge productivity and the supporting learning processes are so closely related, the corporate curriculum has the potential to become the binding force of knowledge networks. These may be characterized as 'smart' communities that heavily depend on shared intrinsic motivation and personal affection as part of the key content of the job.

The management of knowledge

The concepts of knowledge productivity and the corporate curriculum also raise the question as to how far knowledge productivity can be managed. The current interest in knowledge, its complex underlying dynamics and the economic significance that we may attribute to it may imply that we may be seeing the end of the management era altogether.

The origins of management lie in a period of economic activity in which we tried to plan, steer, manage, measure, verify, monitor, assess and evaluate everything we considered important. While knowledge has been important throughout economic history, our desire to manage everything of value to us arose mainly in the previous century. Drucker (1993) argues that the initial application of knowledge to production means and methods gave rise to the industrial revolution. The owners of the means of production were the main players; access to the capital factor ruled economic transactions. Subsequently, the application of knowledge to labour brought about the revolution in productivity. Here, a new category of managers emerged. They cultivated specific knowledge concerning the deployment of production means, use of resources, employee guidance and management of quality and logistics and external markets, clients and the surroundings. Over time, the dominant position of the owner-capital provider shifted to the upper management.

In the current knowledge revolution knowledge is applied increasingly to knowledge itself. The capacity to develop and apply knowledge rests mainly with knowledge workers. These generally highly educated professionals are beginning to prevail over managers. The transition from the productivity revolution to a knowledge revolution might therefore mark the end of the management era.

The ability to develop strategies, procedures and work processes turned top management into the ruling business class of the twentieth century through the power that they inherited from the company owners. In exchange for a salary, security and material support, employees did their jobs in a disciplined and obedient way. In the twenty-first century knowledge productivity is becoming the driving force, and as this knowledge production will be found at every level of economic activity the power then starts to reside with knowledge workers.

The changing role of managers will have specific implications for what is known nowadays as 'knowledge management'. The question is whether the successful management approach from the past is fully applicable to promote knowledge development.

Our desire to manage everything of value to use arose mainly in the previous century. In the line of production management, finance management, personnel management and account management it not surprising that, when knowledge becomes of prime importance, we head for knowledge management.

However, I expect that in a while we will view knowledge management as an anachronism, as the link between two units from different eras. I am not alone in my criticism of knowledge management. In their recent publication Von Krogh *et al.* (2000) are similarly reticent about knowledge management and prefer to promote knowledge development without the 'management' imperative.

Malholtra (2000) deals extensively with the question of whether knowledge management is an oxymoron, a combination of two opposite concepts. He concludes that the management perspective is ineffective with knowledge development. Nonetheless he has high hopes for the self-steering 'knowledge intrapreneur', although this insight does not lead him to abandon the knowledge-management concept.

Knowledge management, control and steering relates more to the 'formal' curriculum, as knowledge productivity encourages the innovation and creativity of an 'open' plan of learning. It will be extremely difficult to organize learning in an open way, especially in a highly competitive environment where predefined outcomes and targeted performances are valued. Therefore strategic capability (as described by Harrison, 2000), knowledge productivity and the quality of the corporate curriculum are less directed towards specific improvements and innovations, as these are not the knowledge that concerns us. The ability to achieve such improvement and innovations matters most. As specific innovation, improvement or invention – possibly patented – may be of great economic value, but the true value lies in the *ability* to generate such improvements and innovations rather than in the actual innovation.

Self-regulation of motivation, affinity, emotions and affections

One of the learning functions in the corporate curriculum supports self-regulation of motivation, affinities, emotions and affections. Nobody can talk somebody else into curiosity, motivation, interest and ambition. The assumption is that people are only clever if they want to be. You cannot be smart against your will. In a traditional economy a manager could say: 'Joseph, work harder, or run faster.' In a knowledge economy it is useless when a manager says: 'Joseph, be smarter or show more creativity!' Being smart and creative depends heavily on personal interest. Affections, affinities and emotions play an important role in knowledge work. I cannot be inventive in a domain for which I am not motivated. I have to ask 'What is meaningful work for me and how do I become committed?' Finding out what emotional and affective drives employees have and how they can regulate these will probably be an important aspect of designing a work environment in a knowledge economy.

Therefore it is important for knowledge workers to identify personal themes and ways to develop them. In view of the earlier statements that knowledge is a personal skill, which can thrive in inspiring knowledge networks and communities of practice (Wenger, 1998; Wenger and Snyder, 2000), we might search for different strategies to develop knowledge productivity.

The core conditions as formulated 40 years ago by Rogers (as cited in Chapter 2) such as self-organization, creativity and open dialogue, individual responsibility, control and authority, extensive and open information exchange, a climate of trust based on mutual respect and genuineness, unconditional positive regard for other people, and an ability to communicate all these to others, have now gained an explicit economic interest.

Promoting knowledge productivity requires the competence to work systematically on the social context as well as on the subject matter component. Previously this was the chief responsibility of instructors, trainers and managers. Over time these roles will have to become those of mentors, coaches, facilitators and inspirers. The desire to guide, manage, control and monitor is becoming increasingly difficult to fulfil. Many curricula, schedules and instructional strategies cannot avert transfer problems. Many knowledge workers do not need their managers and arrange for support independently. The growing interest in self-guidance is apparent in both work and learning contexts. This leads us to ask how we can tempt each other towards knowledge productivity.

The main objective is to acquire the competence to design a workplace that develops sustainable instruments useful for dealing with future issues: the competence to become cleverer, learning to learn, organizing reflection, increasing relflexivity and basically applying knowledge to knowledge development.

Reciprocal attractiveness and passion

Employees are becoming increasingly aware that their economic appeal depends primarily on the power of knowledge productivity. They will see the need to tempt each other and the surroundings they select to cultivate these competencies. This temptation does not result from power, coercion, status or position. Instead it arises from the perceived need to work, design and learn together. This process is not automatic. Tempting for knowledge productivity is inviting rather than imposing. Such competence encourages reciprocal attractiveness and makes judicious use of the the energy contained in everybody's passion.

The moral dimension, as discussed in Chapter 1, sheds new light on the concept of reciprocal attractiveness in a context of knowledge work. It does not only apply to the individual members of self-organized teams, but also to managers and to the firm as a whole. In a knowledge economy values such as loyalty, commitment and trust cannot be bought by paying a salary. It is even questionable whether these values contribute to knowledge productivity. Loyalty and obedience may be welcome and valuable support systems for overcoming a hurdle or an impasse. Without any substantive drive, however, they are likely merely to foster stupidity and at best lead to mediocrity. To develop this substantive drive it is important to explore the relation of individual life themes to meaningful work. Reflective skills are probably crucial in this process as they help to understand what matters in the personal development of a professional. Co-operation and joined knowledge work is feasible when participants each choose their community based on reciprocal attractiveness, passion, involvement and identification with each other's expertise.

References

Drucker, P.F. (1993) *Post-capitalist Society*, Oxford, Butterworth-Heinemann.

Harrison, R. (2000) 'Learning, knowledge productivity and strategic progress' *International Journal of Training and Development*, vol. 4, no. 4, pp 244–58.

Kessels, J.W.M. (1993) *Towards Design Standards for Curriculum Consistency in Corporate Education*, Doctoral thesis, Enschede, Universiteit Twente.

Kessels, J.W.M. (1995) 'Opleidingen in arbeidsorganisaties. Het ambivalente perspectief van de kennisproduktiviteit' [Training in organisations: the ambivalent perspective of knowledge productivity], *Comenius*, vol. 15, no. 2, pp 179–93.

Kessels, J.W.M. and Harrison, R. (1998) 'External consistency: the key to success in management development programmes?' *Management Learning Journal for Managerial and Organizational Learning*, vol 29. no. 1, pp 39–68.

Kessels, J.W.M and T.J. Plomp (1999) 'A systematic and relational approach to obtaining curriculum consistency in corporate education', *Journal of Curriculum Studies*, vol. 31, no. 6, pp 679–709.

Malhotra, Y. (2000) 'Role of organizational controls in knowledge management: is knowledge management really an "oxymoron"?', in Malhotra Y. (ed.) *Knowledge Management and Virtual Organizations*, Hershey, Idea Group Publishing.

Von Krogh, G., K. Ichijo & I. Nonaka. (2000). *Enabling Knowledge Creation*. Oxford, University Press.

Wenger, E. (1998) *Communities of Practice: Learning, Meaning, and Identity*, Cambridge, Cambridge University Press.

Wenger, E.C and Snyder, W.M. (2000) 'Communities of practice: the organizational frontier', *Harvard Business Review*, January-February, pp. 139–45.

Part 2

Developing expertise in learning – individuals and groups

3 The nature of expertise

If I have seen further, it's because I have stood on the shoulders of giants.

Sir Isaac Newton

Aims

The aim of this chapter is fourfold;

➤ to clarify the nature of expert knowledge and expertise;

➤ to demonstrate that expertise is simultaneously an individual and social phenomenon;

➤ to show that the sustained development of expertise requires appropriate means to promote new learning in the workplace;

➤ to illustrate that the limits to the development of expertise are set only by the horizons of our imagination.

This chapter develops a view of specialist knowledge that enables people who depend on their own expertise, or who manage the expertise of others, to take their domain-specific knowledge further and to develop new ideas.

The economics of expertise

The long-term secular trend in the labour markets of the advanced industrial economies is to move from skills based on the manipulation and management of 'things' to work that requires the development and application of knowledge and of ideas. The shift from blue-collar production to white-collar production no longer grasps the complexity of what is involved. The distinction between handwork and brainwork was never an accurate description of what divided the two. People with well-honed practical skills invariably deploy expert knowledge in their own particular domain of competence. Similarly, much brainwork can be tediously routine and uncreative. The distinction we really need is one that grasps the difference between work of a routine, programmed and highly predictable kind to that which requires workers to think in innovative ways and constantly to function at the limits of their understanding. Such knowledge work is becoming ever more important in all of the contexts of working life in modern societies.

The dominant metaphor that underlies all accounts of how this situation has developed is an abstract, organic one. Through science and technology knowledge develops. It develops inexorably and cumulatively, building on what has gone before as if it was some vast, unprogrammed evolutionary outcome stored in the symbols of language or mathematics. Knowledge in this sense becomes that which is consolidated and made explicit in books, journals and encyclopedias. It is a highly specialized, ever-expanding universe requiring complex systems of information retrieval that are well beyond the comprehension of an individual to understand fully. Such knowledge is passed from one generation to the next through the institutions of formal education and can be graded on a complex hierarchy of specialized understanding.

This view of knowledge we describe as 'Big K'. Knowledge here is portrayed as something that evolves by itself, which develops within its specialist domains according to their own rules of logic and evidence. In some fundamental way knowledge in this sense is no longer the property of individual minds. Indeed, 'Big K' is no longer accessible to individuals. It is too vast, too complex and too specialized for individual human minds to know.

'Little K' is different. This is the knowledge that individuals possess for themselves. It is the knowledge that reflects their experience of work and understanding and of their lifelong attempts to consolidate what they know. This is what people bring to the work situation. It is their tacit understanding of what they have to do each day in order to make the machines work or to complete their administrative tasks. 'Little K' is firmly anchored in the realm of individual education and experience.

There are many ways to describe knowledge based on experience. Sometimes we use a property analogy, in which to possess knowledge is seen as being equivalent to possessing property. Indeed the law itself promotes this point of view in the concept of intellectual capital. A powerful element of this image is that knowledge has its boundaries and its unique individual features. The key boundary is that of the individual and what they have come to know and understand for themselves. A further boundary is that of a trade or a profession when the claim is made that only members of that trade possess the true knowledge of its practice. The implications and consequences of this are illustrated in case study 3.1.

Case study 3.1

Company A (see Chapter 2)

To be a welder one needs five years as an apprentice and skill-related training is the norm. Also, the majority of qualified welders in Company A tend to have a long history in which their family members all possess similar or related skills. This 'cultural' influence is a legacy from the ship-building era that so dominated the region in the past. Consequently there is a strong sense of pride in their welding skills.

In its formative years Company A only employed 'time-served welders'. This enabled rapid progress and substantially contributed to its success as a business. However, in the last five years there has been a tendency to employ people without welding qualifications as machine operatives. Our research revealed that this has had the effect of creating a subgroup in the factory – welders and non-welders. Company A professes teamwork as the mainstay of its production and the different groups are placed together in the same teams. On the surface teamwork exists, but the research revealed that teamwork and co-operation is sometimes strained between the welder and non-welder subgroups. It also identified clear differences in responses to research questions between the two subgroups. It was almost as if there were two completely different sets of people working in completely different environments.

In contrast to this view the argument developed here is that knowledge and expertise are best seen as qualities under constant stress of alteration through time. Depending on context, knowledge and expertise either develop or atrophy. The issue is not the nature of the individual minds involved but of how individuals are positioned in the context of their work and the wider settings of their lives. Unpractised skills become rusty. Learning that is not applied and renewed becomes out of date.

A related feature in the dominant metaphor of knowledge in modern society is the western conceit that its rationalized and logical forms carry legitimacy and these represent the pinnacle of human intellectual achievement. This idea not only devalues – and quite illegitimately – other ways of knowing the world, but it no longer describes accurately global distributions of knowledge and expertise. As the global information economy develops the bodies of expertise crucial to its operation are themselves increasingly global. India may not be at the forefront of computer design and microchip technology. The Indian system for training software engineers is, however, decisive for the development of global informatics.

The Unbound Prometheus of western science and technology has clearly transformed the world as we know it. On the other hand, that same system of technological rationality has created a complexity in global social relationships that goes beyond our capacity to comprehend. The cumulative unintended consequences of the actions of millions of individuals and organizations generates a framework of change that cannot be predicted with any precision. Consequently the risks faced by people and organizations in the modern global economy are increasing beyond their ability to control. Ulrich Beck (1992) has characterized modern society as 'the risk society'. Some of the risks, for example those associated with nuclear energy, or global epidemics, or unanticipated meltdowns in key sectors of the global economy, could all become literally unmanageable.

Set against this background the dominant image of the scientific and technological expertise looks to be a fragile one. Knowledge does confer power but maybe not as much as is often assumed. Certainly, the expert knowledge that individuals may possess will never in the circumstances described above be adequate as a description of how the world or specialized parts of it actually work. To understand such complexity or, as Barnett (2000b) describes it, 'super-complexity' requires a different model and image of expertise. That model requires us to see expertise as intimately bound up with the organizational settings and socio-economic frameworks within which experts function.

That wider setting is a highly fragmented one. 'Big K' and 'Little K' are both highly specialized domains of experience and understanding. 'Big K' is driven forward by research and development on a global scale. In all domains of human enquiry – especially those that touch upon the technology of war – research generates new knowledge at an exponential rate. In domains such as pure science, medicine, information technology, engineering, biological sciences and even the human sciences, knowledge productivity has been institutionalized in the work both of universities and private research organizations and government. The modes through which such knowledge develops – pure, developmental or applied – are themselves highly varied. It is important therefore to try and understand the settings in which knowledge is developed.

One recent attempt to do so distinguishes between Mode I knowledge and Mode II knowledge (Gibbons *et al.*, 1994). In Mode I knowledge – typically found in universities and academic life – knowledge is generated by the subject specialists working within agreed frameworks of academic expertise. They work within distinct paradigms that set for them the theory methods and problems of their research. The results of their work is published and is openly accessible.

In contrast, Mode II research is interdisciplinary, often applied, often under the control of commercial organizations, sometimes undertaken in collaboration with universities but always aimed at solving practical problems. Knowledge and ideas generated within Mode II need not necessarily find their way into the public domain. Such ideas can remain commercial secrets. The development of Mode II research represents a profound challenge to universities and traditional forms of academic research. It represents too an important challenge to all our current ideas about the nature of meaning of an open democratic society.

If we combine the categories of 'Big K' and 'Little K' with Mode I and Mode II research we can develop a simple typological map of some important dimensions of knowledge production in modern society as shown in Figure 3.1.

The four quadrants of this diagram define different strategies for generating knowledge. Academic research that is subject based and follows the research questions which are part of the logic of a particular discipline represents an important model of knowledge production in all modern societies. Often publicly funded, this research is published in academic journals and is therefore widely available. The principal audience of much of this research is the academic community within disciplines. It may not therefore be a body of knowledge accessible to non-specialists. Within the traditions of university life such work is held to reflect the important values of objectivity and truth and disinterestedness.

In comparison to this, commercial research and development can often be highly secret. No big company is going to reveal the results of its research before it has found a way to market it in a profitable way or protected such knowledge through patents and copyright laws. Commercial or military research or development does, however, follow the rules of scientific rationality. Or, at least, it does so in principle. There are many examples of commercial research that show it to be of questionable scientific value and often of questionable moral worth. Science- and technology-based industries

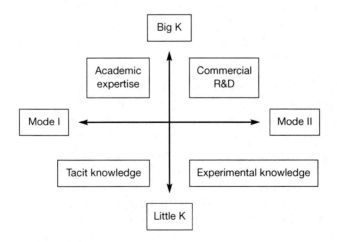

Figure 3.1 Modes of knowledge production

are, however, driven forward by research done in commercial laboratories and research institutes.

Much of the work done in both domains, i.e. the academic and the commercial, have a strong experiential component. Scientists rely on years of accumulative experience to understand what is practicable in research terms. The tacit knowledge of experts is as decisive in shaping the work they do as their explicit knowledge. An important challenge, indeed, for all work organizations is to try and reframe tacit knowledge so that it becomes explicit and therefore available for others to use. For the moment, however, it is only necessary to note that there is a domain of understanding and experience that informs the production of knowledge but which itself does not count as explicitly formulated knowledge. This realm of the tacit needs to be brought into view if we are really to understand the process of knowledge productivity. Case study 3.2 illustrates this combination approach.

Case study 3.2

Fishfeed research and development

Consider the case of a fishfeed company working in the global marketplace of fish farming, a European multinational and lead player in the salmon feed industry. It has grown dramatically in the past five years through successful marketing, strategic takeovers and high quality R&D. Its corporate culture is that of a flexible, devolved organization in which working relationships are generally relaxed and friendly and staff feel secure and valued.

In the summer of 1996 some customers reported disease and slow growth in fish and questioned whether the feedstuff was responsible. Fish were developing eye cataracts that affected their vision. Their inability to feed efficiently resulted in poor growth and behavioural changes when they swam at the surface resulting in sunburn, leading to increased disease incidence and slower growth.

Faced with potentially high costs of litigation and diminished market share the company organized an emergency fact-finding strategy to get to the root of the problem. This brought together the most up-to-date veterinary information from global sources. It involved detailed supply chain investigations to track down possible failures in the quality of the feeds and assessment of a large number of farms where fish were continually tested on a fortnightly basis. This was a huge investigative programme. Careful assessment of the feeding systems of farmers was set in train to establish whether the problem was localized. Further R&D was commissioned from the company's own laboratories, external research organizations and universities. A legal and insurance team was assembled to anticipate the ways in which any litigation might be handled should customers seek to lay the blame on the company.

The outcome, after many weeks of intense meetings, analysis and reflection, was that the cause of problem was multi-factorial. It was possibly the result of changes in water temperature, high levels of ultraviolet (UV) causing stress and also a deficiency in a dietary micro nutrient – a necessary, though not in itself sufficient factor in the equation. This was new knowledge discovered in an organized way requiring international co-operation and high levels of inter-disciplinary working. The scientific information had to be translated quickly into a commercial strategy to deal with customers and with any ensuing legal obligations in ways that were satisfactory to everyone. This was achieved.

Whether an organization structured in a more hierarchical way than this one could have achieved such a result is an open debate. Feed manufactures without the global R&D capacity of this company, or the technical staff in management roles able to act on their knowledge, would not survive in this volatile market for long.

The case study describes a commercially successful, knowledge-productive rather than knowledge-dependent organization and one very aware of the importance of both Mode I and Mode II knowledge. It knows that success is based on the systematic exploitation of scientific knowledge in fish nutrition. But it was not the science as such that solved the problem. It was a necessary but not a sufficient condition. The sufficient condition required teamwork across disciplines, openness, trust and very high levels of commitment to the company to share information, analyse data and working practices openly. Without this kind of organizational climate scientific work alone would not have helped solve the problem.

What was true in this example can be generalized across different sectors and organizations. Those organizations which do not acknowledge that they work in a volatile, knowledge-driven environment and which do not have the means to reflect carefully on their own practice and learn from their mistakes are not likely to succeed.

The nature of expertise

The question of how best to promote knowledge productivity is fundamentally about the issue of expertise. We live in a society with a complex division of labour based on highly specialized bodies of knowledge. Without such specialization it would not be possible to take further the development of science and technology. Without collaboration among experts of different kinds none of the great ventures of modern society would be possible. Space technology, for example, is only possible because of the combined work of physicists, engineers, materials scientists, astronomers and computer experts. Without managers who exercise rare skills in bringing together such diverse groups of people and programmes it would not be possible to launch satellites or put people in space stations. Organizations that wish to remain at the forefront of research and development in their specific domains need to make the best possible use of the experts they employ. But what is the nature of expertise?

The distinction between 'Big K' and 'Little K' provides some of the clues to this answer. A very powerful image of expertise is that of individuals or groups of individuals who possess highly specialized bodies of knowledge, ideas, information and skills. It is as if the body of knowledge itself stands apart from the minds of those who understand it and use it. Expertise in this sense becomes consolidated intellectual property.

On this model of expertise, people become experts through long and carefully guided periods of study. For most of the major professions such as medicine, engineering, law and for any credible career in science, there is a minimum of at least seven years of intensive study beyond the age of 16 before anyone could begin to have the skills necessary to practise in their profession. For those who reach the higher levels of professional competence the years of education and training go on beyond this. In order to maintain the credibility of their understanding such professionals have to undergo processes of continuous professional updating.

In the course of such protracted training experts develop knowledge, skills and understanding and a natural control of the conceptual language of their knowledge domain. They acquire a grasp of the means of communication within that particular domain together with an understanding of the professional ethics which govern their actions. They absorb into their own personalities the professional identity of the subject domain within which they work.

In all domains of expert knowledge there is, after the initial period of training, a process of differentiation that sorts out those people who will continue to higher levels and those who will become mere practitioners in a particular field of expertise. Those who go on to the higher levels develop a critical understanding of the research base of their discipline and become attuned to gaps and weaknesses in their knowledge. They form the nucleus of the people within a given domain who become specialist researchers.

Expertise at this level is not well understood. This is the level at which people break through from the constraints of given disciplines and generate new knowledge. The history of science is one of changes in perspective and understanding – Thomas Kuhn (1962) captured this in his famous phrase, 'paradigm shifts' – and this requires people who can think outside the boundaries of their subjects. The structure of DNA was discovered by young scientists – James D. Watson and Bernard Crick – working in the Cavendish

Laboratory in Cambridge in the 1950s. Their achievement required a deep understanding of chemistry, mathematics, X-ray defraction procedures and biology. Neither Crick nor Watson felt themselves really competent in all of these fields. Each had, however, a highly developed capacity to ask new questions and the confidence to do so.

Peter Medawar's (1986) description of scientists fits Crick and Watson perfectly. 'Mathematicians' he wrote 'are reputed to be rare and special people, exulting in the exercise of a gift far beyond the performance, and perhaps even the conception, of ordinary people' (1986:9). He is quite explicit, however, that scientists are not like this; indeed, in his view 'quite ordinary people can be good at science' (p.9). The crucial quality of a scientist, argues Medawar, is 'disquiet at lack of comprehension' that nurtures in them an exploratory, questioning attitude. At the core of all discovery is hypothesis and imagination. At the boundaries of scientific understanding there is doubt and uncertainty, and those who live their lives at those boundaries are clearly different from people who are merely expert in the application of domain-specific knowledge.

Without the careful detailed work of millions of experts, however, the ordinary business of running a complex civilization would not be possible. Not everyone can be a research scientist. In the field of what Kuhn (1962) called 'normal science' and in the daily practice of experts, much of the work being done is of a routine and highly predictable nature. This is not to denigrate it. This is the domain referred to earlier as Little K. It is the domain of experience. Like the dark matter of the universe, it is a domain that does not come clearly into view. We cannot know easily what knowledge is being discovered in this domain for it remains the private experience of individuals and small groups. What is more, both individuals and organizations differ markedly in their ability to reflect analytically on their own experience. Some organizations will have a clear view of their experiential intellectual capital. Others will have no appreciation whatsoever of what resources they have available to them.

Expertise and ability

The development of expertise requires many years of disciplined training. There has been debate for more than a century about what the qualities are that individuals require in order to undertake such training and education. Are there particular clusters of ability that are necessary for certain kinds of thinking and practice? Can anyone develop expertise in areas that interest them? Or are there limits governing what people can achieve? These are all important questions. The answers to them have for many years shaped our sense of human possibility and organizational practice. The principle of reflexivity discussed previously highlights that our understanding of this matter is not just a more or less adequate reflection of some fundamental psychological realities about individuals. On the contrary, what we believe to be true of the potentiality of individuals to learn and develop will become true in the way in which we organize opportunities for their learning.

Two features dominated discussions about these matters for most of the twentieth century both quite central to main traditions of psychological research. The first is essentialism. This is the idea that human beings are as they are because of their genetic or intellectual make-up and that there is not much scope to develop individuals beyond certain natural limits set by their natural inheritance. The argument applies to both ends of the spectrum, to the very dull, of whom it is often said 'You can't make a silk purse out of a sow's ear' as well as the very bright, who might be classed as geniuses. Both are covered by what the French sociologist Pierre Bourdieu (1974) once called 'the ideology of giftedness'. This is the belief that the intellectual capacity of people is a finite quantum. Some are gifted, most are not. Only the gifted can be expected to reach high levels of intellectual achievement. Those who have achieved in such ways can then think of their success as an outcome of their own intrinsic qualities. Occupational or academic success is then made legitimate as a consequence of the natural order of human abilities.

Related to this is the issue of reductionism. This is the idea that human abilities can be analytically teased out and be seen as clusters of a wide range of discrete capacities. Intelligence can be dissolved into a series of factors, for example spatial ability, capacity for abstract thought, speed of thinking, and each of these in their turn can be broken down into yet further factors that explain them. The danger in such psychological reductionism is that we are blinded to the effects of the social settings in which people both develop and are required to think and act. Essentialist and reductionist arguments about human ability have blinded us to other dimensions of human experience relevant to successful performance at work or learning. The idea of emotional intelligence is a case in point.

Work by the US psychologist Goleman (1996) on emotional intelligence clearly struck a chord among managers and management theorists. His claim is that there is a dimension to intelligence that conventional models of ability do not take into account. That dimension concerns feelings, sensitivities to others, skills in maintaining good inter-personal relationships. At the heart of effective teamworking or successful arrangements that promote inter-professional dialogue among teams of specialists is an ability to see the world from the point of view of the other and to understand the emotional reactions of other people. Psychologists have always known that feelings and emotions are elements of perception and cognition. How we feel affects what we see and how we understand the world around us. The success of Goleman's work is indicative of a realization within management that many of the unsolved problems of organizations stem from a deficit of emotional intelligence rather than an absence of task-specific skills and abilities that can be more conventionally measured through psychometric tests of cognitive abilities.

There are many features of organizational life that militate against the further development of new learning to strengthen existing expertise. They have little to do with the innate or basic abilities of people and a great deal to do with the kinds of attitudes, feelings and patterns of motivation that different work settings nurture. Some organizations develop cultures and working relationships that encourage positive attitudes to new learning; others hold them back.

Consider, for example, just two variables: the willingness of managers in an organization to promote learning and staff development and to make resources available to achieve this and the willingness of employees to approach new learning in a positive, welcoming spirit. These two dimensions open up a number of analytical possibilities for which different organizations will supply many examples, as shown in Figure 3.2.

Quadrant (a) is clearly a situation where one would expect to find evidence of a high commitment among employees to new learning opportunities, a willingness to take risks and to be challenged. Quadrant (b), on the other hand, defines situations where we would expect employees to strike a somewhat cynical attitude to the training and development that might be on offer. If not cynicism, the attitude that might emerge is frustra-

Figure 3.2 Learning and organizational support

tion and anger when people feel denied opportunities for personal growth and development. People might feel that the 'psychological contract' of their employment is no longer adequate for they are not offered any real hope of personal development through new learning and experience. This is likely to be a very serious problem for organizations that employ highly trained, well-qualified staff. There is much evidence that such employees will simply leave, taking their knowledge and expertise with them.

Quadrant (c) is a not untypical one, where a management team is committed to change and development but the workforce appears not to be. Employees content to rely on their old skills often feel anxious about change, uncertain of its outcomes and possibly resistant to it. They strike a defensive attitude in the face of change. Quadrant (d) describes a range of possible settings all with one feature in common: an organizational culture in which no new learning takes place. This is a situation where there is no reflection on experience, no real effort to evaluate current working practices, and it has been described by Watkins and Marsick (1992), two theorists of work-based, experiential learning as 'non-learning.' This is clearly a situation to be avoided for it wastes human potential.

Non-learning or an unwillingness to develop new skills and ways of thinking is not something confined to people with low levels of education or expertise. Thorsten Veblen, that great commentator on the foibles of business life in the United States in the 1920s, highlighted the phenomenon of 'trained incapacity'. Merton (1958b:198) in a famous essay described it as follows:

> Trained incapacity refers to that state of affairs in which one's abilities function as inadequacies or blind spots. Actions based upon training and skills which have been successfully applied in the past may result in inappropriate responses *under changed conditions*.

Merton detected this phenomenon as an all too typical feature of bureaucracy and believed it nurtured a distinctive bureaucratic personality. Individuals so formed are often incapable of appreciating the goals of their organization and become obsessed with administering the means to achieve them. Clients and those they work with often experience this as arrogance, haughtiness and inflexibility.

The key point here is that the structure of work organizations can exert a decisive influence on the character of those who work in them. Depending on the kind of influence exerted, people can be encouraged to think either creatively and innovatively or remain trapped in assumptions that prevent them from doing so. As Gareth Morgan points out, 'ways of thinking tend to generate ways of acting ... limit your thinking and you will limit your range of action' (1997:351).

Expertise and values

Under all the circumstances of normal organizational life in a complex, knowledge-based economy, trained incapacity would be a serious hazard. There are circumstances, however, when it is not the willingness of employees to change that is the problem. When people are forced through the exercise of power to act against their best judgement serious, sometimes catastrophic consequences can occur. The astronauts of Challenger 10 flew to their deaths because NASA managers prioritized publicity over scientific – in this case, engineering – advice. The O-rings in the rocket booster had a design fault. Under the conditions of a severe drop in air temperature the seal did not work properly. The engineers warned against the flight on the unusually cold January morning but were overruled by their managers who had not informed the top-level decision makers in NASA of the problem. The result was catastrophic.

The exercise of power can distort the development and application of expertise. This is an extremely controversial area of public debate. In the United States in the 1960s and 1970s academic radicals castigated US intellectuals for the compromises they made with corporate and state power in the so-called 'military–industrial complex'. Both Chomsky (1992) and C. Wright Mills (1959) claimed that scientists and academics had compromised their values, their commitment to reason and scholarship to service the US war machine. The scientists they criticized had their counterparts in the Soviet bloc and a previous generation had, of course, been willing to apply their expertise to the service of Hitler's Third Reich. German scientists managed a euthanasia programme for mental defectives; they carried out pointless medical experiments on children. German engineers and chemists supplied Zyklon B gas to the gas chambers their civil engineering colleagues had designed.

There is a current debate about whether the needs of industry, commerce and the state are distorting the development of knowledge in modern societies. The environmentalist George Monbiot (2000) has claimed, for instance, that UK universities depend increasingly on corporate finance for their research and that this distorts the work they do. He notes as an example that five times as much is spent on oil and gas research as on renewable energy (2000:289). Biological research is heavily funded by bio-technology corporations. His conclusion is that 'Science in Britain is in danger of being reduced to a search for new applications of existing knowledge' (2000:299). And a key feature of the situation is that the needs of the global environment, and certainly of the poorest people on Earth, are not being met.

These are complex questions but they do highlight that expertise is inseparable from the frameworks of values within which it is nurtured, applied and altered. Values are not just disembodied guides to the rules we should follow. They are woven into the textures of our working lives, shaping both the means and ends of what we do. They are built into the patterns of our working relationships and the ways we value and manage people. In this way they are crucial elements of how people come to think of themselves and, indeed, of how they think and what they think about.

4 Solving problems, situated learning and dominant discourse

The impetus which enables you to fly is our great human possession. Everybody has it. It is a feeling of the connection one has with every source of power. But it is frightening! It is devilishly dangerous! That is why the majority of people are so willing to renounce any idea of flying and prefer to stroll quietly along the pavement and obey the law.

From *Demian* by Hermann Hesse

This chapter discusses problem solving as a powerful activity for 'situated learning'. Problem solving is a central activity in knowledge productivity. All new knowledge derives from finding new ways to handle old problems. The following two elements are covered:

Aims

➤ the rational approach;

➤ the socially centred approach.

Other, now familiar themes are also raised, illustrated and discussed in the chapter. These include the following:

➤ reflexivity, reflection and super-complexity;

➤ power, control and status;

➤ the dominant narrative in problem solving.

The notion of the rational or pragmatic manager discussed in Part 1 is of great relevance in this chapter. We show that this model of problem solving is an inadequate one in the circumstances of the global knowledge economy.

There are many approaches to solving problems and many techniques. Problem solving is a varied and variable activity and as such it offers organizations a real opportunity to start developing a new paradigm for management and a new way of working. This is because problem solving is fundamentally a 'situated activity' (see Chapter 5) and as such offers much potential for authenticity, reality and relevance in learning.

The rational approach

The rational approach to problem solving offers a structured and traditionally 'scientific' approach based on cause and effect reasoning, the elimination of variables and a reductionist paradigm. Here all the elements of a problem in a system are carefully identified, reduced to the simplest descriptions and measured precisely. In certain situations this is absolutely appropriate, in fact this approach has given humanity many gains and advances. It enables us to predict, control, construct explanations and offers the possibility of accuracy in planning. As discussed in Chapter 2, Newtonian scientific method applied to organizational life is the norm for many managers, with measurement and control being the dominant narrative of such thinking.

In part, the interest in Japanese approaches to management (so dominant in the United Kingdom at least during the 1980s and 1990s and still in operation around the world today) could explain this. Since the late 1940s, the Japanese economy has seen exceptional and rapid growth. Japan moved from a bankrupt economy to a major player in the world economy in 50 years.

It is interesting to note that the work of Frederick Taylor (scientific management) was a best-selling book in Japan during the 1950s. The Japanese adapted and developed Taylorism with great effect and some would argue that this played a part in their economic success. However, it is also clear that Japanese approaches are not simply applied Taylorism. They seem to have taken the ideas and developed them with a Japanese logic that is clearly different to that of western peoples.

The central point is that the rational approach alone, particularly as conceived by the pragmatic manager, can sometimes drive out creativity and a sense of real innovation and offer the false comfort of being ethically neutral because it is believed to be 'objective'. The moral implications here are significant for the sense of the rational has the potential to reduce people to be viewed as 'means to an end' rather than 'ends' in themselves. This risks a denial of our very humanity.

Case study 4.1 (which extends the Company A case in Chapter 2) provides one example of rationality in problem solving.

Case study 4.1

Company A (Company A is Japanese owned but managed by Europeans)

Background

Company A, an automotive parts maker, faces two huge technical challenges in the future:

1 the pressure to reduce emissions from motor vehicles;
2 the uncertain future of the internal combustion engine.

It also faces a commercial challenge. Released from a 'tied' contract to an exclusive supplier, the company needs to seek out and build relationships with new customers. It needs to find ways in which it can meet the specific and individual needs of its new customers in the same way that it always has for its long-established customers. In production it needs to develop a more flexible approach and encourage innovation and development. Company A feels that these challenges will be met through a knowledge-productive workforce that has a well-developed strategic capability.

To help meet this challenge Company A makes use of the Kaizen approach to problem solving. The policy is for every member of staff, from senior managers to shopfloor operators, to take part in the Kaizen process in order to improve the way they work. Kaizen is operated at two main levels of activity – Kaizen Team and three-day Kaizen. Because of the imperatives of 'lean production' they are now moving to a one-day Kaizen.

Issues tackled in Kaizen include scrap reduction, health and safety topics, quality improvements, cost reduction on consumables and set-up reductions and efficiency gains. The company sets aside time and resources for this initiative within the normal working week. Kaizen activity is often inter-disciplinary and sometimes involves customers and suppliers.

The tools and techniques of Kaizen consisted of problem solving, PDCA (Plan, Do, Check, Action), teamworking and brainstorming. It appears that Kaizen activity is the model of both efficiency and effectiveness. It also involves people in inter and multi-disciplinary working – a model of Mode I and Mode II knowledge integrated in a knowledge-productive way.

But ...

Managers in Company A readily admit that they are 'Tayloristic' and believe in the scientific methods of F.W. Taylor. Company A is very heavily biased towards the 'objective' and this has served them well in the past. Problem solving is focused on incremental continuous improvement, and while this has been very beneficial in the past it now tends to result in very minor gains.

▶

And ...

There is evidence to suggest that Kaizen activities are declining and the take-up of new projects is reducing. This is partly due to the 'lean production' philosophy that has made Kaizen lean also (down to one-day Kaizen events from three-day Kaizen events).

It may be that the Kaizen logic has served its purpose and has reached a plateau. This is often the case if the rational approach to problem solving becomes a routine or a set procedure. Kaizen has turned Company A into a world-class player but it now seems to be limiting its progress in creativity and innovation because the practice does not allow for alternative methodologies. A new, more flexible approach needs to be developed to problem solving in Company A if it is to make the large steps forward it needs rather than the incremental ones it currently has. Kaizen needs to be revitalized and other, less formalized approaches introduced.

In the Company A case the idea of 'plateauing' through rationality in problem solving is introduced. Case study 4.2 illustrates the concept very well.

Case study 4.2

Engineering Co.

Engineering Co. is a large (in terms of market share, plant and international coverage) multinational engineering company. It is US owned but the case was investigated at a UK site. It is constantly aware of the serious threat of competition.

In order to meet the competitive challenge Engineering Co. created a new corporate 'customer led' strategy. Senior management hoped that this would enable them to maintain and develop further their world market position.

They communicated the strategy to the world sites using a great number of slogans, for example: 'continuous improvement', 'benchmarking', 'learning organization', 'common approach', 'we're in it for the long haul', 'people are our major asset'. They also published numerous manuals, texts and made many presentations. The content of all this was issued by the parent company. Key staff were expected to implement these directives. The contents, while recognizing the need to make operational and structural changes within the organization, also acknowledged the importance of gaining the commitment of the whole workforce. The new strategy involved dramatic changes that revolved around a review and subsequent introduction of new production methods and new management approaches. Engineering Co.'s senior management knew what they wanted and imposed this on all world sites regardless of local custom, culture and practice.

Problem solving was part of this new approach. The concept of the 'Engineering Co. seven-point problem solving plan' was introduced. All problems had to be solved using the seven stages. This had the effect of dramatically improving the employees' ability in problem solving. However, over time this ability plateaued – probably because there was no scope for alternative approaches. The new innovation had become a basic procedure enshrining both good and bad practice together.

Both cases illustrate the need for variety and changes in approaches to problem solving. What starts on one day as a new and innovative process can quickly become an old procedure, confirming the past ways of doing things. Both organizations feel the pressures of pace, time and complexity and respond with rationality (see Chapter 2). The second issue raised by these cases is that rationality enables progress, sometimes quite rapid progress. But, paradoxically, it also restricts and inhibits.

Thirdly, the issue of management power and control is inherent in these cases. In Company A there is a genuine attempt to involve people in working on the problems of the workplace. Problem solving is seen as a major contributor to people's development. Success in Kaizen is rewarded tangibly. However, the gains of a continuous incremental improvement process become limited over time and consequently the desire to participate declines unless new challenges and new approaches can be found to make bigger gains.

Within Engineering Co. problem solving is also seen as an important activity but the management style is one of imposition, almost as if they are saying, 'you will solve problems and you will do it like this'. The response of employees to this style is not necessarily compliance, as managers might assume, nor is it overt antagonism or aggression. In such situations the response of employees is much more subtle and often takes the form of what Gerard Egan calls the 'shadow-side' of an organization. As Egan puts it, 'Because all companies and institutions are both delightfully and infuriatingly human, they have a shadow-side' (1993:33), and

> The shadow-side activities of the business then have two distinct characteristics. They are outside ordinary management processes because they are covert, informal, or even undiscussable; and they are economically significant, they add value, or very often, add direct or indirect costs, including lost opportunity costs, that escape ordinary accounting procedures. (1993:33)

At Engineering Co. UK there is a considerable amount of shadow-side behaviour and much of it comes into the category of 'adding to costs' and 'loss of opportunity'. In addition here, then, is another example of the moral dimension at work. Despite the rhetoric Engineering Co.'s senior management view employees as a means to an end and it is economically costly.

The socially centred approach

Einstein said: 'You cannot solve a problem with the thinking that created it.'

If reason and argument invariably generated new ideas then we would have been living in Utopia for generations! Unfortunately what takes place in organizations has as much to do with underlying structures of feeling and the interplay of micro politics as it has with underlying models of organizational change and individual development. What is more, the proposition that members of organizations can find their own way forward to new solutions if they apply themselves to the task is clearly flawed. The sheer complexity and ultimate unknowability (Soros, 2000) of complex social reality is a reminder that our ideas about how the world functions and changes are inevitably always one step behind the reality we are trying to understand.

Members of organizations therefore have to step outside the constraints of their own thinking properly to understand how they might approach the changes of the future. As raised in Chapter 1, there is also the realm of 'super-complexity'. This is the area of epistemological doubt and of different claims to the validity of knowledge. We live in a world where epistemological validity of science is severely questioned by people who insist that there are 'other ways of knowing'. We live in a world where it can no longer be taken for granted that the output of organizations in the knowledge-based economy – profits for stakeholders, competition, new technology, etc. – are believed to have any intrinsic value. There are real doubts whether or not such an economy is environmentally or socially sustainable. We live in a society where the risks of continuing to work and produce in the way in which we do are conceived of by some as no longer manageable (Adam *et al.*, 2000) There is clearly, therefore, a limit to our rationality. To know this is to grasp something of the idea of super-complexity.

The second idea, again introduced in Chapter 1 is 'reflexivity'. Through the work of Anthony Giddens (1989) and Ulrich Beck (1992, 1994) and, more recently, that of George Soros (2000) this idea has received a great deal of attention in contemporary social theory. The core of it is that the act of trying to understand the world is one which simultaneously changes it. Ideas about social reality do not merely reflect it but actually constitute it. There are, of course, limits. The intellectual force of a dominant discourse can limit the ideas that people have access to. The exercise of power, as illustrated in the previous section, can do the same. Men and women may not always be able to change the circumstances of their lives, but those circumstances are not fixed or beyond control. History and hope, as the poet Seamus Heaney once noted, can sometimes chime together. People denied opportunities to think in fresh ways do, however, find ways to do so. There are moments in history and in the lives of individuals when people transform their view of themselves and their world.

On a social level, the corporate curriculum framework provides a process for problem solving by helping people in organizations to become knowledge productive. The key process is to help them become aware of the ways in which they approach the problems they seek to solve. This can be achieved through intense dialogue that focuses on the deep analysis of dominant narratives which surround a problem. Reflection on practice is a central ingredient of this activity and reflexivity is a common 'outcome'.

Reflection and reflexivity in action

This section offers both an account and a 'model' of the socially centred approach to problem solving incorporating the corporate curriculum framework.

At a recent conference of the Vanwoodman Global Institute, a virtual organization that meets annually, the problems of three organizations were reframed using the corporate curriculum. Delegates (about 30 from the United Kingdom and the Netherlands) came to the conference primed to work on the problems presented by members of three invited case study organizations. They came from a variety of backgrounds with a range of expertise and included academics, consultants, teachers, managers, priests and students.

The first case was the oil company, Shell. A Dutch consultant working with Shell highlighted the elements of a major organizational problem concerned with information and communication technology (ICT). This case study was clearly that of a major global corporation relying on high levels of technology.

The second case study presented was that of a community group in an inner-city area of Gateshead in the north-east of England. St Chad's Family Centre provides services for families in an area of considerable deprivation. The challenge for St Chad's is to sustain development while retaining autonomy from the demands of both local government and the bodies that fund them.

The third case study was an Educational Action Zone (EAZ) in East Durham. EAZ are a major development of public policy in England and are an attempt to boost educational attainments in socially deprived areas. They rely on public–private partnerships and are expected to introduce innovative changes in schools and communities that improve educational performance.

Each case study represented an aspect of organizational change that required new ways of thinking. The challenge for the case study organizations themselves is to find new ways forward to cope with the uncertainties of the future. The challenge for delegates to the conference was to explore how ideas about the corporate curriculum and knowledge productivity could inform the work of the case studies.

Work on case studies 4.3–4.5 was organized in three phases. The first was the case study organizations making a presentation to the conference about their organization and the issues and problems they faced thus presenting a number of questions for the conference to address. Following this, delegates joined focused discussion groups with members of the case study organizations. The task set for them was to work out ways in which members of the case study organizations could learn their way out of the problems they faced. It was also to reflect on the process of managing these discussions within the conference. A third element in the process was for people to mix between the three groups by working in pairs. Each member of the pair took about half an hour to discuss with the other their perceptions and understandings of the process and emerging issues so far. This offered an element of personal reflection and peace facilitated by another person in the mentoring way (see Chapter 5).

Case study 4.3

Shell

Harold Janssen from Overmars Organisatie Adviseurs in the Netherlands presented this case study. The problem, in essence, was how Shell could best integrate its ICT systems into its business operations. The challenge is a global one, for the company operates throughout the world, and one that requires systems which will overcome differences of culture, religion and politics. Lack of success over the past three years in solving this problem has led senior Shell managers to believe that the company needed a 'paradigm shift' in relation to ICT.

In 1998 the company set up Shell Services International, a quasi-commercial institution meant to act as a customer-related business centre to service other business divisions. By 1999 it had 5,200 employees, but the company encountered many problems of communication and of criticism that this service was too expensive. By the year 2000 there was widespread belief that the arrangements were not working, that there were huge losses and great dissatisfaction among staff, with many empoluees leaving. The new structures being proposed 'to stop the bleeding' are to build an IT systems for the Shell community. The idea here is that ICT requires a real human community to make it work. The problem is how to engineer such a shift within Shell. This was a clear instance, argued Harold Janssen, that the problem of being knowledge productive was not a question of acquiring more knowledge but of promoting new working relationships. The challenge was to find methods to promote new ways of thinking and to get a clearer vision of the problem.

Case study 4.4

St Chad's Family Centre, Gateshead

The Rev. Chris Atkinson, chair of the management committee, outlined the problem. He began by framing it historically. During the 1890s the population of Gateshead increased and within ten years was almost 200,000. This was an area for the skilled working class, who built ships on the Tyne. During the inter-war years the area experienced terrible poverty and after the Second World War many women moved into factory work, altering the demography and social geography of the district. During the 1950s working-class skilled jobs in heavy industry were exported to the Far East. High-rise flats transformed the nature of the community. In the 1980s a property slump meant that a third of the houses in this part of Gateshead were bought by absentee landlords, resulting in multiple occupancy and a breakdown of family life. The area has a high rate of pregnancy and one-third of the population is single and unmarried. Drink, violence and drugs are all problems.

St Chad's Church wished to respond to these circumstances. The church community was aware that many women were isolated and that families needed more support. During the 1990s through hard work, organization and bids for National Lottery funding a family centre was built. This centre provides nursery support for children, counselling and a range of other services to help families in the area. The project has experienced rapid growth with a non-professional management committee. It provides training services for its staff and performs a vital function in family support.

The problem for St Chad's is how to move from a community-based structure to one with more effective management skills. It is also how to retain the autonomy and local commitment of the project while working more closely with the funding agencies and local government. As a busy project there is a real problem in finding the space to think strategically and to plan and prioritize. How should this be done?

Case study 4.5

Peterlee Education Action Zone

The director of the EAZ – Jo Williams – presented the case study. Carol Johnson – the literacy consultant – added perspective of a practitioner in working with parents and children. Both were joined later by two head teachers from primary schools in the EAZ.

The Education Action Zone is part of the National Literacy Strategy. It focuses on 24 schools in East Durham. EAZ have developed out of a very changed con-

▶

77

text of educational policy in England. Education has become market led and competitive and schools have to demonstrate success in league tables. On the other hand, in areas such as Peterlee there are severe problems of social deprivation. Peterlee is a 50-year-old 'new' town, drawing its population from families with roots in mining and farming. On national league tables its schools score highly in absenteeism and poor results. The area has a high crime rate, one of the highest rates of teenage pregnancy in the country and a record of poor health and high unemployment. There is a culture of low expectations. There is high staff turnover in many schools and both teachers and parents often have a limited frame of reference in their thinking about education and learning. The cultural capital of the district is seriously depleted.

Head teachers in the district saw the opportunities open to them through Education Action Zone funding and applied successfully for it. The projects that take place within the EAZ involve local schools and cover such things as training, the development of teaching materials, initiatives such as toy libraries and parent and toddler groups. A key question to concerns inter-agency communication. How can staff on the Education Action Zone work creatively with colleagues from other agencies? How can the EAZ sustain innovation in the context of wider social forces that undermine education in the district? Why does change happen in some schools more than in others?

After the presentations delegates reviewed what they had heard and identified what seemed to be common themes arising from them. Discussion of these common themes crystallized into nine main observations, as follows:

1 Political issues are present and are often unique to each organization.
2 Time stress – the pressure to achieve in a short time span.
3 Where precisely does the knowledge-productive challenge lie?
4 Pressure to change and improve.
5 Further micro-political conflicts within each organization as a result of the pressure to improve and change.
6 Tensions between managerial requirements and professional/vocational commitments and values.
7 Key problems centred on patterns of working relationships within each case.
8 Each case study was embedded in a wider organizational and community matrix .
9 Uncertainty about the future, unpredictability in planning and decision making.

Feedback from case study 4.3

Harold Janssen reported on the Shell case study. The practical outcome for him was the realization that the Shell strategy for its ICT framework was unlikely to be successful. The top-down strategy to create an ICT community for Shell ignored the importance of the development of communication and a sense of belonging among the micro communities of different business units and of the IT staff attached to them. There was the deep-seated fear of many large organizations of anarchy. Harold Janssen had come to the view, however, that what was perceived as anarchy was probably one of the necessary conditions for the development of a successful ICT community. The key task was to release the co-creativity of the ICT community in ways that helped them communicate better and meet the needs of business units more directly.

He had been led to these conclusions by the work of the case study group. It had helped him highlight the importance of reflexivity, the relevance of sociological ideas about community and philosophical ideas about the value of human beings. The case study discussions had not been confined to particular domains of expertise but had deliberately crossed many of the boundaries between different disciplines. Harold Janssen noticed that no one was forcing a particular viewpoint, that there was indeed a synergy of ideas. The challenge was to replicate that process in the context of Shell. He felt these ideas provided him with the means to achieve that.

Feedback from case study 4.4

The St Chad's group reported their practical outcomes around two themes. The first concerned peace and stability – one of the key elements of the corporate curriculum. It had been difficult to achieve this and the thinking space it should have created. The St Chad's team had come to realize that many of their problems stemmed from their relationship with funding agencies. They needed to create more space in order to handle this problem more effectively by buying in expertise to leave the key staff to concentrate on their core mission. Chris Atkinson of St Chad's explained to delegates that the process of stepping back, of reflecting, had been invaluable. It had highlighted the need for St Chad's staff to think more widely but above all to create time in their busy lives to do so.

The analytical elements of the corporate curriculum had helped this group think very clearly about the problems of the community project. It helped them focus their questions and look at other organizations of a similar type and define new learning points within their own organization. These outcomes arose not from a process of working down a checklist, rather the elements of the corporate curriculum enabled a fluent, analytical conversation about St Chad's to take place. Crossing the boundary from their own base in Bensham, Tyne and Wear, to the seminar room of the university had enabled them to establish some useful critical distance upon which they hoped to build new ideas.

Feedback from case study 4.5

The group working on the Education Action Zone had to cope with a number of difficulties. At times the discussion became intense and indeed on one occasion the case study team were asked to leave the room. This crisis point proved to be a productive one. It broke down the division between insiders and outsiders and cleared up some confusions about the role of the group itself.

The two head teachers from the EAZ took a very positive role in reporting back. This was evidence in itself of the group having taken ownership of some of the ideas examined. They reported that they had used corporate curriculum tools to help them stand back from their situation and had identified the main problem. Changes in education that had set up market principles and systems for measuring school performance had been painful for staff teams. The process of explaining what this felt like to delegates clarified for the head teachers that they themselves had taken on too much responsibility to solve the problems at the schools. In order to protect their staff they had paradoxically undermined the ability of their colleagues to co-create and contribute new ideas to solve problems. What they had done, in effect, was to empower the problem and not the staff to help solve it. One head reported that she now regarded her perception of the busy school as somewhat misleading. Her concern to see everyone occupied and active had limited the amount of time available to colleagues for inter-professional communication and reflection. She was determined to solve this problem as soon as she returned to work. The case study team felt that the conference had been extremely useful in enabling them to reframe their sense of what the problems in the Education Action Zone were.

Comments on the problem-solving process

Although the groups had different problems to work on they followed some common methods of doing so. All groups used the corporate curriculum framework as both a focus and a monitor of progress. All groups asked questions, challenged information and pushed boundaries. There were moments of crisis where the case study organizations felt very challenged. The element of self-regulation played a crucial and very necessary part here. Participants could have become defensive and entrenched. They could have simply defended their positions and held on to the dominant narratives they had arrived with. But they did not. Through the high levels of creative turmoil, as well as periods of peace and stability, colleagues were helped to think through their arguments and reframe the narrative.

All of the working groups were skilful at reflection in action. There were times when the groups took a break and pairs were seen walking and talking together, providing high levels of mentoring support for each other. There seemed a tacit understanding among the groups that the solution to the problems lay within the organizations themselves. This committed them to a great deal of open communication and support for the case study staff in ways that presented them with challenging questions and also helped them towards new solutions. In all of the groups there was a high degree of energy, laughter and fun.

Initially there was a tendency in each group to focus on the more technically specific 'how' questions. It soon became apparent that 'how' questions are strongly 'solution' oriented. While this may not be a problem, all groups were seeking a solution, asking 'how' tends to focus on the problem and encourage the thinking that created it in the first place. The groups moved into asking a range of open-ended 'who', 'what', 'when' and 'why' questions. This had the effect of shifting the group away from immediate solutions to an exploratory process aimed at deeper understanding, full participation and engagement in the dialogue. This ultimately led the case organizations to start both to 'own' the problem by reframing it through intense dialogue and viewing it differently. People's dominant narratives changed.

Few of the groups relied on domain-specific subject expertise. In fact the domain-specific knowledge widened beyond the obvious as the meeting of a variety of minds from mixed domains collectively created a new way of 'knowing'. This experience resonates with the case study of the fish food company presented in Chapter 3.

The extent to which these discussions have an 'output' can be measured by the responses of the members of the case studies themselves. They engaged in a problem-solving process of reflection in action and their judgements on the utility of the conference represent evidence of its success. At the same time, the process of reflection in action by conference members on the ways in which the problems presented through the case studies were handled enabled us to identify several areas where our prevailing understanding of the corporate curriculum and knowledge productivity needed further development. In particular, people's values play a crucial part in their motivation and commitment, and in valuing people and accepting diversity open communication becomes possible. We argue very strongly that it is this that enables people to really understand the issues and problems they face, and in understanding them they are able to identify and commit to a new way forward and a solution with which they can identify. This is reflexivity in action.

The key ideas highlighted in this chapter concern values, boundaries and the process of co-creation. On the question of boundaries, it is clear that people concerned with the corporate curriculum and with learning organizations need to reframe their understanding of the boundaries around and within organizations. In particular, the two potent ideas of 'reflexivity' and 'super-complexity' highlight that there is a complexity to the ordinary work of most people in most organizations which prevailing conceptions of the learning organization have not yet grasped. Secondly, it is clear that all forms of learning are inescapably bound up with values. No credible account of learning in organizations can be given without a description of the values that the learning is expected to sustain or reflect.

Finally, since learning is a social, situated and essentially creative process, it is essential to explore in any organization the ways in which people are either helped to work together creatively or hindered in doing so (Lave and Wenger, 1991). Significant change and transformation in how organizations work can only come from people working together in ways that allow them to understand and communicate with one another better. Once people are aware of the meta-cognitive dimensions of their learning they become more effective learners. This proposition was most powerfully demonstrated in the responses of case study participants to the processes of being engaged in this conference. The methodologies involved in the ideas of the corporate curriculum – the ways of thinking and approaching problems and of asking questions – proved to be a powerful tool of thinking and analysis. When this tool is refined to include in a systematic way the elements of values and co-creation it proves itself to be a robust method of knowledge productivity. Alternatively, we may just 'prefer to stroll quietly along the pavement and obey the law'.

5 Generating new knowledge

Knowledge can be communicated, but not wisdom. One can find it, be fortified by it, do wonders through it, but one cannot communicate and teach it.

From Siddartha by Herman Hesse

Aims

This chapter is structured as follows:

➤ Introduction

➤ The backdrop

➤ Mentoring

➤ Situated learning

➤ Complexity at work and learning to be knowledge productive

➤ Conclusion

This chapter is based on two articles: Alred, G. and Garvey, B. (2000) Learning to be knowledge productive: the contribution of mentoring, *Mentoring and Tutoring*, December, vol. 8 no. 3 pp 262–72 and Garvey, B. and Alred, G. (2001) Mentoring and the tolerance of complexity, *Futures*, vol. 33, July pp 519–30. Reprinted with permission from Elsevier Science (Website for *Futures*: http://www.tandf.co.uk)

Introduction

Knowledge is the cornerstone of the knowledge economy and yet acquiring knowledge is not sufficient in itself. Wisdom is important for it is through the experience of knowledge that a person becomes wise. Wisdom, we argue, is akin to the idea of 'alertness' and the awareness of possibilities.

This chapter is a discussion of what is at stake as people and organizations move towards being knowledge productive, towards individual and shared perceptions of knowledge productivity. It is also about the generation of knowledge and the development of wisdom. In the main it focuses on the social setting of the workplace and in particular suggests that mentoring activity holds much potential as a way of developing not only knowledge but also wisdom.

We start with a number of key assumptions. First, knowledge productivity is a valid and valuable perspective. Linked to this is the idea that the creation of new knowledge 'depends on tapping the tacit and often highly subjective insights, intuitions, and hunches of individual employees and making those insights available for testing and use by the company as a whole' (Nonaka, 1996:19). In addition, 'the key to the process is personal commitment, the employees' sense of identity with the enterprise and its mission' (1996:19). Knowledge, as opposed to information, arises as much serendipitously as through planning and standard practices. Learning to be knowledge productive is a potential present in all aspects of employees' experiences, motivated by personal commitment to the opportunities and demands encountered at work.

Secondly, the concept of a corporate curriculum captures the complex, diverse nature of learning in organizations. The application and use of the corporate curriculum framework can and often does lead to the production of knowledge. Thirdly, knowledge is the result of the process of learning. Learning, in all its richness and manifestations, becomes the central activity in a knowledge-productive environment. Hence a theory of learning is essential to make explicit how learning is perceived, understood, enhanced and applied. However, learning as a process, disembodied and general, does not go far enough. What is required is a view of learning that helps us talk about the *person* of the learner – the employer/employee as a learner, powerfully and constructively self-aware and optimally engaged in the organization's activities. It is this that shifts us into the realms of wisdom.

In addition to this, 'it is groups, not individuals, that adapt to their environments and .... this is the basis for the peculiar genius of the human species. We are a successful species because we cheat; we tell each other the answers' (Emler and Heather, 1980). One important 'answer' we learn is how to learn, and we do this essentially with the help of others. From birth onwards, we learn in the context of relationships, including acquiring the ability to learn independently.

The backdrop

Learning and experience

Illustration 5.1

'What did you learn at school today, Steve?'

'We read a story, and played in the gym, and I did some writing about my holiday.'

'Yes, but what did you learn?'

'I finished a page in my maths book, and I've got a new friend, he's called Tom.'

'Yes, but did you learn anything?'

'Can Tom come to my house?'

Saying what you have learned from experience is not always easy. Describing what you have done comes more readily. Translating description into awareness of the lasting effects of experience is a challenge of a different order. It is one that could be seen as a central aim of formal education, if going to school is to prepare people for going to work in a world where knowledge is a key resource, and uncertainty and 'super-complexity' a certain feature.

Illustration 5.2

'What did you learn at work today, Steve?'

'Most of the morning was taken up with discussions with suppliers. After that, I finished the annual report. It was difficult and I could have done with more time, but it had to be in today. I arranged an appraisal interview with my line manager and then couldn't stop thinking about it when I should have been getting on with the latest development project. And just before I was coming home, a colleague wanted some help with a customer.'

'Yes, but what did you learn?'

'That's the second time you've asked me that! I don't know really, it was a fairly ordinary day, much like any other. I suppose I was surprised the report took so long, and I was pleased to be able to make some helpful suggestions about dealing with the customer.'

'Yes, but what did you learn that was new, what knowledge did you produce?'

'What knowledge did I produce – that's a strange question! I don't know, but it has made me think about how I interact with customers. Why do you ask?'

In contrast to Steve the schoolboy, Steve the employee has more to say about the day's activities. He reveals some insight into how he learns, a sense of something he is good at, how he can be distracted, how he needs to give tasks sufficient time, his ability to work under pressure. This second snippet of conversation touches upon a number of issues that are the province of learning. These issues come to the fore in understanding organizations when they are looked at from the perspective of knowledge productivity. These issues include, for example, time management, relationships, communication skills and sharing what you know, problem solving, creativity, emotions, meta-cognitive skills and a capacity to reflect upon behaviour and experience. In a knowledge-productive organization Steve will ask himself the question – 'What did I learn at work today?' – and will have several answers.

The above illustration highlights the need for dialogue and discussion about the things we encounter in the workplace. We believe in the old maxim that 'we don't know what we think until we discuss it with someone'. This leads us to the practice of mentoring. Mentoring is one way of developing a meaningful dialogue with another person and has the potential to shift experience from 'knowing' to wisdom or knowledge in action.

Mentoring

Mentoring is an important type of learning relationship, found increasingly in a range of occupational settings. We speculate that this is because mentoring activity encourages and facilitates informal or 'open' learning. More traditional formal or 'closed' approaches to learning are increasingly being criticized for not delivering enhanced capability and performance to organizations. Against this background it becomes inevitable that alternatives to the 'formal' are investigated by organizations.

Mentoring is versatile and complex. It is used for a variety of purposes in organizations and often where transitions are necessary. We propose that inherent in mentoring is the capacity that one person has to help another and that this capacity needs to survive and thrive in the complex environment of the knowledge economy. However, there are challenges. Despite the many acknowledged benefits of mentoring, it is not always recognized as a legitimate activity and is not always valued sufficiently within the work environment. For example, organizations sometimes mix up the roles of line manager and mentor. The authority that comes with a direct line-management position is not appropriate in a mentoring partnership. Mentoring is not about power and authority differentials but about learning and development within a trusting relationship. Therefore the mentor is best situated between the organization and the mentee, knowledgeable about both and responsive to both.

There are many factors that influence mentoring in an organization. These include the perceived purpose of mentoring, organizational culture and management style, and the 'dominant logic' (Bettis and Prahalad, 1995) and organizational environment. Each of these will be discussed in turn.

Purpose of mentoring

The purpose of mentoring is not always made clear to people. Some may associate mentoring with the concept of fast tracking employees with exceptional talent. Here, mentoring is often conceived in an instrumental way with it being viewed as a 'management tool'. This tends to encourage mentor control, an emphasis on giving advice and, in some cases, manipulation. This form is more akin to coaching behaviour.

Another view on the purpose of mentoring is to take a more holistic perspective, with development of the mentee as the central objective. The argument here is that financial success in an organization is a consequence of having developed and capable people. Where the development of the mentee and organizational goals coincide it is appropriate to talk of a 'mentoring organization', where employees use a number of people to assist in different ways to enhance their learning at work. Where the mentee's agenda and the organization's goals do not coincide, this becomes acceptable also as a recognition that diversity means a pluralistic agenda. This takes us beyond the instrumental approach (often associated with training and coaching) and into the realms of capability building, where people are able to exercise judgements, make decisions and develop wisdom in their work. Here ideas of 'one best way', 'singing from the same hymn sheet' and so on seem rather simplistic objectives – an optimistic misjudgement of the reality of the workplace.

Culture and management style

There are organizations where mentoring and other supportive behaviours work against the grain of organizational culture. Much learning at work, and much of the nature of organizational culture, stems from informal rather than formal activities. An effective mentor knows this and is effective by virtue of understanding how the organization works and how to get on in it. The mentor is in a key position, standing 'off-line' between the organization, its values, culture and practices, and the developing employee.

Dominant logic

In general, the informal learning that takes place in mentoring and other learning processes is affected by what has been referred to as 'the dominant logic'. This is an outlook that reflects organizational culture. The 'dominant logic' emphasizes the power of the organizational influence on individual thinking. This can be subtle and indirect as well as overt. Bettis and Prahalad (1995) argue that 'the dominant logic' influences both behaviour and thinking, and has the potential to both inhibit or enhance learning capabilities.

To sum up, the form mentoring takes is influenced by the perceived purpose of mentoring, the 'dominant logic', management style and culture of the organization. Paradoxically, mentoring can be both constructive and destructive, helpful and manipulative, confirm cultures and change them. Mentoring is about learning and learning is complex, paradoxical and associated with change. Mentoring also involves iterative learning, reflexive and reflective learning. These are essential learning processes in the complex environment of the knowledge economy.

Situated learning

In the context of workplace learning, concepts discussed in previous chapters such as 'situated learning' (Lave and Wenger, 1991) take on particular significance in relation to knowledge productivity and the generation of new knowledge. There can be little doubt that the message of 'situated learning' is very clear – learning is a social activity.

We suggest consistently through this book that the workplace is the context of knowledge productivity. It is very important for organizations that are concerned with knowledge productivity to appreciate the influence of the context or situation of *being* at work. It is also important to recognize that the knowledge produced starts out simply as an inevitable consequence of being at work, of doing the job. This may include such things as subject matter expertise leading to the design of a new product or procedure, or something less tangible, such as communication skills, or rapport with customers, or the ability to use turmoil creatively.

The significance of the current emphasis on workplace learning is not that learning did not take place until this new emphasis came along, but lies in the recognition that learning can and should be made more explicit. It lies in the idea that people can become more aware, and hence, potentially at least, more in control, of *what* and *how* they learn.

New learning may be refined and elaborated by subsequent reflection and rumination (Kolb, 1984), but learning *from* experience is at its centre, learning *as* experience. This is a central point of the theory of 'Situated learning' (Lave and Wenger, 1991). 'Situated learning' theory perceives learning as a form of participation and is therefore complementary to and supportive of the concept of knowledge productivity:

Learning viewed as situated activity has as its central defining characteristic a process that we call *legitimate peripheral participation*. By this we mean to draw attention to the point that learners inevitably participate in communities of practitioners and that the mastery of knowledge and skill requires newcomers to move toward full participation in the sociocultural processes of a community . . . A person's intentions to learn are engaged and the meaning of learning is configured through the process of becoming a full participant in a sociocultural practice. This social process includes, indeed it subsumes, the learning of knowledgeable skills. (Lave and Wenger, 1991:29)

The key notion is 'legitimate peripheral participation'. *Peripheral* contrasts with *full*; it is a positive term and its conceptual antonyms are *unrelatedness* and *irrelevance*. It is a dynamic concept, suggesting an opening, a moving forward to greater participation in a sociocultural practice. This aspect of the theory of 'situated learning' provides a basis for critically challenging the role of formal training in organizations and at the same time it gives impetus to the value of informal, 'situated learning'.

The consequences of 'situated learning' are manifest in relationships with other members of the organization, for example through engagement in the organization's social practices, by contributing to the achievement of the goals and aspirations of the organization, and in the ways in which people relate to their concept of *self*. This is a positive outcome where employees develop a sense of belonging and of being valued in the organization. Employees develop diverse competence and a confidence in being *themselves* at work. In addition, 'situated learning' acknowledges the *person* of the learner, their sense of themselves as a learner, in relationship with others, and at large in the learning landscape where 'personnel and teams find their way and construct knowledge' (Kessels, 1996a:10).

In tying learning into authentic participation 'situated learning' highlights the importance of certain qualities of the learner, such as preparedness, tenacity, flexibility, alertness, resourcefulness, self-regulation and self-knowledge. To develop the 'self-knowledge' theme a little – self-knowledge, as a description of a concept, is an inadequate word. Self-knowledge is knowing what's out there (rather than what's inside, as if one might be transparent) – but as a participant. It feeds into the fantasy that all forms of judgement, wisdom and right feeling are really cognitive modes of knowledge. Self-knowledge is not practised in isolation. It is a quality that exists only in practice; small wonder that we do not find it (as 'self-knowledge' suggests we might) in internal scrutiny. Self-knowledge is developed in relation to the others and within an organization by reflection and dialogue and as a result of reflexivity. As a consequence of all this learning is a way of *being* in the social world, not a way of coming to *know* about it, let alone an extra to the 'real' business of work. It is a disposition or a cast of mind. Without this engagement, or participation, there is no learning and no knowledge productivity.

We have introduced in previous chapters the idea of language and talk as powerful mediums of social practice. Lave and Wenger (1991) cite the importance of stories in their studies. They make an important distinction between talk *within* a practice and talk *about* a practice. For people at work the purpose is not primarily to learn *from* talk as a substitute for legitimate peripheral participation but to learn *to* talk the language of the organization as the key to legitimate peripheral participation (see Chapter 8). This is of crucial importance in the creation of new knowledge.

The view of learning as situated acknowledges that individual motivation to participate goes beyond task knowledge and skill, i.e. being able to write more efficient software, or to develop new products. A deeper sense of the value of participation to the learner lies in *becoming* part of the organization, and in moving towards a greater sense of identity and self-confidence within it, hence the relevance and importance of the learning functions of the corporate curriculum – 'peace and stability' and 'meta-cognitive awareness and self-regulation' (see Chapter 2).

Mentoring is one way in which benefit can be developed from the situation of work, developing a sense of the *self* at work, learning the language of the organization and being valued through active participation in talk.

Complexity at work and learning to be knowledge productive

First, it is our understanding that learning to be knowledge productive is a social activity, influenced by the social setting. In the organizational setting we understood that learning is a process and activity which addresses a combination of short-, medium- and long-term goals. It is a complex activity and process with a moral dimension. We have argued that if people are viewed as a 'means to a commercial end' rather than 'ends in themselves' this is an immoral stance. Against this background we speculate here about complexity at work and learning using three organizational states. We draw these from Ralph Stacey's (1995) ideas, introduced in Chapter 2, on the application of complexity theory to organizations. He recognizes three types of organizational system: stable, unstable and complex. All are non-linear feedback systems, where there are many outcomes to any action. Group behaviour is more than the sum of individual behaviours, and small changes can escalate into major outcomes.

Learning in stable organizations

We speculate that learning in a stable organization takes place against a background of relatively clear paths, both short and long, that the learner will tread in the organization. Here there is an emphasis on means rather than ends, such that learning may involve largely instrumental teaching, perhaps in the form of the 'formal curriculum' (see Chapter 2). Activities such as coaching may relate well in this situation. In coaching the outcome of the learning intervention is often known in advance and the agenda for learning is either set by the coach or by the organization. We suggest that stability within an organization at the beginning of the twenty-first century is likely to be a short-lived reality. This brings with it some significant challenges as some organizations may behave as if they were stable but in reality their environment may be unstable or complex. Consequently, activities to support and encourage learning may be based on faulty assumptions. These assumptions, based on a concept of stability, may include a clear and recognizable career path and a continuity and stability of employment within the same organization. People with such assumptions may see learning activities or perhaps training as a way to maintain the existing system and thus be disappointed when training events do not match their expectations. This is not a knowledge-productive environment.

Learning in an unstable environment

Learning, as described above, we suggest, is severely challenged in an unstable environment. Learning activities are likely to become focused exclusively on short-term goals and the kind of interpersonal relationships necessary for 'situated learning' to flourish may disappear or be displaced by friendships between people sharing a common difficult fate (Rigsby *et al.*, 1998). Conversation may slip into the 'shadow-side' (Egan, 1993) where it has the potential paradoxically to be both destructive or add value. The outcome of conversations falling into the 'shadows', we suggest, depends on the prevailing management style and culture. The pragmatic manager may be pragmatic about learning in unstable times and therefore learning activities will be reduced, cut or dispensed with altogether. Survival may become the sole preoccupation within the organization and often this bid for survival has an individual focus rather than a collective one. Everyone for themselves – the ingredients of social disintegration and conflict.

Consider the case of Financial Institution B, illustrated in case study 5.1.

Case study 5.1

Financial Institution B

Financial Institution B is a large player. It has a long history and the management's thinking is rooted in its history. In recent times Financial Institution B found itself in an unstable situation. Its customers were leaving, its market share was shrinking and the competition was offering a whole range of different services. One of Financial Institution B's responses was to cut all 'unnecessary management development' and to focus only on 'technical' training. The idea was that management skills and behaviours were a luxury, and by focusing on the technical they would be able to improve product knowledge among employees and therefore regain market position.

It did regain its market position, but by merging with another financial services provider. However, five years on, with no management development activities, the company found itself with a huge knowledge and skills gap in management. All levels of management, whether newly appointed or aspiring, were finding it difficult to cope. They simply did not have the knowledge of skills necessary to perform the job.

This is a further example of a seemingly rational decision resulting in unforeseen consequences. It also illustrates the folly of short-term thinking and a misunderstanding of the importance of the knowledge-productive process.

Learning in a complex environment

A complex system is both stable and unstable. It is a dynamic system at the edge of instability, characterized by short-term predictability and long-term unpredictability. At the individual level, an employee may work in teams that have a short lifespan. A new team may make new demands so that previous learning needs to be revised: for instance, an individual may contribute by taking the lead in one team but find this approach is counterproductive in another. But while adaptation is important it is far from the whole story, as a complex system is dynamic and will change yet again as parts of the system act. There are few, if any, contented cows ruminating in complex systems.

Stacey (1995) describes a complex system as being in a state of 'bounded instability'. He suggests that there are limits in such a system but they do not operate in a deterministic fashion; and there are rules, but these are local and other rules are found in other parts of the system. Hence following rules does not ensure predictable outcomes, and is not always intelligent behaviour. The effects of actions of one part – an individual, a team, a department – arise in complex interactions with the actions of other parts. The best course of action is difficult to discern because the final outcome emerges in an unpredictable way from a multiplicity of actions by others. Hence decisions need to be coupled with a capacity and a readiness to deal positively with whatever ensues from the complex interactions of the whole. This includes the ability to compromise, to be resilient and to accept that there may not be a 'right' answer.

Boolean algebra gives a helpful formal description of complex systems existing in nature (Waldrop, 1992). Complex systems have also been modelled by arrays of interconnected light bulbs, where switching on and off is governed by simple local rules. The resulting patterns are the unpredictable result of multiple actions in complex interaction within the system; they are not planned and do not originate from any particular part of the system.

When the system is a human system, such as a manufacturing company or a hospital, and the capabilities to respond to what emerges are present, then there is potential for emergent innovation that is beneficial. A single light bulb in a Boolean array makes a difference because it is part of an open system, it is well connected, responds unambiguously to other light bulbs and sends clear messages. Contributing in a complex human system rests in part upon the equivalent human qualities such as being open, a good communicator, sensitive and empathic towards others and also being part of a broad network of people at work with both strong and weak connections.

Other examples of complexity, such as the performance of music (see Chapter 6), are perhaps more intuitively analogous to learning at work. The nature of a particular performance is complex: there are rules set by the score, the notes, the instruments and the limits of the performers, hence the instability is bounded; but the music collectively played is unique to that performance, to that occasion. The good conductor is one who knows he or she cannot control everything that happens but rather will allow the fullest participation of each player within the vision and spirit of the music. The classical recording industry thrives on the variety of performance that arises from the complexity of performing groups of musicians. What is new in a performance, the emergent innovation, is heard most explicitly when musicians improvise and it is striking that Drucker (1992) and Barrett (1998) have used the improvising jazz band as a metaphor for learning at work. The point made by these writers reminds us again of the importance of informal learning, of learning that departs from the rules, away from overt training and instruction, and within the daily flow and flux of experience at work.

Being knowledge productive in the complexity of the corporate curriculum

If a learner works in a complex environment we suggest that they will prosper and contribute if they can remain knowledge productive within a state of bounded instability. This requires perception of the situation for what it is. If the situation is a 'rich landscape of learning' then the successful learner will have an appreciation of themselves in respect of all seven elements of the corporate curriculum as well as their learning and performance at work. See illustration 5.3.

Illustration 5.3

Steve

Steve has difficulty with problem solving at work. Most of the problems that occur need to be resolved collectively.

One solution would be to put Steve on a problem-solving skills course run by the training co-ordinator. He would be instructed in the ways of solving problems and hopefully would return better equipped. But he may not. The training course may be interesting, but does it address Steve's difficulty? It probably addresses Steve's manager's issue and the training manager's agenda. If Steve attends the course both can tick a box to say that Steve is competent in problem solving.

Problem solving may be the manifesting difficulty but what else is here? Steve has to work in a group. Could this be the issue? Solution – put him on a teamworking course. Steve has to communicate with people when working as a team. Perhaps this is the issue? Solution – put him on a communication skills course. Steve may feel uncomfortable with certain members of the team. Solution – put him on an interpersonal skills course. Steve has to make presentations as part of problem solving. Perhaps this is the issue? Solution – put him on a presentation skills course.

The list could go on but would Steve, the team or his boss be any further forward? Maybe they would, maybe they would not.

The concept of a corporate curriculum may be able to help Steve, his boss and the team. All or several of the elements of the corporate curriculum interact in complex ways. Using both a 'situated' approach and the elements of the corporate curriculum framework may help the various parties to explore Steve's issue. For example, discussing the issue in the context of 'peace and stability' at work may help. Exploring the issue from the perspective of 'domain-specific knowledge' or working towards improved 'self-awareness and self-regulation' within the team environment may help. Applying 'creative' thinking could assist. Offering Steve the opportunity to explore his specific

---

condition and context may be more beneficial than a training course. This may need facilitating by a third party or through a team discussion. So, instead of focusing on problem-solving skills through the 'formal curriculum' the discussion may focus on the value of reflection, of drawing breath, of standing back and viewing a situation afresh. It may involve open and honest feedback, genuine collaboration and mutual support.

So, Steve's difficulty with problem solving may be ameliorated by the exploration of some other part of the corporate curriculum that initially seems far removed.

(See Chapter 4 for a more detailed example of problem solving in a corporate curriculum.)

Illustration 5.3 shows the importance of understanding oneself and others as learners. The opportunity here is to learn to view work as a place to learn and to appreciate that learning to generate new knowledge is a complex business within a complex environment. Steve's case and others like it in the day to day of work offer the potential to apply a complexity-informed perspective so that complexity becomes lived with and accepted, tolerated as normal rather than fought against or simplified. In turn, it is *toleration* that enables people to suspend their judgement (as opposed to close down their thinking) and continue with their development (see Daloz, 1986). Of course individual efforts in this direction are likely to be subject to the organizational constraints and the 'dominant logic' of the culture.

What if complexity is not accepted as normal?

We suggest that when complexity is not accepted or tolerated as normal both an employee's learning and generation of knowledge in the corporate curriculum and mental health suffer. Then the employee may resort to any of three sorts of response.

First, they may 'run faster', in the belief that doing more of what appears to 'real' work will resolve the situation. Garvey (1995) describes this as the 'time pressure culture'. Here a person works long hours, becomes task oriented and often becomes stressed and ineffective. In such an environment learning gets squeezed out. The learner will have difficulty in surviving because there is little time to participate in anything other than the immediate work in hand.

Secondly, they may deflect from their own responsibility and attempt to get what they want from others through manipulation and playing political games. Thirdly, they may retreat from complexity in a major way and become cynical, alienated, tired, stressed, burnt out or ill. In short they will cease to be knowledge-productive, let alone wise.

Facilitating knowledge productivity

As we have argued, learning is a social activity and therefore knowledge productivity is dependent on the social context. Helping another person be knowledge productive requires certain personal qualities. It is important, for instance, to be tolerant, patient and generous towards others. In a complex organization the emphasis on 'ends' remains but, as is seen in Steve's case, deciding on the 'means' is in itself far from straightforward. The various elements of the corporate curriculum may come into play to enable a greater understanding of the situation that can eventually lead to a new approach being adopted. This is when learning to generate knowledge requires persistence and resilience.

Sometimes there will be value in looking in detail at specific incidents or events and exploring the individual's or group's experience of these. This may involve discussion around and analysis of the particular narrative of the situation to develop greater insight and greater wisdom. This is 'situated learning' in action.

Within the knowledge-productive organization people need to be alert to learning opportunities and aware of the need to facilitate learning for groups and individuals. This becomes everyone's responsibility and therefore understanding the learning process and knowing about and applying the appropriate learning skills becomes the province of all people within the workplace. There are clear implications here for the core abilities of people at work, and 'facilitating learning' in the knowledge economy could become a new core competence. This would include understanding various pedagogic methods such as: action learning, mentoring, coaching for specific outcomes, situated learning, future state visioning, scenario planning, open space process, dialectic facilitation, co-operative and collaborative dialogue.

Developing awareness

In complex organizations a high degree of self-understanding and a recognition of the importance of restoring oneself is important. This may enable a true toleration of complexity in the sense of 'sustaining' rather than tolerating as merely 'putting up with'. To be restored is to achieve a measure of the necessary 'peace and stability' in one's position at work, despite the complexity all around. Being restored helps individuals to appreciate those talents and qualities that are exchanged for employment, and to renew their personal commitment and 'sense of identity with the enterprise and its mission' (Nonaka, 1996:19). In this sense healthy personal relationships are at the core of a knowledge-productive organization.

Conclusion

The corporate curriculum is not a panacea which will guarantee that organizations will negotiate successfully the transition to being first and foremost knowledge productive. Recent research reveals that most companies which believe themselves to be knowledge intensive do not, in fact, use knowledge well:

> They do not capitalise on ideas and creativity. They lose knowledge through staff turnover and downsizing. They have knowledge assets they do not exploit. They buy in expertise that they already possess, because they do not know what they know and no large organization has effective knowledge management, let alone knowledge management practices, embedded throughout its organization. (Skyrme and Amidon, 1997)

Moving towards knowledge productivity will require cultural change at all levels of the organization, if the metaphor of a corporate curriculum as a rich landscape of learning is to be more than just metaphorical.

If this is achieved it then becomes appropriate to talk about a 'knowledge-productive' organization. This can be characterized by the compatibility of individual and organizational aspirations, high employee commitment, a focus on collaboration and team development, and a complex web of practices and relationships that are supportive and developmental, both of the individual and of the organization. Above all, a 'knowledge-productive' organization is populated by a diverse group of people who have developed an enthusiastic sense of themselves as learners. When learning spreads in this way new knowledge is produced and the individuals within the organization become wise and capable.

Critique of Part 2

Jussi T. Koski, Ed.D. *University of Helsinki, Finland*

Shadow-lives and corporate creativity

If you think you know what is going on, you haven't got a clue about what's going on.

Jane Bryant Quinn (in Howard Gardner's *Extraordinary Minds*, 1997. London: Phoenix)

Introduction

In this critique I will comment and build upon ideas presented, implicitly or explicitly, in the Introduction and Chapters 3, 4 and 5 of this book. Rather than criticize assumptions that may be faulty or irrelevant, I will formulate and elaborate ideas and points of view that I consider to be of fundamental importance in today's and tomorrow's knowledge-intensive work. These ideas include the nature and centrality of learning, the social nature of expertise, dangers of trained incapacity, the role of power in organizations, and the often serendipitous nature of knowledge creation and productivity. As core concepts I will refer to creativity and creativity management, because it is through these that I have been reflecting on organizations and knowledge-intensive work in my recent research.

I personally find creativity (as a wide, general concept) more relevant and fruitful than restricting oneself to notions such as knowledge creation or knowledge productivity. This is not least because in knowledge economy creative imitators often overcome the original knowledge producers in terms of business success. The ultimate question for business organizations is, then: how can we develop our creative potential and performance per se, i.e., how can we increase our innovativeness in all aspects of our work and in all our operations, including but not restricted to knowledge production?

According to a well-known creativity researcher, Mihaly Csikszentmihalyi, 'to be human is to be creative'. This means that for we humans creativity has an inherent value in itself. It is also, however, increasingly a means to individual and organizational success and prosperity. In this instrumental sense I use Leonard and Swap's (1999:6) definition of organizational creativity: 'Creativity is a process of developing and expressing novel ideas that are likely to be useful.'

Managing creativity may sound like a paradox, but it definitely can and must be done in order to release and enhance the potential of individuals, groups and organizations. To manage creativity we must first conceptualize and then carry out a systemic and comprehensive model of enhancing it. In this critique, I will deal with three essential dimensions of creativity management. First, I will briefly describe some 'generic' creatogenic and creatopathic (see Barron *et al.*, 1997) features of organizations. Secondly, I will outline a few essential and basically down-to-earth elements of creativity management. And thirdly, I will portray some characteristics of creative individuals that managers need to be aware of.

Creatogenic and creatopathic features of organizations

Creatogenic features of a given organization are values, beliefs, commitments and habits that enhance the creativity of both individual employees and groups. These features include the following (creatopathic features are of course their opposites):

- Top management is explicitly committed to enhancing and releasing creativity throughout the organization.
- Employees are simply expected to be creative; according to many research results this simple message to employees can alone make them more creative.
- The mission and vision of the organization is clear to everybody. This creates the necessary alignment (Robinson and Stern, 1998), which is of fundamental importance to any collective creative endeavour.
- A creative organization or group is genuinely mission based (Senge, 1998): decision making is guided by the leading ideas of the organization; it is not linked to formal positions of authority and power. In this kind of organization managers understand that, to use Russell Ackoff's (1994) set of concepts, *power over* (the authority to command and thereby make people do things they do not want to do and would not do voluntarily) is not the way to sustainable creativity. Rather, what is needed is *power to* make people do things voluntarily by means of leadership – with encouragement, motivation and conditions conducive to efficient work – not with commands.
- There is a playful and even 'adolescent' attitude to work.

An important creatogenic feature of an organization is the condition that there is a widely shared epistemological manner (a term used by Ikujiro Nonaka) within that organization. To illustrate his point Nonaka (2000) has compared the epistemological manners of US company General Electric (GE) and the Japanese Honda (see table). According to Nonaka neither of these approaches is 'better' in itself. The point is that an organization has to be aware of its own inclination. However, my view is that 'the Honda way' as described here is a more fruitful way to innovation, quality, knowledge productivity and job satisfaction and harmony of employees.

GE	Honda
People live to compete	People live to create
Winning means everything	Life should be a joyful experience
People are difficult to change	The potential of people is limitless
Everything is based on winning the competition	Everything is based on finding our own purpose. Why do we exist? What is the core concept of our work?
Knowledge production is based on comparison. Am I/are we better than the others?	Knowledge production is based on self-reflection. Who am I/who are we? Why do I/we want to do this?
External motivation	Internal motivation
Goal: to be number one	Goal: to serve the customer
Relation to knowledge: exploitation (using the existing knowledge)	Relation to knowledge: exploration (building constantly new knowledge)

One potential pitfall of the GE approach as described in the table is a benchmarking sort of attitude. When understood in a narrow way it can hinder learning and creativity. I remember someone having said, insightfully, that benchmarking is the fool's way of learning. Nonaka himself comes close to this view when he stresses that if you only compare your own performance (business processes, management practices, knowledge-creation practices, products) to that represented by the so-called best practices you never really get to create something truly unique and novel. So behind quality learning and genuine creativity there may be benchmarking, but there is definitely also something more, namely self-knowledge and self-reflection combined with serious playfulness and creative craziness.

This problem has its equivalent within the academic research arena (cf. Thomas S. Kuhn). Especially when we deal with complex and emerging issues whose importance has only recently been more widely recognized, as is the case of knowledge research and the issue of knowledge productivity, we need to seek for alternative research practices, i.e. we must not get stuck with 'best practices' approach too early on.

However, when we are dealing with knowledge productivity it is also important to realize that if an organization focuses solely on exploration it is usually incapable of profiting from its knowledge and know-how. If, on the other hand, an organization concentrates only on exploitation, its products and processes will soon be out of date. Here, too, the balance is the key. (See Levinthal and March, 1993 for the importance of the balance between the exploitation and exploration modes.)

Elements of creativity management

Corporate creativity manifests itself either in the form of improvements (incremental creativity) or as innovations (radical creativity; see Robinson and Stern, 1998). In the everyday life of organizations improvements and innovations most often happen without planning, and happen unexpectedly. According to Robinson and Stern, a company can never know in advance who will be creative, what creative acts will take place and when and how those acts will happen. They have formulated a special 'no-preconceptions principle of corporate creativity' that, I think, is a sound starting point for developing comprehensive creativity management for a firm: 'A company's creativity is limited to the same extent that it acts on preconceptions about who will be creative, what they will do and when and how they will do it'.

Implicit in this no-preconceptions principle is the same kind of criticism toward an (over)rational planning approach that characterized Peters and Waterman's modern classic *In Search of Excellence* (1982). In other words corporate creativity must be empowered and nurtured with a light touch, not directed or commanded from above.

As Robinson and Stern have said, the six essential elements of corporate creativity (aspects that have to be taken special care of) are alignment, self-initiated activity, unofficial activity, serendipity, diverse stimuli and within-company communication. Here I shall reflect more closely on the ideas of self-initiated and unofficial activity; I shall use the concept of self-initiated activity to denote them both.

Let me first sketch an analogy. In schools there are official, written curricula that guide the schoolwork. But there is also what the educational sociologists have called 'the hidden curriculum'. This refers to activities, interactions, power relationships and learning that really takes place. The content of the hidden curriculum can sometimes be quite far apart from the official, written one. Correspondingly, within any organization there is the official side and the 'shadow-side'. The inevitability and potential benefits of the shadow-side are often poorly understood. Far too often this side of an organization is seen, at least from the managerial perspective, as being only something negative.

However, for organizations, self-initiated and unofficial activities offer much wider possibilities for exploration than can ever be set up officially. These activities constitute the hidden and often relatively cheap 'underground R&D department' of a firm. (See Robinson and Stern, 1998.)

But the most important thing is that at the heart of self-initiated activities is what is called internal or intrinsic motivation of an individual employee, as opposed to external (extrinsic) motivation. So, when talking about self-initiated activities we are dealing with worlds of personal passion, enthusiasm, commitment and aspirations. In other words we are dealing with the most essential ingredients of sustainable individual and corporate creativity.

Douglas McGregor stated in his classic work *The Human Side of Enterprise* (1960) that managers far too often neglect individual employees' intrinsic motivation and their needs for self-actualization. Even today employees are still regularly managed according to the premises of what McGregor called theory X: people are unreliable, unable to make commitment and they are (externally) motivated to work just to receive their regular pay-cheque. So, according to the principles of theory X, people are managed by means of control, explicit rules and regulations and external motivators. The shadow-side of the organization and employees' self-initiated activities are controlled and suppressed to the very minimum. The effects of this approach are, however, extremely counter-creative.

Peter Drucker (1993) reminds us that in every organization there always exists simultaneously both manager culture and intellectual culture. To put it more pointedly, from the manager-culture perspective employees are no more than means to achieve corporate goals. Thus they can and must be treated instrumentally, not as whole personalities. On the other hand, from the intellectual-culture perspective, individual employees see the organization only as a means to practise and cultivate their own professional expertise and to increase their market value as employees.

From the knowledge-productivity and corporate creativity point of view, neither manager culture nor intellectual culture must dominate. Both cultures have to appreciate the balancing effect of the other. Employees must add value to the organization, but also the other way round: organizations must add value to employees by letting them cultivate their passions, even in the shadow of official corporate practices.

Characteristics of creative individuals

In my opinion finding and comprehending research describing personality characteristics, working habits, motivational structures, etc. of creative individuals must be part of any serious systemic approach to creativity management. Because space here is limited, let me just sketch out what Csikszentmihalyi (1996) has discovered about creative personalities.

Csikszentmihalyi has come to the conclusion that if we were to use one word to describe a typical creative personality the word would be complexity. By a complex personality he means that such a person is able to move from one mode of behaviour to the complete opposite as the occasion requires. I feel sure it would enhance our capacity to learn and innovate if we could understand and cultivate these kinds of polarities within each other and ourselves. The exemplary complexities Csikszentmihalyi found include the following:

- Creative individuals have a great deal of physical energy, but they are also often quiet and at rest. They usually sleep a lot.
- Creative individuals tend to be smart, yet naive at the same time. They are good at playing with ideas in a childlike way. A playfully light attitude is typical of creative individuals. They understand that, as George Bernard Shaw put it, finally 'all progress depends on the unreasonable man'. For the most part, due to their playful quality, creative individuals are good re-framers. They understand that, no matter how important experience is, sometimes we 'lack inexperience' and, consequently, a fresh point of view.
- Creative individuals are very disciplined and responsible, yet also playful and 'irresponsible'.
- Creative individuals alternate between imagination and fantasy at one end and a rooted sense of reality at the other.
- Creative individuals have both introvert and extrovert tendencies.
- Creative individuals are humble and proud at the same time.
- Creative individuals have both masculine and feminine aspects in their temperament (psychological androgyny).
- Creative individuals are traditional and conservative, yet rebellious and iconoclastic.
- Creative individuals feel passionate about their work, yet they can be extremely objective and critical about it as well.
- Creative individuals are capable of feeling a great deal of enjoyment, yet also suffering and pain.

It was another time and another context when, back in the 1960s, Herbert Marcuse coined the term 'one-dimensional man'. This term itself, however, should warn us not to restrict our spiritual, personal and professional growth to the obvious. To a smaller or greater extent, everybody can be creative. And, as Csikszentmihalyi sums up his findings, creative personalities are never just individuals, but rather multitudes. Let's all be like that!

References

Ackoff, R.L. (1994). *The Democratic Corporation: A Radical Prescription for Recreating Corporate America and Rediscovering Success*, New York, Oxford University Press.

Barron, F., Montuori, A. and Barron, A. (eds) (1997) *Creators on Creating: Awakening and Cultivating the Imaginative Mind*, New York, Tarcher/Putnam.

Csikszentmihalyi, M. (1996) *Creativity: Flow and the Psychology of Discovery and Invention*, New York, HarperCollins Publishers/HarperPerennial Division.

Drucker, P.F. (1993) *Post-capitalist Society*, New York, Harper Business/HarperCollins Publishers.

Leonard D. and Swap, W. (1999) *When Sparks Fly: Igniting Creativity in Groups*. Boston, MA, Harvard Business School Press.

Levinthal, D.A. and March, J.G. (1993) 'The myopia of learning', *Strategic Management Journal*, vol. 14, pp 95–112.

McGregor, D.M. (1960) *The Human Side of Enterprise*, New York, McGraw-Hill.

Nonaka, I. (2000) 'A new paradigm of management and firm: a shared epistemological manner of a firm', presentation at Helsinki School of Economics and Business Administration, 29 February.

Peters, T. and Waterman, R.H. Jr (1982). *In Search of Excellence: Lessons from America's Best-run Companies*, London: HarperCollins Publishers.

Robinson, A.G. and Stern, S. (1998) *Corporate Creativity: How Innovation and Improvement Actually Happen*, San Francisco, CA: Berrett-Koehler Publishers, Inc.

Senge, Peter M. (1998) *The Practice of Innovation*, WWW document, derived September 1999 at http://www.leaderbooks.org/leaderbooks/l2l/summer98/senge.html

Part 3

Developing expertise in learning

6 Creativity

If it were not for the Poetic or Prophetic Character,
the Philosophic & Experimental would soon be at the
ratio of all things & stand still, unable to do other than
repeat the same dull round over again.

William Blake, *There is no Natural Religion*

Introduction

Successful organizations in the modern economy work under the imperative of the need constantly to be creative in what they do. Global competitive pressures act in different ways on private and public sector organizations but the competitive pressures are nevertheless intense. Change and innovation are the only constant features of work organizations in today's society.

The aim of this chapter is to examine the ways in which organizations respond to this imperative to be creative. The aim of the chapter is to do the following:

Aims

➤ examine the current dominant discourse of creativity in the realm of contemporary management theory;

➤ develop a view of creativity which demonstrates that creative organizations are those which seek to be open to the world around them;

➤ illustrate that creativity requires high levels of domain-specific skills and appropriate group dynamics to translate these into new achievements;

➤ explore the ways in which creative thinking can be applied and developed through innovative practice.

The chapter seeks to engage readers in a dialogue that will encourage them to think critically and reflectively about their own organizations. The development of an ability to do so is the very first step in helping people develop creative organizations.

Creativity: the dominant discourse

There are two bodies of literature, thought and reflection in which the problem of creativity stands out. The first concerns competitiveness in the global economy and the requirement of all work organizations continually to adapt and change to competitive pressures. The pressure to innovate – to find new products, new markets and new ways of doing things – is intense. To achieve success for the organizations in which they work people have to become ever more creative in the ways in which they do their jobs. The success of different organizations, indeed of national economies, in achieving these goals is something that is precisely measured in the global economy. Success or failure in the creativity stakes reveals itself in data on productivity rates, market share, profitability and economic growth.

Though they may wish to, governments cannot compel creativity in the economic and social organizations of their societies. It is for this reason that a literature has grown up concerning the promotion of creativity in the workplace. Management theorists have attempted to clarify how creative change is possible in organizations. Their work has resulted in the development of a wide range of techniques for achieving creative thinking. A whole new language of creativity has entered the managerial vocabulary. The language is a description of techniques. Management theory has given us a range of powerful tools with which to help organizations improve their performance in the writings of Handy (1991), Senge (1992), Csikszentmihalyi (1997), Gardner (1997), Seltzer and Bentley (1999) and many others. It is a literature that urges managers to be creative and to develop new techniques for their subordinates to think in new ways.

Consider the list of managerial techniques shown in Table 6.1. These are some of the instruments that constitute the toolkit of managers who believe they are in touch with the times. These are the techniques to promote innovation and change in both people and organizations.

Table 6.1 Managerial techniques

Brainstorming	Mind mapping
Benchmarking	Kaizen
Team building	Buzz groups
Learning styles	Networking
Conferences	Management development programmes

Alongside such technologies of change there is a vast and growing literature that is almost spiritual in its aspirations for self-improvement, creativity and innovation. The bookshops at international airports where the world's executives purchase their travel literature are full of titles concerned with how to release the potential of people to achieve business goals. These are the 'sacred texts' of the dominant discourse, which binds together the management elite, whose work catalyses the global informational economy. The language of creativity in the context of what Zygmunt Bauman (2000) has called 'liquid modernity' – our modern world of global business, mass consumption and the effortless crossing of national and cultural boundaries – is a challenging one, which shows little respect for tradition. Young managers are urged to 'step outside the box', to 'reframe the problem', to 'think the unthinkable', to 'push the boundaries out'. Such groups are encouraged to learn a language rich in the vocabulary of flexibility, adaptability, innovation, new ideas, challenge, incentive and success. The language describes the boundaries of a mental world full of opportunity, challenge and the possibilities of commercial redemption through high earnings, global economic success and an open-ended tryst with the global corporations that employ them, to commit their working lives to endless change for the reward of high salaries.

The icons, rituals and organizational techniques of this corporate world define both the skills and the social identities of its managers. These identities crystallize around a number of beliefs about the ways in which human beings can become creative. It enables managers to see themselves as having a creative role in their organizations.

The claim developed here, however, is that the tacit models of creativity that are embedded in this literature and the outlooks associated with it can be misleading. When the errors of this way of thinking, to use the words of production engineering 'stack up', then the cumulative consequences can be serious indeed. The proposition explored in this chapter is that the current discourse of creativity rests on a false model of the creative person and also of the innovative organization. This false model, with its insistence that creativity is essentially an aspect of the quality of individual minds, has shaped both the understanding of private sector managers and government policy throughout the developed industrial world in respect of promoting innovation and change in the workplace.

There is, nevertheless, a global market in the provision of postgraduate business courses that encourage their students to learn about promoting creativity. There is not a manager in the western world who has not engaged in creative game playing in business schools or hotel conference suites, to learn about how to think 'outside the box' or to release the potential of others. We wish to argue, however, that there are three main weaknesses to this dominant discourse of creativity.

The first is that creativity is conceived of in a reductionist way, in that it is seen as a facet of the minds of individuals. In fact, as the perspective of social learning running through this book would indicate, it is a social process dependent for its success on the kind of support it receives in organizations. Secondly, the model focuses too narrowly on what takes place inside particular organizations and does not explore sufficiently the complex interactions between organizations and their environments. What we show here is that really innovative organizations are those that sustain strong networking and relationships with other organizations and are open to ideas and influences that arise from within those networks.

Thirdly, the dominant model rests on a rather inadequate view of the nature of creative experience. As we shall illustrate, real creative experience involves a sense of transcendence and mutuality among human beings that goes well beyond the cognitive experience of developing a new idea. All creative thought involves transformation in how people experience themselves and others. The feeling of going beyond conventional understanding and of discovering something new is what drives creative people onwards. They experience a constant sense of newness at the boundaries of known worlds. The insights they experience and the understandings they reach require them to rethink everything they had previously understood about a particular area of work or enquiry. The past therefore is opened to new interpretations, as entirely new futures become conceivable. Such people experience a new sense of possibility in their lives.

Taken together, these three main arguments highlight that the process of being creative is not one which can be mechanically managed or compelled. It is one that has to be nurtured and acknowledged. Organizations must remain open to change in response to new ideas coming from the people who work within them. If they do not, then the flow of ideas will dry up and people will leave the organization and take their ideas with them. Where, for example would IBM be now if it had retained Bill Gates?

Creativity: beyond psychological reductionism

Ordinary language once more gives the clue to the nature of the dominant discourse of creativity. Those believed to be creative are often described in terms that emphasize their innate, unique and destructive differences from others. Consider the list shown in Table 6.2.

Table 6.2 Descriptions of creativity

He/she …	is a genius.
	has a first-class mind.
	has exceptional attributes.
	is gifted.
	has something special.
	stands out in the crowd.
	has a unique ability.
	is a high flyer.
	is running in the fast lane.

The terms apply indiscriminately across a range of human endeavour and seek to capture the special qualities of the people described. Behind the descriptions are tacit theories of what makes creative people different. Discussions with different groups of employees – in this case supervisors, managers, miners and nurses – reveal a strong assumption that creative people in the main are born, though their abilities have been nurtured by careful training (Williamson 1998, 2001). There may be, as Thomas Gray hinted, millions of 'mute, inglorious Miltons' lying unacknowledged in country churchyards, but they do not count. The creative people conjured up as the dominant discourse are invariably Samsons, unique from birth onwards and exceptional. Asked to provide lists of creative people, most groups of people we have discussed this theme with mention Shakespeare, Einstein, Mozart, Brunel and other 'geniuses'. They also often suggest people from the past, from the 'big' domains of science, the arts, sport and business, and they are commonly white, European and male.

While this may reflect the dominant culture in which we ask the question, the main consequence of this is that it is very difficult to acknowledge the creativity displayed by a diverse mix of 'ordinary' people in a range of ostensibly ordinary contexts. The achievements of ordinary workers – in paid employment and in the home – in arriving at innovative solutions to problems is not often acknowledged. There is a real loss here, both to the self-regard of individuals and in the knowledge capital and that of communities and organizations. If there is indeed far more creative work and achievement taking place than is recognized, then the result of such work will not be translated into new products, procedures or policies.

There is a danger, too that, believing creative ability is a quality only of exceptional people, most people place artificial limits on their own ability to act and think in creative ways. They develop no belief in their own potentiality as human beings.

The grounds for believing that the dominant, highly individualized model of creativity is misleading are twofold. The first is that psychological research shows that creative people require years of disciplined training, effective support and appropriate stimulation (Tardif and Sternberg, 1988). The second argument is that creative thinking and work require support for it to continue. There has to be a framework of values, resources and organization that nurtures and acknowledges it. Without such sound and organizational support creativity will falter. In any case, it is not a quality that results in continuous activity throughout a lifetime. The Salzburg Court was no place for Mozart. He felt stifled there and was compelled to leave.

Such an observation might seem light years away from the hard technical and practical world of business and commerce. In fact the statistics of labour turnover, with some firms or universities unable to hold on to highly achieving staff, are a consequence of the poor management of people with creative skills and ability. This is the brain drain phenomenon that is potentially so damaging in the global information economy.

Networks of creativity

In so far as the dominant discourse of creativity focuses on the qualities of individuals, it fails to bring into view a range of conditions at the inter-organizational level that either sustain or inhibit creative work.

Much has been written in recent years about the conditions of knowledge productivity in organizations and the changed conditions of R&D in the global information economy. From the work of Gibbons *et al.* (1994) and of Etzkowitz *et al.* (2000) there has been a growing recognition of the importance of networks in knowledge generation throughout the world. Their focus, and the focus of others, has been on the changing links between industry and universities through international co-operation and collaboration in science and technology. This has included programmes such as the Fifth Programme of the European Union to promote international co-operation in R&D.

There have been, too, important changes in approaches to economic development and regional regeneration. As explained in Chapter 1 regions of growth in the global economy such as Silicon Valley, Baden-Wurtemberg, the Thames Valley corridor, Paris-Sud are those that display high levels of co-operation between business, government and higher education, particularly in scientific research and development. Different countries promote these developments in different ways, some rely on the market while others are more interventionist. Market frameworks can nurture regional developments that promote creative work in business and commerce. There are many examples in the United States of close co-operation between business and higher education through its science parks and dialogue centres. The University of Colorado at Boulder, for example, is playing a major role in business development in the regional economy, and there are many similar examples elsewhere (Jacob and Hellstrom, 2000).

The Economic Development Board (EDB) of Singapore does not leave economic development to the uncertainties of the marketplace. Through policies to promote creative thinking skills in schools, and a high level of scientific and technological inward investment, Singapore plans to move its economy up the added-value chain and to be no longer dependent on low unit cost manufacturing. Recently the EDB entered into contracts with the world's ten best universities to strengthen through research and postgraduate training Singapore's high-level skills base and capacity for business innovation. This is an example of long-term strategic thinking and is a key element in the success of the Singaporean economy.

In western societies there have been occasions, especially in wartime, when the same kind of strategic approaches led to astonishing creative developments. The cold war was the spur to much of this in the fields of rocket development, the space programme and thermonuclear weapons. Big programmes such as these depended for their success on the integration of organizations, leading-edge science and technology and political vision backed up by the resources needed to realize it. But why do we need a crisis to be creative?

Creative experience

The dominant model of creativity probably contains within it a rather false view of the nature of creative experience. The common language for describing it is once again telling. How often have we heard of 'the Eureka experience'? How often have we heard expressions such as 'the idea just came to me' or 'I had this flash of insight'? People who report creative experience in this way are not setting out to deceive. Rather they are drawing upon a powerful dominant narrative that enables them to describe their experience meaningfully. Our point is that this narrative is in many ways a misleading one. It reinforces the belief that somehow creativity is an individual achievement whereas, in fact, it is inseparable from the social setting in which it takes place.

The realm of scientific creativity provides many examples of institutions that seek deliberately to create the optimum conditions of scientific productivity. The Salk Institute for Biological Research in the United States has been deliberately designed to recruit and bring together the best brains in biological research that money can buy. The premise on which the Institute is built is that such people need complete freedom to follow their own scientific muses. There is no attempt to predetermine the programme of work that they should follow. Salk scientists are evaluated to see whether or not they have achieved results, but the prime responsibility for their success rests with the scientists themselves.

The Institute of Mathematics at Cambridge University in Britain has redesigned its building so that social interaction among colleagues is maximized. Even in the toilets there are blackboards on which people can write to develop ideas. It is not possible for people who work there to enter the building and go to their own rooms without first passing through a common area where they will meet other colleagues. The point is this: the conditions for creative thinking can be engineered. They involve the right combination of resources, people, organizational support and appropriate recognition for achievement.

The conditions for creativity set out above may be necessary but they are not sufficient. Creative thinking involves new ideas, new thoughts. Once again, these mental events cannot be thought of as discrete experiences. First, they are invariably social because they take place within a social and organizational context and, secondly, they evolve and develop through time. High-level meta-cognitive skills are at their centre. Creative people not only live at the boundaries of knowledge, they monitor their own work highly effectively. They know what they do not know. They are people skilful in what Gardner (1997) calls reflecting, leveraging and framing. They constantly reflect on what they do. They actively turn their own weaknesses into strengths. And through framing they turn their experiences into something positive that they can build on to achieve their goals.

If not consciously learned, these abilities can be developed. Whether they develop fully, however, depends very much on how they are experienced by the individuals involved. Csikszentmihalyi (1997) has tried to capture one aspect of this experience in the concept of *flow*. This term he applies to a set of experiences that people often encounter when, through almost effortless action, they feel they are living out the best moments in their lives. Such activities go beyond normal experience. From climbing mountains to painting works of art or seeing a machine one has designed meet all its functional requirements there is a common thread: they all involve an experience of being stretched, challenged and successful. The positive feedback from the experience is immediate.

In Csikszentmihalyi's analysis, such experiences are what he calls 'a magnet for learning', an opportunity to rise to new levels of challenge and skill. He argues strongly that creative people have a capacity to so order their lives that they create in their ordinary working conditions that which will help them achieve their most creative work. Some will move from one country to another to achieve these conditions. Others change companies or universities. Studies of creative individuals invariably highlight the importance of the context in which they work and of their need to experience that sense of transcendence, of living at the boundaries.

Some of the implications of these propositions for the way in which creative people can be either motivated or inhibited can be conceptualized as shown in Figure 6.1. The figure is no more than a tool for speculation. What it suggests is that when organizations both value and resource creative activity then the motivation of people to try and be innovative in how they do things is likely to be high. When neither resources nor organizational support for new ways of doing things are high the response on the part of employees will be indifference or perhaps cynicism. The point to consider is this: irrespective of the innate ability of particular groups of employees, the context in which they work will be decisive in shaping whether or not people apply their minds creatively to the work they do. Support for creativity, its acknowledgement and reward, as well as the resources to enable it to happen, are all issues for management. Managers do not themselves need to be scientific or technological experts in order to create the conditions under which science and expertise and new ideas can flourish.

In addition to understanding that there are important organizational supports for creativity, managers also need insight into how the creative process itself unravels. A good example of this is provided in case study 6.1

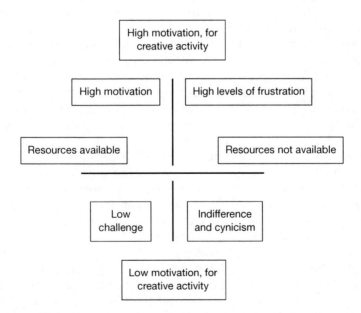

Figure 6.1 Motivation, support and creative activity and organizational support for creative thinking

of Concert Royal, a small chamber music ensemble. The account provided here has been discussed with key members itself and is intended to capture the experience of being creative. What stands out is that creative work rests on a firm bedrock of domain-specific skill, well-rehearsed practical competence and a strong sense of being part of a group whose members work for one another.

Case study 6.1

Concert Royal – creativity in performance

Concert Royal is one of the United Kingdom's longest-established chamber music ensembles. It is a quartet of musicians consisting of Peter Harrison, flute, John Treherne, harpsichord, Rachel Gray, cello, and Margarette Ashton, soprano. The ensemble aims to recreate the sound world of the eighteenth century using original instruments and performing in the style of the period.

Many people have used the performance of music as a metaphor for creativity and knowledge productivity. In relation to Concert Royal and the performance of 'early music' this raises some very interesting points.

During the eighteenth century it was common for composers to write a melody and a bass line and then indicate the harmony through a series of numbers known as figured bass. Performers would interpret the music following a broad set of guidelines that were the conventions of the day. For example, the continuo section could make choices about which harmonic variations it opted to play, the soloists could ornament and embellish the music. The performers were expected to listen carefully to each other and echo and repeat the various embellishments when it came to the appropriate point in the music. Some composers wrote only a melody and bass and allowed complete freedom to the performers to create the harmony. John sometimes improvises in the eighteenth-century way around well-known themes. During one performance he attempted to weave the song 'Ten Green Bottles' into every piece he played! In effect, the performers were operating in a state of 'bounded instability' (see previous chapters). Here there are rules but aspects of the performance are emergent and spontaneous.

Concert Royal is a vastly experienced group of performing musicians. Their 'domain-specific' knowledge is built on many years of studying eighteenth-century treaties on the performance and interpretation of English music of the time. Initially, this knowledge is embedded through and during individual practice sessions. These are sometimes intense and very repetitive. At other times Margarette says that 'the practice goes on in my head, giving the music meaning, it is not just about playing the notes in the right order'.

Practice in music is very important, every musician knows this. The function of practice is to deeply embed the process, the techniques and the music in the minds of the performer so that, when the performance happens, creativity can flourish, the spontaneous can happen. During the performance the professional musician can be in a state of 'flow'. According to Peter, 'it is this that makes the difference between a professional performance and an inspired one'. Practice depends on high levels of 'self-regulation' and meta-cognitive awareness.

When the members of the ensemble meet together they talk about the music, discuss the 'weight' of the notes, the pace, the tone, the 'feel'. They practise together – listening, performing and talking. 'Communication' is crucial during practice and during the performance but, in performance, they cannot talk to each other. They have to communicate through gesture, eye movement and through the sounds they are making. The main reference point for communication is the 'lead' performer. Rachel, the cellist, tends to keep the 'pulse' of the music going.

Sometimes they practise the ornamentation but often in the live performance one of them may change it quite spontaneously as the mood takes them. The other members of the ensemble have to respond. It keeps everyone 'on their toes' and alert, aware of each other in the moment of creation. The members of Concert Royal learned to do this from reading the ancient treaties on performance. In one volume, the author talks of 'risk' as being an essential ingredient in creativity. 'That small element of risk adds "spice" to the performance', says Margarette. 'it raises the adrenalin and with it the levels of flow'. It is 'problem solving' in the heat of the moment but this is based on deep 'domain-specific knowledge' of the music, the period and each other.

Before a performance the musicians prepare themselves mentally and emotionally. To do this they follow routines and rituals and often there is a high degree of 'peace and stability'. This offers valuable mental orientation to the task. And when the performance is over, there is the inquest! The details are discussed, the errors identified, the escape from errors laughed over and the highs and lows explored. The audience will rarely know, unless they also have 'domain-specific' knowledge, that something has gone wrong. This is true 'reflection' in the spirit of progress and development.

The members of Concert Royal begin every performance with a creative challenge before them. They trust their skills to rise to it. In the course of the concert they solve a range of musical and communication problems. If they failed to do so some members of the audience would leave disappointed, but the evening would not have been disastrous or life threatening.

There are other contexts when creative problem solving is literally a matter of life and death. Case study 6.2 of Apollo 13, the NASA flight to the moon, is an indication of problems that required creative solutions if total disaster was to be avoided. Everything about Apollo 13's mission was planned and rehearsed in meticulous detail. NASA drew upon the best skills in science and technology available. With all their planning, however, the space team could not cover every eventuality. Indeed it was not science and technology that saved the mission. It was something else: a coming together of skills, teamwork, communication and a practised determination to approach problems innovatively. This was a team of people structured to work well together. Without that degree of commitment, who knows what the outcome might have been?

Case study 6.2

Apollo 13 – a lesson in creative problem solving

Among some of the most famous words in history Jack Swigert's statement 'Houston, we've had a problem here', probably stands as one of the greatest understatements of all time!

The Apollo 13 flight had little public interest or support, but when oxygen tank no. 2 blew up, causing both no. 1 tank to fail and the loss of electricity, light and water 200,000 miles from Earth, the public became very interested. What followed was probably one of the greatest pieces of creative problem solving ever.

The astronauts made their way into the Lunar Module for safety. The Lunar Module could sustain the crew for 45 hours – they had to stretch it to 90 hours but re-entry was calculated as around 151 hours. Water was a problem – they would be out of water 5 hours before re-entry. The oxygen supply was sufficient but the removal of carbon dioxide was a concern. Power was a major concern.

After a day and a half the carbon dioxide levels in the Module were dangerously high. The crew had to devise a way to connect the spacecraft to the lithium hydroxide canisters so that the carbon dioxide could be removed, but the connections were incompatible. There then followed an exploration into the absurd! The astronauts gathered all the spare materials they had on board. This amounted to plastic waste bags, cardboard and a limited amount of sticky tape. Houston engineers gathered exactly the same materials together and experimented continuously with the components to make a connecting device. They then had to communicate this information through the radio to the astronauts so that they could construct the device on the Lunar Module. It was a success.

To return the Module to the right flight path to get back to Earth with limited power was a major problem. Houston had 2 hours to solve it. Without computers and with debris floating all around them in space they had to orient the craft using only visual alignment with the Sun through one of the windows. This proved accurate to a variation of less than 1 degree. The ground control could then calculate the exact timing of the thrust of the engines to fire the Module back to Earth. During this time everything was controlled and calm, but some years later the Mission Control Director said that his writing in the log was almost illegible because he 'was so damned nervous'.

The success of this rescue was truly remarkable and was marked by creative thinking and innovation based on a genuine sense of urgency, focus, teamwork, discipline, mixed domain-specific knowledge, excellent communication and co-operation.

Creativity and innovation

Creativity is one thing; innovation is another. It is the difference between idea and application, between imagination and action. Successful innovations in organizations require skills beyond those of being creative. Managers have to be aware of their operational environments and of the ways in which new ideas might propel their work forward. Creative ideas translate into innovative practice only with careful management and evaluation. This is a requirement that goes well beyond the responsibility of individual firms. National investment in science and technology and in the development of a strong R&D base is another precondition for successful innovation and change in individual organizations.

Countries that do not provide the policy framework within which organizations can flourish are unlikely in the long term to sustain innovative economic development. It does not necessarily follow, however, that organizations will respond to a supportive environment provided by government. Successful and sustained innovation requires both appropriate public policies and adequate responses to those by managers of economic organizations.

These observations suggest a number of important analytical distinctions to help us think through the nature of innovation. Some organizations will approach development from within a long-term perspective. Others are much more driven by short-term, market-led considerations. Some organizations are much more prepared to take long-term risks than others. Some will invest heavily in planned research and development, others will not. Some organizations will rely on buying in the expertise their innovation plans require. Others will try to nurture their employees to develop such ideas themselves. There are no simple formulae that explain how successful innovation can be achieved. It does, however, involve a balance of long-term planning, investment, staff development, hard work and both the willingness and ability to think new ideas and act upon them.

Case study 6.3 contains many of these elements.

Case study 6.3

Tallent Engineering

Tallent Engineering is a company in the automotive industry based at Newton Aycliffe in County Durham. In the 1940s the company specialized in pressing metal to form ladies' powder compacts. In the 1950s it extended its production to build the body shells of washing machines and other white goods. In the 1960s it developed, on the basis of heavy metal pressing, a market niche in automotive subframes. In the 1980s and 1990s Tallent Engineering grew to become a global multinational player in the automotive industry.

The company has recently been taken over by the German conglomerate Thyssen but remains nonetheless very committed to its County Durham base and labour force.

In presentations about its development and its plans the company highlights that much of the change it has achieved in the past quarter-century was realized through the work of a relatively stable staff team. It is a company that attaches a great deal of importance to in-house training and skill development and to total quality management. The company is very proud of its investment in training and education and is willing to support employees who wish to take up further studies.

There is a widespread belief in this company that it has been well led by a senior management team over many years. The prevailing narrative among company employees is that this is an organization committed to innovation, development and change, but also strongly supportive of the existing labour force. It is a company very skilled in a range of management techniques to improve its production processes, benchmark its position against competitors, measure its performance and keep ahead of market trends in the industry. Employees have a very strong sense that this is a good company to work for, that their futures are secure and that change and innovation are valued. The career of its managing director has become iconic of the company's corporate culture. He has risen from an apprentice to his current position with the company and firmly believes that this is a career pattern in principle open to all. True or not, he is widely admired for his achievement and takes an active part in the local and regional economies through business networks and government policy initiatives.

There are many successful companies such as the one in case study 6.3. There are, however, unfortunately many more that have not succeeded in responding to the new economic environment. The economic history of most societies is littered with stories of business failure, closure, takeovers and amalgamations in which unsuccessful units have been closed down. There are many public sector organizations that through poor support from government, inefficiency and bureaucratic overload have failed to develop and respond in new ways to the needs of clients and citizens. Too many young people have failed in schools and colleges that have not enabled them to experience the joy and achievement of learning creatively.

There is a real challenge for managers in all organizations to think these issues through. It is now a cliché to highlight that people are the most important asset of any organization. What we have shown in this chapter is that it is the creative potential of human beings that is their most important quality. William Blake, who began this chapter, should end it. Science and technology – the philosophic and experimental – are not enough. Without creative imagination we are all condemned to repeat the same dull round over and over again.

7 Environments for learning

I keep persuading younger colleagues to whom I teach script-writing or directing to examine their own lives. Not for the purposes of any book or script but for themselves. I always say to them, 'Try to think of what happened to you which was important and led to your sitting, sitting here in this chair, on this very day, among these people. What happened? What really brought you here?' You've got to know this. That's the starting point … I'm frightened of anybody who wants to show me a goal, me or anybody else, because I don't believe you can be shown a goal if you don't find it yourself. I'm fanatically afraid of all those people.

Krzysztof Kieslowski, Polish film maker, in Stock (1993:35–6)

The idea of an environment for learning would conjure up in many people's minds a school (perhaps a film school of the sort referred to by Kieslowski cited above), a college, a university lecture theatre or an open-learning centre in a company. The learning environment that we are concerned with in this chapter is much more subtle than any of these and refers to the cultural and psychological contexts which provide a climate for motivation to learn and set the expectations that engage people or alienate them from learning and thinking. The experience of having lived under a repressive, censor-controlled regime led Kieslowski, one of post-war Poland's most important film makers, to question all attempts by those with power to impose on others their ways of thinking. It was not only that it was an offence against freedom to do so. His concern was that it ran counter to how human beings think, create and live: people who claim to know what should happen, what should be, are necessarily wrong, because no one can know what the future will be or how ideas will change. The future and new ways of thinking are there to be constantly discovered. The first step on the road is critical self-awareness.

The aim of this chapter is to clarify the necessary conditions for successful learning and critical self-awareness in organizations and to identify the elements of successful learning environments. These will be seen to include the following:

➤ resources and skill development;

➤ organizational cultures open to new ideas;

➤ arrangements in organizations that promote reflection and analysis;

➤ a wider cultural climate that attaches importance to learning and personal development.

Environments for learning

It is a well-established proposition in the field of lifelong learning that learning takes place in a range of different contexts. Adult human beings learn in the contexts of formal education, the workplace and in the communities in which they live. As Daloz says, 'To understand human development, we must understand the environment's part, how it confirms us, contradicts us, and provides continuity' (1986:68).

Those with personal computers are connected to a wider network – the World Wide Web – that brings them into contact with resources, communities of interest and practice that extend well beyond the boundaries of their own nation states. These contexts provide opportunities and stimulation for people to learn across a range of different domains and at different points in their lives.

Whether people take up such opportunities for learning, however, is not something determined by the supply of them. People have to want to learn. Their willingness to do so is something shaped by their previous educational experience, their position in society and the actual opportunities open to them. It is the interaction of supply and demand that shapes the form, content and pattern of learning opportunities of any society. The analytical elements that would help us think through the complex relationships hinted at here includes the elements shown in Figure 7.1.

This simple device opens up a number of important questions, as follows:

■ How far do the organizations of which people are a part encourage them to take up new learning opportunities?

■ Is the wider social and cultural environment in which people live conducive to and supportive of the idea of continuous learning?

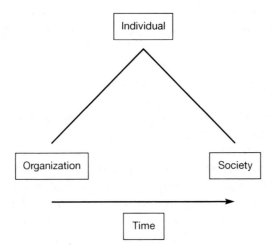

Figure 7.1 Telling inter-dependencies

■ How far do organizations respond to the changing circumstances of their environment to perceive the need to promote the learning of their members?
■ How have motivations, opportunities and circumstances for learning changed through time?

These questions break down into many more, each one probing in more detail the resources available to people for learning. For the advanced industrial societies there is a great deal of evidence that these opportunities and patterns of learning follow lines of social demarcation which relate to social class, gender, generational and racial inequalities. A range of public bodies have highlighted that this differentiation of opportunities is dysfunctional for modern economies. The European Union memorandum on lifelong learning (2000), the G8 Group Cologne memorandum on lifelong learning (2000), the work of the OECD and of nearly all of Europe's national governments has, in the past few years, highlighted the importance of further education and training to promote global competitiveness.

This is not only a European phenomenon. Pacific Rim countries such as Japan, Singapore, Australasia and Taiwan, to name a few, are all committed to a public policy agenda that promotes lifelong learning in the workplace (see Field, 2000). Global competitive pressures exemplify themselves in many ways. They can be seen in the development of work-based training strategies and policies to attract particularly well-qualified staff across national boundaries. There is an international market emerging in high-level skills. Countries and organizations that fail to keep abreast and indeed ahead of these developments will find themselves at a competitive disadvantage in the future.

Behind the globalization of labour markets there are long-term cultural shifts in attitude and expectation. Throughout the world people are taking a more strategic view of their career development and are investing personal capital in the acquisition of academic and vocational qualifications. As the demand for qualifications increases so does the phenomenon that Ronald Dore (1976) presciently identified as the 'diploma disease'. This is the phenomenon of qualification inflation. Given the importance of qualifications it is also not surprising that more and more employees negotiate into their labour contracts opportunities for further training and professional development. Organizations that can respond to these expectations are likely to attract highly qualified staff. Those that cannot will disadvantage themselves in an increasingly complex labour market. Given this, it is vital that managers in organizations think strategically about the longer-term development of their human capital. The successful ones are those who create learning environments that nurture personal and professional development.

Resources and skills

The changes and pressures identified above can be examined from a number of different angles. The first of these that stands out concerns the individual employee.

At each point in their working lives individuals have strategic choices to make about their personal development. Career planning can never be a precise art and the future is intrinsically unknowable. In any case, individuals do not approach these decisions as rational choice theorists would have us believe. They are not economic calculating machines, their understanding of their careers is refracted through a whole series of assumptions about their social status, their gender, their religion and through the prevailing values of the communities in which they live their lives. It is hardly surprising, therefore, that many people make choices about the future which are based on inadequate information or on intensely local considerations. Nor is it surprising that some people make decisions that are simply irrational and wrong. Culture, class division and social deprivation can severely damage the possibility of some groups of people taking long-term views of their own working lives. Those blessed with a good education, good careers advice and supportive working contexts can do so, though never with real certainty about the outcome.

The experience of people who live and work in the developed centres of the global economy is different from that of those who struggle for survival at its periphery. People who live in the technologically developed societies have access to information and learning resources barely imagin-able to those who live in the underdeveloped societies. It does not follow, however, that these resources are well used. The statistics of educational failure are a terrible indictment of the failures of formal education to pro-mote the educational life chances for everyone. And it is ironic that a significant proportion of young people in the developed societies of the world reject education and fail to invest their time and resources in long-term personal development.

It is not surprising either that many young people in the developing soci-eties have high expectations for education. It is their only hope of escaping poverty and unemployment. It is these aspirations that lie behind global patterns of labour migration and a changing global division of labour. East Asian societies produce more engineers and mathematicians than those in the west. The Indian city of Bangalore is a world centre of excellence in computer software engineering. Singapore seeks to develop its economy around high-level skills. The oil-rich states of the Middle East must import many skilled workers and professionals. There is a need, given this back-ground, for both governments and organizations to take a long-term strategic view of their labour supply, education and training needs.

It is clear, therefore, that a full understanding of the logic of global labour markets requires deep cultural, political and economic insight into the life experiences of different groups of human beings. We cannot attempt that here. On the other hand we cannot ignore this background because it does affect the way in which people make decisions, and through that it sets the constraints in which government policies to promote effective learning environments must develop.

A number of analytical distinctions help identify the problems faced by individuals in thinking about their long-term professional development. Consider the list of options presented in Table 7.1.

Table 7.1 Individual career planning

Short term	Long term
General education	Specific vocational skills
Personal needs	Organizational requirements
Theoretical	Practical
Individual learning	Group learning
Sector specific	Sector non-specific
Incremental learning	New learning domains
Non-accredited learning	Accredited learning

Each of these distinctions can represent opposite ends of a spectrum of choice. Particular individuals or groups of individuals will display different patterns of choice against these profiles. Some will think about their futures only in a short-term way. Others plan and invest in their own human capital on a much longer timescale. Some will focus their work-based learning in particular economic sectors, others will seek generic skills.

What people actually do, however, is not just a matter of choice. Choices have to be modified against opportunities available. In the world beyond compulsory education for most people these choices are constrained by the labour market. People are positioned differently in relation to the labour market. Some have access to employment and to job opportunities that entail training and career development. Others face unemployment or at best marginal employment in the secondary labour market.

When training and development opportunities are available people develop strong expectations about themselves and their future. They develop what Manuel Castells (2000) has called project identities. They can picture themselves at some point in the future realizing in their lives values that matter to them. If the organizations in which they work allow them the training opportunities their life projects require they will experience work as a domain of practice in which they continue to learn and to develop.

Those denied such opportunities are likely to realize their life projects in other domains, not necessarily relevant to the workplace and from which the workplace does not benefit. In working with groups of managers we are often struck by the rich variety of activities people pursue outside of their workplaces. These activities often require high levels of commitment, knowledge and skill, determination and creativity – the very qualities organizations are seeking to recruit. This suggests that people make choices about when and where they offer their skills and abilities. Such differentiation of opportunities therefore touches in subtle and profound ways on the kinds of expectations that build up within an organization and which therefore decisively shape the character and commitment of its human assets.

Richard Sennett (1998) has noted that short termism and fragmentation in the management of the labour market in western developed societies has meant that people do not build up a strong sense of obligation towards their employers or their work colleagues. He goes further, arguing that contemporary working arrangements corrode the moral character of employees and strip work of its moral dimension. Because they are not valued, many workers do not value the organization for which they work or feel a personal obligation to be interested in and support other colleagues with whom they work. There is therefore a moral dimension to work-based learning. It concerns the value placed upon people by employers and the ways in which people value themselves. As case study 7.1 shows, when people feel that their contribution to an organization is a worthwhile one, for which they gain suitable reward and recognition, they are much more likely to take a positive attitude to their own self-development and be open to seek out new ideas.

Case study 7.1

Oil Company Co. – rewarding development

In the case study on Oil Company Co. in Chapter 2 it was mentioned that Oil Company Co. rewards its staff for meeting commercial performance targets and for development activity. On the basis that most individual performance-related pay schemes fail because the reward is not worth having, Oil Company Co. makes the performance and development payment worthwhile. In total it is worth 30 per cent of an individual's pay.

Performance targets and development plans are agreed through the appraisal process and, in review, people are expected to provide evidence of both. This is translated on to a multi-dimensional measurement chart (rather like a spider's web). This includes both hard measures and qualitative assessments translated into rankings on a 1–10 scale and is used to 'map' progress against previous achievements and the percentage reward is given accordingly.

This system of reward has made a major positive change in the way people view and participate in development activities; and financial performance has also increased.

A tradition of educational research probing the nature of successful schools provides important additional clues to define the elements of the productive learning environment. The core idea is expectation. Irrespective of the level of resources available to them, the message from successful schools is that those that have high expectations of their pupils, and learning contracts between teachers and pupils in which these are made explicit, are the ones that succeed. When pupils are valued they respond to the valuation placed upon them. When their teachers have high expectations of them and monitor whether these are being achieved, pupils typically respond with interest and motivation. Case study 7.2 illustrates this very well.

Case study 7.2

A true story – Terry

Terry was born into poverty in rich, middle-class West Sussex, England. Nobody talked to him. He was left to play on the street and bring himself up.

School was no better. It was alien. He didn't fit in. All the other children could read. They talked differently. Could do sums. Could draw. Play instruments. They were good at sport. Terry wanted to be good at sport. But nobody took any notice of him. But he showed them. He could fight. He could shout and push the other kids over. They didn't fight back very often. He got into trouble with the teachers. So what? He didn't care. Why should he? What could they do to him that was worse than he had? The teachers talked about Terry in the staff room. He was a nuisance and difficult. He would never make anything of himself they said.

Terry developed ways to cope in school to survive. He would draw attention to himself for negative reasons: but at least it was attention. He was learning to cope within a hostile and alien environment in which he could not participate. Over time the gulf between Terry and the other children deepened. Eventually he reached the final year. He was to have a new teacher. Terry didn't know what to expect from this new teacher. The new teacher talked to him, asked him questions, found out what he liked, and Terry found himself talking to him back.

The class were 'doing' the First World War as their project. Terry had his big chance, he could make a dreadnought battleship. This new teacher had loads of balsa wood and all the tools. The teacher talked to Terry about his model, asked him about size and proportion they talked about scale and looked at pictures of the dreadnought together. The new teacher was interested in him, listened to him and treated him with respect. Terry started to feel quite good about school.

The rest of the children in the class started to take an interest in what Terry was doing. The new teacher set them all interesting problems. He let them set their own problems. He joked with them and talked to them about their work. He joined in with their projects. He took photos of them working. They took photos of their work. They made films. Wrote music. Told stories. Solved problems. Did real sums. Found out things. Looked at things. Drew 'real' pictures of 'real' things. Did science. Did projects in groups. Talked to each other. Had a great time.

Terry's model progressed well. It was the best thing he had ever done. He knew that. The teacher said it was 'brilliant'. The kids in the class said it was 'ace'. Terry felt good. Good for the first time. The other kids let him play cricket in the playground. They said he was good at it. Terry started to ask about reading. And found he could do it. He started to ask about sums and found he could do them. Terry's behaviour in the playground improved. There was no need to fight anybody.

When he had finished his model the new teacher asked him to show it to the whole school. All the kids said 'brilliant' and gave him a clap when they saw the model. The other teachers couldn't believe what was happening. The new teacher was fearful of the future for Terry in the next school. But, here and now, Terry was a hero.

What was happening to the well-established pattern of winners and losers, failures and successes?

How had Terry achieved something when his destiny was to be a waster?

Our proposition is that it is the same in the workplace. As we have noted, all workplaces are sites of learning. They are what Lave and Wenger (1991) call communities of practice. In the course of everyday working people come together to solve problems, to talk and to think about how things can be done more effectively. Whether such experience is translated into new learning and new kinds of practice depends upon whether the organization enables this to happen. Whether people remain motivated to continue to work and to think and to develop depends crucially on whether they are valued for doing so.

This is not rocket science. In some ways it is common sense. Common sense, however, is a pattern of thought and action often embedded in false and bizarre propositions about how social reality is constituted and changes. It is too often an elaborate framework of old saws, clichés, prejudices and unexamined convictions that lock people into unproductive ways of doing things. The common sense of much contemporary management thinking is too often a closed system of thought based on unexamined nostrums that make sense only to those who believe them.

The challenge is to go beyond this and to tease out the subtle elements of learning environments that bear directly on how people think and act in relation to one another in the communities of practice of the workplace. Those we have identified concern personal identities and social expectations. When much is expected of them people in general respond with effort and enthusiasm. Whether anything is expected of them is a matter of the culture of the organizations in which they work.

Organizational cultures

A central theme running through this book is that all organizations teach, whether consciously or not. Some have explicit training programmes and human resource development strategies. Others do not. This is not to say that they therefore necessarily do not help promote their staff. Many organizations without formal HRD mechanisms nonetheless provide communities of learning and environments of practice that are extremely productive and developmental. The problem does not lie with structures. It lies with attitudes and expectations and commitments. It lies in the way in which particularly managers in organizations value the people with whom they work.

Structures cannot be ignored. It was noted 30 years ago by Burns and Stalker (1961) that, in the then dynamic environment of the electronics industry, the most successful organizations were those which had management structures featuring flexible teams that in some way reflected the variability, complexity and change taking place within the marketplace of their operations. Those companies studied by Burns and Stalker that retained more bureaucratic structures of management were less successful in this volatile context. In any domain of human practice – commerce, the military, public administration, community organization or health care – structures have to be appropriate.

The literature of management is littered with examples of the damaging consequences of inappropriate structures. Charles Handy (1995) has noted that the organizations of the future will be very different to those we currently understand. When intelligence and knowledge are the assets of an organization its structure will reflect the key task at hand: to be innovative and flexible. 'Organizations' he writes, 'will organise, but to do so they will no longer need to employ' (1995:39). This observation marks out a new kind of future in which organizations become virtual rather than real, temporary rather than permanent. The future implied in this for employees is that they, too, will be under enormous pressure to be flexible, mobile, innovative and possessed of transferable skills and an ability to monitor their own skills development.

Some people will do this for themselves, especially if they have had a good school or college education. The millions who have not will be dependent on the opportunities open to them in the workplace or in the communities in which they live. The real danger is that the work-based skills will be too narrow, too instrumental and tied to the needs of today's technologies rather than those of tomorrow. Training outcomes are too often measured by calculations that assess their contribution to 'the bottom line', i.e. short-term financial profitability. Training too often focuses on a narrow understanding of occupational competencies.

John Garrick (1998) has unmasked the weakness of such approaches, which dominate so much management thinking and human resource development: they rest on an inadequate view of learning and a concern for instrumental rather than questioning knowledge. 'Contemporary work-based learning strategies' he writes, 'rarely deal in self-criticism, paradox, irony or doubt, yet it is precisely these qualities that give substance to learning'(1998:79). On this account, learning takes place in a successful, knowledge-productive way when there is a high tolerance of ambiguity, doubt, questioning and tolerance of differences. Under these conditions, new demands are made upon the ways people think (see Chapter 5). In short, it requires high levels of self-reflexivity.

Yet this aspect of thinking is often muted in organizations that have set ways of doing things or which rest on false claims that managers and other experts (inside or outside the organization) always know best. Such tacit assumptions of an organizational culture inhibit learning and the development of new ideas. Even in organizations with a well-developed corporate rhetoric that stresses empowerment, teamworking, participation, there is a danger of a learning tokenism which will eventually lead to suspicion and mistrust. It is only when organizations are willing to change in response to new ideas that the language of empowerment has meaning. As we have shown (in Chapter 6) and will show (in Chapter 9) the development of such organizations requires new forms of communication and of leadership that help them become learning organizations really open to and responsive to new ideas. Whether such organizations develop is as much a problem of the structure and exercise of power as it is of the ways in which work-based learning is conceptualized and understood.

Structural reflexivity

Knowledge is power. All commercial organizations trade on their expertise. All professional groups justify what they do on the grounds that they are possessed of distinctive, validated bodies of specialized knowledge. Some organizations become identified with the bodies of knowledge upon which they depended. It is for this reason that commercial organizations – and certainly many departments of the modern state – keep their knowledge secret. They must protect their knowledge from competitors who seek it but who are unwilling to spend the time and money to gain it themselves.

The importance of knowledge in organizations is widely recognized. The knowledge capital of organizations is widely seen as their most important asset. The growth of human resource development from the older practices of personnel management is an acknowledgement that continuously successful organizations will require continuously developing employees. This cliché of modern management is, however, misleading. There is no necessary connection between the development of individual skills and talent and the growth of knowledge capital in an organization. For that link to be sealed mechanisms are needed that enable organizations to identify, consolidate and test out the knowledge and experience of employees.

Much has been done recently to help people in organizations articulate what they know, to help them transform tacit knowledge into something that is explicit (see Chapter 8). The Scandinavian academic and consultant Engeström (1996) has developed the mechanism of the learning laboratory to enable employees to investigate systematically what they have come to know about a problem. His work has many similarities with that of Senge (1990), who has also developed programmes of learning laboratories to help managers think analytically about the problems they are solving and become critically aware of how they and other members of their organization typically solve problems.

A market in learning technologies has opened that promotes organizational learning in ways that would have been unimaginable even a decade ago. Web-based learning, video-conferencing technologies, electronic learning platforms and multi-media packages, open learning centres and so on enable communication across continents and levels of inter- and intra-organizational learning that were simply not possible before. International bodies such as the European Union promote work-based learning and involve businesses in cross-national programmes of staff exchange and learning. E-learning has become a symbol of the new, competitive culture of the 'weightless economy' (Leadbetter, 2000), with its growing dependence not on manufacturing – men, women and machines – but on the 'intangible assets' of information, understanding, knowledge and networks of people with expertise.

Again there is a moral issue here. Some (Rajan et al., 1998) show that 'KM knowledge management initiatives in many firms are concentrated on elite groups of knowledge-workers making up no more than 20 per cent of the workforce' (Scarborough et al., 1999:50). This is a clear case of potential new levels of exclusion within organizations as a new power base of knowledge workers becomes established. Rajan et al. (1998) also add a further social caveat to the knowledge management agenda in that as companies store up the knowledge of their employees in IT systems and knowledge bases this may put more people at risk of redundancy. We believe that short-sighted and morally bereft companies may well follow this line of argument but, in our view, this clearly shows a fundamental misunderstanding of the nature of knowledge and knowledge creation in a social context. It is also based on the mistaken assumption that codified knowledge is a fixed point and that the knowledge and people's collective experience is of little value. Perhaps this is further evidence of the inappropriateness of the knowledge management concept? (See Chapter 8.)

There is no doubt that this new environment for knowledge is well supplied with the means to disseminate information and ideas. It is certain, too, that those organizations that do not keep abreast of these developments will be disadvantaged and succumb to competitive pressures.

However, whether the flow of information translates into new knowledge, into new assets, is a matter for debate. Ronald Barnett (2000) has made the telling point that without open and critical debate, and without a framework for this 'working knowledge' to be tested out and assessed, the vast accumulated experience of today's knowledge practitioners will not translate into new knowledge. For that to happen there has to be what Barnett calls 'structural reflexivity'.

With the model of discipline-based science as his guide, with its framework of peer-reviewed journals, conferences and an open climate of criticism and debate, Barnett makes the point that much 'working knowledge' (and often the creativity that is part of it and which is encouraged by those who urge companies to become 'learning organizations') is not really open to scrutiny. It is not tested out in the way that professional knowledge can be. It is not made transparent in the way that science is. Consequently, claims to knowledge that are based on experience or on 'working knowledge' are flawed. All claims to knowledge must be tested and this requires more than procedures for doing so. It depends on a cultural and political climate that is open both to new ideas and able to embrace the changes that would flow from them.

Just as non-distorted communication (see Chapters 6 and 8) requires a balance of power between the participants in a conversation, the development of new knowledge requires open organizations in an open society. New communication technologies certainly facilitate such openness, but in themselves do not alter the micro-political climates of work organizations to enable new ideas to be translated into new actions or products. For that to happen there has to be a critical engagement with ideas themselves.

The philosopher Karl Popper (1992) has provided an account of the need for such critical dialogue that has major implications for all thinking about learning organizations. That account centres around the idea of a third world or what he calls 'world 3'. There is a world of facts and of physical objects that he calls the 'first world', a world of subjective experience he terms the 'second world' and one of statements – of propositions and ideas and theories – that he calls the 'third world' or 'world 3' (1992:181). World 3 is the product of the human mind and it feeds back upon and changes the other two. It is a world that changes, and the changes in it are recorded in the history of ideas. It is a history of dialogue and debate and of critical questioning that generates a world which is in some senses independent of the people who make it up.

This way of thinking stands in sharp contrast to views of the creation of knowledge that see it as a matter of individual people possessed of great gifts applying their minds to a problem. 'In opposition to this' writes Popper:

> I suggest that everything depends upon the give-and-take between ourselves and our task, our work, our problems, our world 3; upon the repercussion upon us of this world; upon feedback, which can be amplified by our criticism of what we have done. It is through the attempt to see objectively the work we have done – that is to see it critically – and to do it better, through the interactions between our actions and their objective results, that we can transcend our talents, and ourselves . . . This is how we can lift ourselves out of the morass of our ignorance; and how we can contribute to world 3. (1982:196)

This perspective on the nature of human knowledge highlights the importance of communication, openness, the value of all human experience, of dialogue and criticism.

World 3 knowledge only develops under this regime, to use another term from Popper, of conjecture and refutation. The tragedy is, of course, that there are still too many states of the world in which this is not possible and too many organizations in which employees are either prevented from or are fearful of joining in the debate. The loss to world 3 knowledge is incalculable. It leaves us free to conjecture, however, about what would happen if the communication and educational and training resources of the modern world were deployed to engage everyone. Against this test our scientific civilization is still a pale shadow of what it yet might be. And the problems that we currently struggle with – and often through our own ignorance compound – will have solutions very different to those imposed on us all at the moment.

Climates of learning and development

The analysis of learning climates set out in this chapter is founded in an image of the different levels through which learning in organizations needs to be conceptualized. Learning is something that people and only people do. Organizations do not learn. They do not have minds. To speak of them as if they did is to commit the fallacy of 'misplaced concreteness'. Organizations can be said to learn only in a manner of speaking. Learning requires a brain, a purpose, a memory, a language; it depends upon communication between different human minds. Only individual human beings can learn and each does so in different ways with varying degrees of enthusiasm, ability and commitment.

It is for this reason, of course, that any credible account of how knowledge is created has to rest on a model of how the human mind works. Changes in our understanding of this – changes that are part of the development of world 3 – have resulted in great new insights into human abilities and potentialities. The idea, for instance, that there are many different forms of intelligence – such as linguistic, spatial or interpersonal (Handy, 1994) – or that there are different learning styles (Honey and Mumford, 1992) opens up the entirely new idea that, if people were helped to learn in ways that suited their unique mental profile, more would achieve their potential than currently do so. Managers in organizations who can acknowledge this are more likely than those who do not to see the full potential of their employees and concentrate on their future potential and capability rather than on more limited, present-day competencies.

Propositions about individual potentialities slide inexorably, however, into others about the social settings in which people learn. This chapter has established that people are shaped by the climate of expectations under which they work. These, in their turn, are shaped by the micro-politics of the organizations in which they are employed and the opportunities for learning that are open to them. It is for this reason that any account of the learning organization must embrace descriptions of the models of learning and of human development held by those with power to shape the learning opportunities of employment.

It is clear, however, that no account of this could be given that did not place such understanding against the prevailing interpretations of a culture about what people are capable of. A hundred years ago women were denied access to the medical profession on the grounds that they were thought to be not psychologically suited to it. Management remains a male-dominated activity. There are many structural arrangements in labour markets that deny opportunities to social groups which are disadvantaged. Age, gender, class and ethnicity still constitute grounds for holding back people from opportunities for learning and personal development. These are cultural and political closures that must be challenged by the public (especially legal) institutions of modern society.

Whether that happens or not is something dependent on the structure of the distribution of power in society. The point, however, is this: such structures do change. They can be changed. Through politics and the development of public policies education and training opportunities can be developed that were once previously denied to people. International comparative studies of education and training policies drive the conclusion that appropriate frameworks of public policy can nurture positive attitudes in companies towards training and development and shape the prevailing expectations within a society about education and training at work.

Debates about what such policies should be are debates in the realm of world 3. They are reflexive. They feed back into the worlds of things and impressions. Whether they do so depends on whether people are both enabled to and are themselves actually engaged in the process of thinking. In this way the circle becomes complete. A vibrant and productive world of ideas requires thinking people in environments that encourage them to think.

8 Communicating knowledge

I'll not throw away good knowledge on people who think they can get it by the sixpenn'orth, and carry it away with 'em as they would an ounce of snuff.

Bartle Massey the Teacher, in *Adam Bede* by George Eliot

The above quotation suggests many things. First, a central theme of this book that knowledge has value. In fact, in the context of the story of Adam Bede, it is highly precious. Secondly, knowledge *needs* to be valued and respected. Thirdly, knowledge has to be developed, worked on in context and embedded for its value to be realized. Fourthly, knowledge is also about power and status. Finally, communication, as an umbrella term, plays a crucial role in the acquisition, development and embedding of knowledge.

Aims

The aim of this chapter is to explore the following themes:

➤ Ideas on communication?

   (a) Lego brick house or plant?

   (b) dominant discourses

   (c) training for effective communication?

   (d) formal or open?

   (e) vocal tone, language and non-verbal communication;

➤ the influence of power and politics in communication;

➤ making the tacit explicit;

➤ values and communication;

➤ the idea of 'journey' in communication.

It is difficult to offer a model of communication and perhaps 'models' are the wrong way to conceive of communication. Here we offer descriptions, perspectives and approaches to communication drawn from a variety of sources. This chapter is an attempt to express the complexity of the subject, its importance in the development of a knowledge-productive organization and the very 'situated' nature of communication.

Ideas on communication?

Communication establishes meaningful distinctions between, and among, people, objects and behaviours. It also defines the structure and goals of interacting events. Therefore communication in this sense is the active, or dynamic, aspect of the social context. Fundamentally communication is concerned with the relationship between the intention and the result of the communication. This is a very complex issue. It is bound up with the inter-actions between language, meanings, emotions, histories (see earlier chapters, particularly Chapter 2) assumptions, values, agendas, power, status, systems and structures.

As the psychologist Jerome Bruner says:

> we shall be able to interpret meanings and meaning-making in a principled manner only in the degree to which we are able to specify the structure and coherence of the larger contexts in which specific meanings are created and transmitted. (1990:64)

Meaning making is a crucial importance. Illustration 8.1 offers just one perspective:

Illustration 8.1

Different meanings ....

Recently I was talking to a general manager (GM) of a business. He had just come through a merger and was expected to work closely with the managing director (MD) of the other business in the merger. The GM didn't have a problem with this at all. He knew and respected the MD.

However, friction developed. The MD said that he wanted a business with 'no secrets' and that 'all information needed to be shared and open'. The GM had no problem with this until he started to realize that 'no secrets' and 'open and shared information' was understood differently by the MD.

The GM thought these words meant that people could discuss issues when they arose and dialogue would be generally welcome. He thought in essence it meant 'let the people get on the with job and when there are things to discuss we will discuss them'. The MD meant that there would be weekly progress meetings where each person presented their activities, achievements, progress and future activities. He thought that this would help to build good rapport and an understanding of work activities.

The GM believed that this rather draconian approach to management would mean that people would be demotivated, that 'real' dialogue would go 'underground' and that in the 'public progress meetings' people would make things up and put a positive spin on their activities. He believed that it was an unnecessary control and pressure on people and that it would do the opposite of the MD's intentions.

In general there is broad agreement as to the importance of communication in organizational life and its paradoxical nature – 'Communication is the knitting which holds organizations together – and the thread which keeps coming apart. It is the greatest single influence on organizational effectiveness ..... it cannot be perfected' (Misteil, 1997:2). As suggested by the 'sting' at the end of this quote developing communication, particularly in a knowledge-productive environment, is highly problematic.

The issues behind these problems could be expressed in many ways. The communication specialist John Shotter (1998) has a view:

> there is an increasing recognition that the administrative and organization systems, within which we have long tried to relate ourselves to each other and our surroundings, are crippling us. Something is amiss. They have no place in them for us, for our humanness. While the information revolution bursts out around us, there is an emerging sense that those moments in which we are most truly alive and able to express our own unique creative reactions to the others and othernesses around us (and they to us), are being eliminated. In an over-populated world, there seem to be fewer and fewer people to talk to – and less and less time in which to do it'. (from web site http://pubpages.unh.edu/~jds/SCJ99_fin1_pap.htm)

Perhaps in our quest to compete we are at risk of losing sight of what is important. Shotter's perspective is that we are losing the ability to 'engage' or 'participate' on the level of our very humanity. He implies that we need to rethink and reframe organizational life in order to restore ourselves so that we can truly participate and become engaged in it.

Illustration 8.2 offers a perspective on this point.

Illustration 8.2

Lego brick house or plant?

I recently attended a seminar. The presenter used two visual aids. He held up a Lego house together with an impressive houseplant and asked us to look at them both.

'If you wanted to change the Lego house, what would you do?' he challenged.

'That's easy,' replied a keen member of the audience in the front row 'you just redesign it by taking it apart and putting it back together again and maybe you would buy some new bricks and add them to the construction.'

'Yes,' replied the presenter, 'and what of the plant?'

'Oh that's different,' said Mr. Keen .'That's alive.'

'Yes, indeed it is,' replied our presenter, 'just as the organizations in which we work day in, day out, are alive. Alive because they are full of people who are alive. We are not like Lego bricks, we are like the plant, we must be nurtured, fed and watered and have the right conditions for growth. Why then do the people who run our organizations insist on treating us like Lego bricks? Pull a bit off here, stick a bit on there and buy a new brick if one won't fit!'

The Lego brick house is, perhaps, the objectivist's (see Chapter 2) perspective while the plant image provides a powerful metaphor of a living organization in need of careful attention. A plant requires certain conditions for life, the Lego house is inanimate. Managers who perceive their organizations as 'dead' will behave without consideration or respect for the 'life' of the people living and working within the organization. The business world is littered with human tragedies, badly handled, poorly managed, because of the 'Lego house' perspective.

Many of us feel and believe that managers make decisions about our lives with no reference to us at all. We may feel that we play no part in their strategy. We are not consulted or asked for our views (this is particularly disempowering when we in fact have a clear view based on deep knowledge). Managers tell us that their (often self-constructed and self-justifying) strategy means that we all need to restructure and reorganize for the 'fourth' (think of a number!) time this year (Chapter 2). Jobs are put under threat, we are made to feel anxious, stressed and unwell, and then challenged for not performing well. Many of us may feel that the organizations we know and work in are indeed viewed as 'dead' and that management is doing a good job of killing them some more!

The fact that we need to reorganize and restructure for the 'fourth' time is not evidence of an emergent strategy. We believe that it is evidence of a gross misunderstanding of the nature of the complex social system of the organization. This misunderstanding is constantly communicated to us not only by the words but also by the deeds of management. This point is explored further in case study 8.2 on Engineering Co. later in this chapter.

Shotter's view on this is that we do not need to invent something new to deal with this problem, which many of us feel in our daily lives. He believes in the theme which runs through this book, that the solution lies within us (see Chapter 4): 'to understand human communication better, we do not need any new theories. We need to critically elaborate the spontaneous theory of language we already possess' (Shotter, undated, from website http://pubpages.unh.edu/~jds/SCJ99_fin1_pap.htm).

Dominant discourses

To probe deeper, in previous chapters we have raised the issue of dominant narratives. So, what are the dominant narratives associated with communication? Current discourses in organizations about communication include statements such as these shown in Table 8.1.

Table 8.1 Common communication statements

Top down	Bottom up
Cascading the message	On message
On song	Off song
Singing from the same hymn sheet	On board
Copied in/Copied to/Copied out	In the loop/Out of the loop
Grapevine/Rumour machine	Run it up the flag pole to see if it flies

Language like this creates a shared meaning. This is then backed up by behaviour and organizational structures and the dominant discourse creates a narrative. In the above discourse the meaning can be associated with insecurity, compliance, power and status differentials. This point is also considered later in the Engineering Co. case study.

In the rich landscape of a corporate curriculum communication plays an essential role in linking the features of the landscape and may assist us in creating a new discourse and a new narrative for our organizations (see Chapter 9). However, there are many complexities affecting the communication process. These include the following:

- unstated assumptions;
- incompatibility of cognitive schemata (approaches to thinking, often influenced by 'culture');
- confused presentation;
- distraction/noise/interference (Blakstad and Cooper, 1995).

- inaccurate decoding of the message;
- doubts about the true intention of the sender;
- perception and perceptual selection processes;
- semantics and the meaning of words;
- channel selection;
- inconsistent verbal and non-verbal communication (Kelly, 2000).

In the organizational context are the following:

- physical distractions;
- information overload;
- time pressure;
- technical and 'in-group' language;
- status difference;
- task and organization structure requirements;
- absence and formal communication channels (Kelly, 2000).

It is a wonder we make any progress at all!

Training for effective communication?

One way to tackle these issues is through communication skills training courses. The challenge here is that training courses in communication skills can be of benefit but they often do not tackle the whole issue. For example, we often talk of 'listening' as a key communication skill. In fact many of us have probably been on 'listening skills' courses. This is fine, and the truth is that skills are employed when listening and are necessary. In listening it is important to remember the importance of eye contact and 'congruent body language', or of asking open questions, summarizing and reflecting. It is equally true that a listener will also draw on other qualities and capacities in order to listen. These include attitudes, emotions and intentions towards the other person. Rogers' core conditions of learning (as expressed in Chapter 1) are relevant here. These elements interact with each other and influence the 'tone', the feeling and ultimately the outcome of any communication. We are sensitive beings and any person has the capability to be aware of true intentions and motivations in communication. The notion of 'unconditional positive regard' for another human being is of particular significance. This suggests that a climate of mutual respect is of vital importance in the communication process – a factor often missing in workplace communication. This is discussed later in this chapter in relation to Habermas's concept of 'ideal speech situation'. We are also suggesting that communication in this sense is a form of and a vehicle for learning in itself.

These abilities are not predominantly technical skills of an esoteric sort that have to be acquired from new. They are capacities that we use in our ordinary daily lives as human beings. Thinking of them as skills carries the risk that we regard them as new things which we need to acquire. In turn this lays down an implied threat that, when engaging in learning dialogues we may have to go and be trained first or we shall be found wanting (after Alred *et al.*,1996:4-5). The idea of 'assumed incapacity' (Chapter 3 raise the idea of trained incapacity, this is a linked concept) is a strong feeling and is often found among highly motivated and experienced managers, when they come forward to act as mentors for example. It is another illustration of Shotter's comments on the organization 'crippling' us through the imposition of technical rationality – the 'you can't do that until you are trained' mentality.

There is agreement among researchers that one of the main ways of improving communication within organizations is to tackle it at the level of the individual. Here there is an attempt to improve an individual's awareness of personal values, beliefs and attitudes and how they affect his or her perception (Kelly, 2000). To communicate knowledge productively with another person requires high levels of this type of self-knowledge. Knowing oneself is a step towards knowing others. This point is strongly stated throughout Shotter's work.

The concept of self-knowledge or self-regulation, as discussed in Chapter 5, plays a vital role in helping us move beyond training and recognizing that, as humans we possess many abilities simply by virtue of living in a community. The challenge is that often we are unable to make the links and connections between our various skills and abilities and different contexts. We find it difficult to think in terms of 'transferable skills and abilities'. This, we suggest, is a consequence of the dominance of the 'formal or closed' curriculum.

As discussed in Chapter 5, mentoring-type activity can make a substantial contribution in improving the self-knowledge that is a necessary part of knowledge-productive communication. Here we believe there is a distinction between communication as 'information giving' and communication as a means of learning to be knowledge productive.

Formal or open?

Communication can be seen as being about both the 'formal or closed' elements of the curriculum and the 'open or informal'. Although there are many 'formal or closed' approaches to communication within an organization that are helpful and valuable, they can often be based on a one-way system of communication, and the one-way is often top down. The 'one-way' approach is fine for delivering information, but it offers little opportunity for checking meaning and exploring assumptions. This point is illustrated by Figure 8.1:

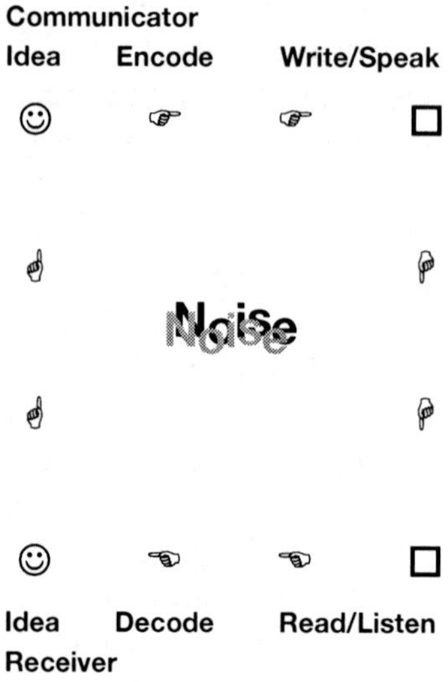

Communicator

Idea   Encode   Write/Speak

☺   ☞   ☞   ▢

Noise

☺   🖎   🖎   ▢

Idea   Decode   Read/Listen
Receiver

Figure 8.1 Communication cycle

The 'communicator', the transmitter of the communication, has an idea. This may be in the form of a feeling, an image, and sometimes words. To communicate it the 'communicator' has to 'encode' it into language and then write or speak it. The 'receiver' needs to listen or read the piece of communication and 'decode' it back into feelings, images or words. Hopefully the 'receiver' will then have the same idea as the 'communicator' and respond. Sadly this often fails because of the 'noise' in the process. 'Noise' is related to emotions, skill levels at speaking, writing, reading and listening, background knowledge, context and status. The 'communicator' has his or her agenda and 'history' that influences the communication and so does the 'receiver'.

In the context of knowledge management, information is often communicated via the written word. This raises many 'noise' problems and assumes that the reader is sufficiently skilled at reading to interact with the material or to engage in what Frank Smith (1994) refers to as having a conversation with the text.

The important element in all forms of communication is 'shared meaning'. In a knowledge productive environment it is both the 'communicator's' and the 'receiver's' job to develop 'shared meanings'. This involves the 'communicator' in understanding the 'receiver's' history and agenda and adapting the communication accordingly. In the same way the 'receiver' needs to be aware of the 'communicator's' history and adapt accordingly. The participants' intentional states become important and status without respect in either direction provides another layer of 'noise' in the process.

Vocal tone, language and non-verbal communication

Further elements in the communication process include the vocal tone, the language and the non-verbal element of all human interactions.

The vocal tone is an important element as it offers scope for misunderstanding. Often this has cultural significance as non-native speakers or writers may not appreciate the subtleties of the language in use. It is easy to be rude without meaning to be! Vocal tone on written communication is very difficult to detect and easily misunderstood. The 'tone' of a piece of writing is often a matter of opinion and relates to the emotional state and the assumptions made by the reader. One person's innuendo is another's honest assessment of a situation.

The language of communication is also important. In groups, people develop ways of talking to each other. This defines the group and creates a sense of belonging. It also excludes those who do not have the language. Some sociologists call this 'restricted codes'. As Gigliogi (1972:567) states: 'We share a linguistic repertoire with members of our social networks and failure to fit in linguistically may have far reaching consequences.' Within a pluralist, complex organization this has the effect of creating sub-groups and 'in' groups and 'out' groups. In John Shotter's terms this is known as 'otherness'. This creates a social challenge for any organization and is a challenge that cannot be met through conventional management controls because it is often in the 'shadow side' (Egan, 1993) (see Chapter 1).

The elements of non-verbal language also play an important role in the communication process. These include facial expression, gesture and body language. None are so precise as to avoid confusion and comprehension failure. Business people who work across national boundaries often encounter real difficulty in multi-cultural communication because of social differences in non-verbal communication.

If we examine the basic ways in which we communicate – face to face, telephone, writing – only face to face includes all of the three elements of tone, language and non-verbal communication. The implications of this are not completely clear but may suggest that written communications may be better for information exchange and that telephone conversations are second to face-to-face dialogue if developing shared meanings is the objective.

All these elements of communication combine to make important contributions to the construction of shared meanings. They are often spontaneous and as such happen in specific contexts and specific situations. We argue that they represent basic elements of our humanity and are difficult, if not impossible, to 'train' (in the formal curriculum sense) into people but are acquired through participation and social engagement and perhaps through a form of role modelling. As Shotter (undated) puts it 'new understandings can emerge in our spontaneous living relations with the others ... which teach us something which cannot be learnt in any other way' (from website http://pubpages.unh.edu/~jds/SCJ99_fin1_pap.htm).

The message is clear: there are some things we learn in the 'heat of the moment' or, put another way, in the 'open curriculum'.

Case study 8.1 is an exploration of communication within a corporate curriculum framework.

Case study 8.1

Oil Company Co.

Oil Company Co. UK Ltd was a division of Oil Company Co. Following a recent merger, it is now part of the Oil Company Co. group. The division offers a 'total package' to its clients of specialist technical know-how as well as a range of specific lubricants for a variety of industrial applications. The majority of 'field' staff work from home.

Over the last five years Oil Company Co. has been on a journey of development, at the heart of which has been a range of people policies. These have included the application of sophisticated recruitment and selection techniques and extensive training and development. Both performance and development activities are rewarded through the pay scheme. The measurable performance benefits of this approach have been substantial.

The project

A group of five people with different interests and responsibilities within Oil Company Co. and a researcher were brought together for a series of discussions held over a four-month period.

The corporate curriculum formed the framework for the discussions. The overall aim was to develop a learning strategy for the diversion that will enable the people in the business to be knowledge productive.

Following a discussion session (which generally lasted a full working day) the main group members undertook to relay its content to their team members and to return to the next main discussion group with feedback from their teams. In this way the methodology itself created change within the various teams as the process unfolded and progressed.

Communication, as an element of the corporate curriculum, was discussed with the following results:

- The idea of communication for knowledge productivity offers great potential.
- Communication is about giving and receiving, interpretation, impact and action.
- Communication is not primarily about disseminating information.
- The quality of communication has implications for approaches to learning.
- There are close links to other elements of the corporate curriculum.
- Communication needs to be about encouraging learning.
- Communication has the potential to motivate, enthuse, build relationships and develop 'passion' in and for people's work.
- Qualities such as empathy, understanding and emotional impact are important aspects of communication.
- Understanding communication from someone else's perspective is important.
- Communication carries with it responsibility and it needs to be clear and focused on the recipients' needs.
- There is a need to prioritize communication to avoid overload and inefficiency.
- Currently in Oil Company Co. there is a tendency to 'blast' people with information or to assume 'mental telepathy' – that people 'just know'.

While homeworking has many benefits and helps to create a more 'open' curriculum, the communication networks it creates sometimes manufacture 'in' groups and 'out' groups. This is not deliberate but for various reasons some people are not in the 'informal' communication loops. Consequently they cannot participate in knowledge-productive communication.

The discussion group identified the need for a greater integration of the division's individual functional areas through knowledge sharing and mutual understanding, i.e. sales and production. In this way it would be possible to develop a 'one team' philosophy rather than a regional or functional team orientation. The participants agreed that there were organizational and functional conflicts between groups and that the 'homeworking' approach for people in the field presented a social challenge for learning and knowledge productivity.

▶

Ideas for action

- Develop an interactive information system for basic current information.
- Develop an interactive information library for archive knowledge and case studies.
- Develop an understanding of communication approaches and philosophy through dialogue and education.
- Enhance and develop the existing measurement system to include communication.
- Develop a 'code of conduct' for communication to minimize overload.

The influence of power and politics in communication

From our own experience of working in a range of organizations it is clear that the topic of communication often dominates the management agenda. In climate and attitudinal surveys it is nearly always an area for concern for managers. Time after time these surveys point to the issues of 'status' and 'power' as key to people's perception of how well communication is working in their organization. For example, the more senior the respondents, the more positive the perspective on the timeliness and accuracy of information. The more junior the respondents, the less positive the perspective on the timeliness and accuracy of information.

For many 'ordinary' people working in organizations this finding is not a surprise. Daily they are exposed to the influence of the complexity in communication that comes from status and power. Under some circumstances communication becomes distorted. The German sociologist, Habermas, has discussed this extensively (1989). His idea is that differences in power and status between people and groups can distort the communication between them. This leads to mutually suspicious interpretations of the other's meaning. In some settings, for example political propaganda, distortion is built into the communication process. Habermas's remedy for distorted communication is the 'ideal speech situation'. Here genuine dialogue is nurtured between people who possess the same information on a topic, the same skills to debate it and who agree before they discuss the matter to follow the precepts of logic and reason and to respect one another. The model of the 'ideal speech situation' is rarely enacted in practice; it represents a standard to be achieved. In the absence of these conditions communication can be one-sided, confused, and can breed resentment and suspicion.

The thrust of our argument is that knowledge-productive communication requires open dialogue and respect for persons. It relies equally on the distribution of information and the acknowledgement of the right of people to hold different opinions. The search for truth, in this sense, requires both justice in human rights and social equality. Case study 8.2 illustrates these points.

Case study 8.2

Engineering Co. (see Chapter 4)

To implement the changes required by its new corporate stratergy success-fully Engineering Co. recognized the need to change the management culture. To do this they introduced a new management philosophy to *implant* the concepts of 'learning organization' and 'continuous improve-ment'. The philosophy was dominated by the 'customer-led' concept. The senior management of Engineering Co. recognized that the change was only achievable through the involvement and commitment of the whole work-force. *'The battle for supremacy in the market place will be won on the factory floor'* was the international corporate statement.

In the past at Engineering Co. authority, responsibility and control were firmly in the hands of management. This encouraged an autocratic manage-ment style, which focused primarily on the task and ignored the motivational and developmental needs of the staff. The main challenge of the Engineering Co. Production System was to change this management style.

A programme of education and training was used to help achieve this change, and central to the whole international programme was the notion of 'the common approach'. This meant that all training inputs, development systems and evaluation processes were underpinned by constant reference to Engineering Co.'s objectives.

Language and communication

The changes were heavily communicated through documents and slogans posted around every site. It was a 'top-down' approach. Senior management recognized that change could be achieved if the language was changed. So they changed it. However, this did not go far enough. On the shopfloor the change of language was linked to the past perception of autocratic manage-ment and, although the slogans appeared and management language changed on the surface, the 'real' language of management and its behav-iour remained the same as it had always been.

So managers, when in 'manager role', talked of 'people are our most impor-tant assets', 'we're in it for the haul' and 'it's people who make the difference.' But, when they were 'themselves' they talked of the workforce as 'the animals', they were going to 'break their backsides' and 'hold their feet to the fire'. In terms of the behavioural change, this can be summed up by a supervisor: 'You can talk about development as much as you like, but if the product is not out of the door on Friday you still get your backside kicked.' In sum, here is a complete contradiction between the espoused language and behaviour of change and the reality of true underlying values. The autocratic

▶

'mindset' dominated the implementation and the workforce knew this. Consequently the change was a failure and the autocratic 'mindset' dominated the narrative.

This case raises many moral, ethical and practical questions. Here are just three.

1 Is change and development in the commercial context focused on people as a means to an end or ends in themselves?
2 Can the two, seemingly opposing, agendas of commercial progress and valuing people ever be compatible?
3 Many organizations use the language of development, but management action and behaviour rarely matches the rhetoric. Can we learn a new way? Or are we simply providing nineteenth-century solutions dressed up in 'new' language?

Making the tacit explicit

The Oil Company Co. case study illustrates the problems encountered in making explicit the tacit. The term 'tacit knowledge' has been used throughout this book and is an important concept. Some explain it by saying that it is the sum total of an individual's experience, fully internalized and more than they can express. Tacit knowledge is a combination and coming together of the technical and rational and the personal, emotional and intuitive. As Nonaka (1991:98) suggests, it 'consists partly of technical skills – the kind of informal, hard-to-pin-down skills captured in the term 'know-how'. A master craftsman after years of experience develops a wealth of expertise 'at his fingertips'.

Boisot (1995) suggests that tacit, uncodified knowledge is that which is internal to an individual but that this is only of any value if it has become explicit. Tacit knowledge becomes explicit through social interaction. The environment in which the social discourse takes place is a significant influence on the ability of the participants to exchange and develop their mutual understanding. The participants 'make sense' of their worlds through social engagement. Piaget's theory of decentration is helpful here: 'An adult person's repertory of possible perspectives entails as experiential possibilities aspects that are immediately visible only from the position of her or his conversation partner'(Rommetveit, 1985:189). Communication is clearly central to making the tacit explicit. But here is a paradox. Boisot (1995) suggests that the tacit is the knowledge with real commercial value, but once it is explicit through socialization the competitive edge is naturally lost. If this is the case, knowledge management systems, the current manifestation of making the tacit explicit, may be the source of competitive failure and not the source of advantage some would have us believe!

To return to Oil Company Co., one response to their challenge is to create an interactive database of field cases for colleagues to share and learn from. This would help to make the tacit explicit. This may be helpful in putting into the public domain certain experiences but, unfortunately, it would not guarantee the development and acquisition of any type of knowledge. The information would be communicated but that would be all. This type of explicit knowledge needs facilitation, grounding and transferring into other domains, and this can only happen through a different type of communication not based on information alone but also on dialogue and learning conversations between individuals and groups of people. A knowledge management system is a good start but the socialization process also needs to be present. As Nonaka (1991:98–9) puts it:

> Sometimes, one individual shares tacit knowledge directly with another. For example, when Ikuko Tanaka apprentices herself to the head baker at the Osaka International Hotel, she learns his tacit skills through observation, imitation, and practice. They become part of her own tacit knowledge base. Put another way, she is 'socialised' into the craft.

Through knowledge-productive discussion, perspectives are modified and developed and sense is made. The participants engage in 'an intersubjective world, common to all of us' (Schutz, 1945:534). The dialogue point is crucial. As Bruner says, 'language is a way of sorting out one's thoughts about things' (1985:23). We cannot emphasize enough that the knowledge-productive way in organizations means that meaningful dialogues, as the medium of communication, are essential. Once the tacit has been made explicit we continue to build new tacit knowledge grounded in meaningful, purposeful and relevant experience.

Values and communication

So far we have examined the social and psychological dynamics of communication and only touched briefly on the relationship between communication and values. This theme needs to be made explicit for it is crucial to the task of understanding how organizations can improve the ways in which people in them communicate with one another.

The organization of scientific work provides us with one of the most successful models of knowledge generation known to humankind. Science is organized to promote open communication of information and ideas. Of course a great deal of scientific work carried out for governments or commercial organizations is secret, but this does not detract from the main point: scientific ideas that have come to be accepted have been openly debated and discussed and thoroughly tested. The US sociologist, Robert Merton (1958a) suggested half a century ago, during the Second World War, in a famous essay 'Science and democratic social structure' that science was as much informed by an underlying moral commitment to truthfulness as it was to its methodological principles to discover new knowledge.

What Merton called the 'ethos' of modern science was a combination, in his view, of four 'institutional imperatives' (1958:553). These were, first: universalism – the idea that science is impersonal; truth does not depend on the status of the person claiming to know it. Secondly, there is the norm of what he called 'disciplinary communism' – the idea that science is a collaborative enterprise that eschews secrecy and celebrates the common ownership of ideas. Thirdly, there is 'disinterestedness', the presupposition that truth claims are based on evidence and not self-interests or group loyalties. Finally, he cited 'organized scepticism', an attitude of suspended judgement until all the facts are to hand.

This excursion into the moral suppositions of science was written during the Second World War when the excesses of Nazi science were already well known. National Socialism created an institutional science that dedicated itself to the service, not of science, but the state. The essay was written before the explosion of atomic weapons in Hiroshima and Nagasaki but the force of Merton's argument nevertheless remains: all the institutional imperatives of science – and therefore of the growth of knowledge – are threatened by the politics of power. His essay was a timely reminder to democratic politicians that science required an open society in which ideas can be tested; that science was a value-governed activity and that its most important institutional imperative was openness of communication. Without that it cannot flourish.

The openness of communication is not just a technical matter depending upon whether communication channels are free and accessible. It is much more a problem of values and of whether or not people in an organization share a sense of its purpose and its values and whether there is an underlying commitment to truthfulness informing the communication that takes place. Two further illustrations from the period of the Second World War illustrate this point. Illustration 8.3 concerns Viscount Slim of Burma, the British general who pushed the occupying Japanese Imperial Army out of Burma while Illustration 8.4 tells of Adolf Hitler, whose distorted communication led to military disaster in Russia.

Illustration 8.3

General Slim was called to India from the Middle East in 1942 to organize the fight back to recapture Burma. In his book *Defeat into Victory* (1986) he explains the principles that governed his approach to this problem. First, he diagnosed the problem. Burma was overrun; British military intelligence was poor; troops had no training in jungle warfare. They were below combat strength, seriously ill with tropical diseases, stretched across a long battle front and suffering very low morale. Such was Slim's diagnosis. His solution centred on morale and, as he considered the role he had been given, he set out the principles that would guide him. 'Morale' he wrote 'is a state of mind.'

> It is that intangible force which will move a whole group of men to give their last ounce to achieve something, without counting the cost to themselves; that makes them feel they are part of something greater than themselves . . . The foundations are spiritual, intellectual and material, and that is the order of their importance. (p.182)

By the term 'spiritual' he meant values: the troops needed to know why the war was worth fighting. The intellectual requirement of high morale was that everyone should know and understand what their role in the war effort was. Material resources included machines and weapons and supplies. Without a commitment to the values that informed the task and a clear, checked-out understanding of their role in the enterprise, no amount of equipment would have helped British and Burmese troops to achieve the recapture of Burma. Slim made a point of open communication, both up and down the lines of command. He discouraged written communications because they could be ambiguous. All communicated messages had to be clarified and checked that they had been understood.

Slim was held in great trust by his men. They felt he worked for them. His views on leadership are still an important part of the training of senior British Army officers. Though he did not use the language of management theory his insights are entirely modern and telling: communication is the key to finding new solutions to problems. The task of leadership in an organization is to remove the barriers, both structural and emotional, to effective, inclusive communication. Slim was the author of the phrase used by the British Military: 'Serve to Lead'.

It took two years to recapture Burma; a job was done that would have seemed unimaginably impossible at the outset for it required tactics, ideas and actions unknown at that point to the troops. Slim was able to put together the organizational and communication pre-conditions of a successful campaign.

Illustration 8.4

In contrast, Anthony Beevor's (1998) recent and much-acclaimed book, *Stalingrad*, is a vivid account of the defeat of Hitler's armies on the Volga. It is a chilling military history informed by recently available Soviet and German archive materials. The outlines of the defeat at Stalingrad are well known: an overstretched, exhausted, undersupplied, demoralized army was no match for Soviet strength and the Russian winter. Beevor's book can be read, however, as a study in organizational communication. What it reveals is a German High Command structured to insulate Hitler from bad news, to deny him the truth about the conditions on the ground. His refusal to allow General Paulus's 6th Army to surrender and his insistence that Stalingrad should be held at all costs were completely irrational and an unsustainable position. German generals kept information from Hitler in order to ingratiate themselves or pre-empt his angry responses to failure. Communication in the High Command became ever more distant from the realities of the armies on the ground. Senior staff were prepared, in effect, to write off the quarter of a million men in the 6th Army to protect themselves in the paranoid politics of the Third Reich.

These illustrations from military history have a clear analytical message. The values that inform the work of an organization are crucial to the quality and effectiveness of the communication that takes place within it. Where there is openness, trust, respect for people and an overarching moral commitment to truthfulness, communication is likely to be effective and productive of new ideas and new ways of doing things. When these conditions do not apply there is a real risk of failure and of repetition of old mistakes.

The wartime examples, as well as that of the institutional imperatives of science, that have been mentioned here should not be dismissed as out of date or merely of historical interest. A key message that is directly relevant to the present day is that the moral requirements of the growth of knowledge and understanding are under constant threat. Science remains the most powerful model of knowledge productivity in our society. Yet the scientific enterprise is threatened by military and commercial pressures, secrecy, and competitiveness. In an open society there should be – and, indeed, there is – an overt debate about the values that govern scientific research, the interests that predominate in it and its consequences for the way we all have to live our lives.

What is true for science is true also for the work of all organizations that generate ideas, perspectives, ways of thinking – discourses – that shape the ways in which different groups of people conceive of and find the solutions for the problems that they regard as important, public and urgent.

The idea of 'journey' in communication

As a summary and a conclusion to this chapter we return to the concept of 'journey'. In Chapter 2 we quoted a section from Cavafy's poem *Ithaca*. This poem very clearly expresses the idea that travelling on a journey is of greater value than the destination. The journey is the experience and not the end point. In Laurent Daloz's book *Effective Teaching and Mentoring*, he suggests that 'development is like a journey from the familiar to confusion, adventure, great highs, and lows, struggle, uncertainty . . . towards a new world in which nothing is different but all is transformed, its meaning is profoundly changed' (1986:Ch.3).

We can conceive communication as 'information giving', with its end point being 'the information given'. We can also think of communication as developmental, as a journey of discovery in a learning landscape where 'personnel and teams find their way and construct knowledge' (Kessels, 1996:10) (see Chapter 5).

The scientific world has a long tradition of debate and dialogue based on openness and inclusion. A scientist writes up his or her work and presents it at a conference. The conference then debates the work, challenges it and tests the knowledge. It is only then that information becomes knowledge – when it has been put to the test. This is often retrospective, but the knowledge produced is viewed as 'in transit'. Science has learned that knowing is not a fixed point.

We put forward the idea that the 'destination' concept is the current dominant discourse, that organizations are obsessed with the arrival rather than with the travelling and this creates a narrative that locks us in the present. In one of the case studies in this book Company A, UK has a slogan – 'A company on the journey to excellence'. The challenge for all of us engaged in organizational life is to live the slogan.

Critique of Part 3

Harm H. Tillema, *University of Leiden, the Netherlands*

Knowledge-productive learning; what is it all about?

Concepts and conceptions may turn out to be walls, obstructing the view on the actual space of what really matters.

Denzo Genpo Merzel, *The Eye Never Sleeps* (1993)

What is needed to promote knowledge-productive learning in organizations? This question might summarize the effort undertaken in the last three chapters where some informative answers were given and some new and challenging perspectives outlined. The central message delivered may perhaps be phrased as follows: reaching knowledge productivity in organizations is the arrangement of learning environments that will stimulate people to develop, exchange and communicate their knowledge. The social contexts in which people work are inseparably related to their achievement and development. Therefore setting the conditions for active engagement in self-study, collaborative inquiry or creative teamwork may help people to reframe their thinking and encourage them to make their tacit knowledge explicit, to the benefit of both the employee as a learner and the organization as a productive entity. This perspective could be labelled knowledge-productive learning (KPL) in organizations, and deals with 'engineering' the conditions for creative thinking and critical awareness within organizations. It acknowledges the social and communicative nature of persons learning in organizations who are constantly aware of and reflect on what they do – 'through knowledge-productive discussion perspectives are modified and developed and sense is made' (Chapter 8).

The achievement of KPL in organizations, however, is fraught with all kinds of inherent tensions. The authors are quite explicit about this: i.e., there are tensions between openness and closure, between dialogue and keeping information to oneself, between power and being yourself between stability and risk taking between commitment and expediency and between destination and journey.

KPL may become a challenging concept in human resource development and a fruitful idea to pursue in organizations, and as such may frame our thinking on engineering the conditions for learning, but it still is, I believe, underdeveloped as it stands. That is why, instead of simply reviewing and reflecting on what has been put forward in Part 3, I would like to take a more constructive stance. I would like to build further on the notion of achieving KPL by adding the concept of authenticity. This, I believe, may have good prospects for integrating some of the major points the authors make.

My position will be that alongside the elements of creativity, structural reflexivity, innovative thinking and open communication, as put forward by the authors, knowledge-productive learning can be comprehended more explicitly and coherently by taking the perspective of authenticity as a frame of reference to incorporate the different notions and to point out the mechanisms by which KPL can be attained. This thereby retains the authors' focus on people as the heart of an organization, integrating the elements of tacit knowledge exchange and dialogue, self-directedness and personal free-dom as conditions of learning. It also uses the social communicative dimension of collaboration in teams to create, reframe and renew the knowledge base of the organization. How, then can organizations create environments that provide for and enhance knowledge-productive learning?

Caution is warranted, however, and the above-mentioned tensions might illustrate this. Evaluation studies of stimulating learning processes in organizations (Katzenbach and Smith, 1993; Winslow and Bramer, 1994; Probst and Buchel, 1997) reveal the early adopters' uneasiness and the many uncertainties about broadening the workplace to become a site of learning. They emphasize the potential threatening nature of open and discovery-oriented approaches to knowledge construction. There are people learning in organizations who themselves remain inert (as, for instance, in the case of the Engineering Co. in Chapters 4 and 8); and there are organizations that learn without their employees developing or changing.

Starting from a dilemma that most employees experience in developing competence in their work, I would like to explore what authenticity means as the active ingredient for KPL in organizations.

A central HRD dilemma: engaging in knowledge-productive learning while working under pressure. How can workers become learners as well? Acknowledging the inherent potential of employees as knowledge workers, we have to realize that they predominantly possess highly encapsulated and implicit (or tacit) knowledge (Fenstermacher, 1994; Probst and Buchel, 1997). Furthermore, it has to be recognized that people often work in isolation, with not much opportunity for exchange (Huberman, 1995), and are most of the time under pressure (Winslow and Bramer, 1994). Moreover, organizational conditions often provide little opportunity to renew explicitly and (re)create their knowledge base (Eraut, 1994). There are in fact few, if any, tempting learning conditions available in regular work, and most work requires people to configure their response to given or fixed formats. In order to develop and constantly build on their existing knowledge (Butler and Winne, 1995), explicit formats and apparent settings of exchange have to be erected in order for persons to unfold as knowledge-productive workers (Drucker, 1993). Knowledge-productive learning would require a dynamic interchange between the implicit, i.e, tacit knowledge and the explicit, i.e., intentional, goal-directed learning (Nonaka and Takeuchi, 1994). New ways of creative thinking (Cobb, 1994; Anderson, 2000) are needed to enhance knowledge-productive learning. These may use formats such dialogue, reflection, inquiry and self-regulation as vehicles for exchange of knowledge between persons, thus creating settings that will take into account the learners' interests, beliefs and practical theories to arrive at authentic contributions in work (Wallace and Louden, 1994).

It is therefore essential to be able to revert to a mechanism that can convert the dilemma into a positive circumstance. The authors rightfully point to creating the necessary conditions in organizations (instead of depending on an individualized model of creativity in learners) and establishing formats that support and sustain learning in organizations. However, we again face the questions of what mechanisms can make this transformation feasible?

The perspective of authenticity

Achievements, and productivity of persons for that matter, depend to a large extent on the opportunity to demonstrate what one can do (i.e., the Oil Company Co. case study in Chapter 8). Studies of performance in organizations (Brooks, 1994; Winslow and Bramer, 1994) point to the importance of the contexts in which people work. These determine their motivation to engage in new, challenging activities, and enhance their productivity as well as their innovative potential, which would otherwise remain tied to fixed routines and eventually lead to a gradual drop in productivity. The preceding chapters have made it abundantly clear that it is the organizational environment and its embedded management thinking which promotes (or denies) the basic elements of humanity and spontaneity in learning. However, these chapters still lacked an appropriate concept through which this point could be explained in a coherent and captive way.

Taylor (1991) argued for a culture of authenticity in learning within the workplace, which was based on the argument that authenticity is a moral ideal of which an integral part is self-determining freedom: 'There is a certain way of being human that is my way. If I am not, I miss the point of my life, I miss what being human is for me' (p 29). According to Taylor:

> authenticity (A) involves (i) creation and construction as well as discovery, (ii) originality, and frequently (iii) opposition to the rules of society and even potentially to what we recognise as morality. It (B) requires (i) openness to horizons of significance and (ii) a self-definition in dialogue (1991:66)

Authenticity on the one hand is about 'finding my own design of life and work', and on the other hand about finding relationships to fulfil ourselves; it is a 'dialogical feature of our condition without which human desires are self defeating, and can destroy conditions for realizing authenticity itself.' (p 35). The notions of difference, originality, of acceptance of diversity is part of the modern understanding of authenticity (Van der Westhuizen, 1993).

Discovering one's authenticity means not working in isolation but negotiating work through dialogue, partly overt, partly internalized, with others.

> To come together on a mutual recognition of difference that is, of the equal value of different identities [it] requires that we share more than a belief; we have to share also some standards of value on which the identities concerned check out as equal. (Taylor, 1992:52)

Authenticity as a concept may condense in features of knowledge-productive learning, resembling what Shuell (1990) called 'active meaningful learning', i.e., denoting a constructive, cumulative and goal-directed learning process (Pintrich *et al.*, 1993; Claxton, 1996) learning environments and organizational conditions promoting creative solutions to daily problems instead of routines or trained responses, and a culture of communication and collaboration in teams.

This knowledge-productive learning not only requires an orientation towards the learning needs and (prior) work experiences of the worker/learner, but also requires a work context in which communication evokes relevant explicit knowledge (Engeström, 1994).

The concept of authenticity may provide a benchmark for the evaluation of frequently mentioned principles for designing interventions to stimulate KPL. These may include interventions such as conceptual dialogue and exchange among peers (Wilson and Cole, 1992; Spiro, 1990) in which reflection and dialogue between collaborating learners are taken as the starting point for exploring new ideas or strategies. Learners/workers are using ideas such as collaborative learning in teams (Katzenbach and Smith, 1993; Wallace and Louden, 1994) as platforms for generating new knowledge, self regulated learning and inquiry (Zimmerman, 1990; Claxton *et al.* 1999).

Here the study *into* and discovery *of* the analysis and design of work, as part of practice, is being used to assist people to become more knowledgeable about their own work environment.

These principles constitute important elements of the concept of authenticity, which may help us to interpret and design interventions in organizations suitable for knowledge-productive learning. A brief evaluation of these principles from the perspective of authenticity is called for, in addition to what has already been elaborated in Part 3.

Building blocks of KPL

Conceptual exchange and reflective dialogue, as ways of making explicit the tacit knowledge, have an enormous potential impact on action, as is apparent in the work of Engeström (1994) as well as others (Cobb, 1994; Eraut, 1994). Existing beliefs and embedded conceptions lie at the heart of self-regulative action (Wallace, 1995). Critics (Gilroy, 1993; Eraut, 1994) of the concept of the reflective practitioner (Schon, 1983), however, point to the problem that reflection in learning may remain implicit and local, and may even lead to idiosyncratic knowledge, not open for scrutiny (Egan, 1997). From an authenticity point of view implicit beliefs and conceptions must be challenged and opened for external debate in order to become of relevance for professional action; and this occurs only when they can be communicated and shared with others. Exchange and dialogue together with reflection, and conceptions together with exchange, are therefore central features in knowledge-productive learning. Engeström (1994) studied the process of exchange (among engineers, technical operators and teachers) and showed that unfolding ideas in a discourse allows for multiple perspectives and value-added solutions which contribute to better and mutual understanding and to the productive generation of new knowledge.

Self-directedness in learning

A second principle that contributes to knowledge-productive learning is the self-regulation of learners. Essentially this is a process by which one directs and controls learning to attain one's goals (Zimmerman, 1990; Claxton *et al.*, 1996), using several learning strategies as well as meta-cognitive monitoring in developing knowledge.

From an authenticity perspective it gives the learner freedom to learn, but also a greater degree of responsibility for accomplishing one's goals. It requires an active and personal involvement in learning and the setting of personal standards that can be reached in a realistic way. Knowledge is seen as a tool or a vehicle, not as an object for study and inquiry, i.e., attached to issues that are at the core of one's performance. In this respect the person becomes a manager of his or her own learning. This learning is not necessarily equated with individual learning per se; it also implies learning to operate in teams and co-operate with others.

Collaboration in teams

Wallace and Louden (1994) described some of the dynamics of collaboration as related to authenticity. They describe a picture of the 'deeply personal nature' of the qualities of successful collaboration. They base their analysis on the personal characteristics of knowledge, and on the central place of biography and experience in work lives. In the supplement to the *International Encyclopaedia of Research in Education* collaboration is defined as 'a relationship that involves 'receptivity of the other', one that pays careful attention to the other's voice. In their description of faculty research collaboration Baldwin and Austin (1995) have identified six dynamics of collaboration as follows.

1 a degree of jointness (distinctive roles vs shared responsibility);
2 definition of roles and responsibilities (explicitness vs openness);
3 flexibility of roles (rigid vs flexible);
4 similarity of standards and expectations (uniformity vs different perspectives);
5 proximity of partners (local vs distant involvement);
6 depth of relationship (personal and professional vs strictly work relation).

In this description of dynamics some of the elements of authenticity, described above, may be recognized again.

Organizational support of KPL

Baldwin and Austin's intervention of conceptual exchange entails four stages.

1: recognition and attention in order to explicate one's knowledge and beliefs

Originally great value is attached to discrepancy and confrontation as a way of arriving at a point where the learner experienced a 'cognitive conflict'; which was thought to provide a starting point for the introduction of new ideas (Posner *et al.*, 1982). However, more incremental ways of motivating and interesting people in to new knowledge may lead to attention and explication (Tillema, 1997; Pintrich *et al.*, 1993).

2: evaluation and investigation or study

The best way to decide whether new ideas are plausible, fruitful and intelligent is to experiment, study and investigate. Creating opportunities to get acquainted with new information and to try out new ideas (in a non-manipulative, non-threatening way) is an important condition for knowledge-productive learning. But only in so far as one is encouraged to handle new information in one's own way and to test the tenability of one's existing ideas.

3: decision to change or generate new knowledge

This stage is in fact composed of the actual moment at which new information is perceived to be acceptable, i.e., coherent or reconcilable with the pre-existing knowledge, and as such it is prepared for in the previous stages. Instruction can bring a person to this point; it is, however, up to the learner to make the decision to change and allow a reconstruction of his or her knowledge base.

4: reconstruction, or building up a revised knowledge structure

The way in which organizations may use authentic ways of developing expertise in personnel is certainly rife with tension, as the previous chapters indicate (see also Probst and Buchel, 1997). There are, however, some powerful learning interventions that may open up encapsulated knowledge and bring about authentic contributions in organizations. Approaches to knowledge-productive learning (Wallace, 1995; Anderson *et al.* 2000) have assigned a prominent role to conceptual exchange, self-regulation and collaborative inquiry of learners. They stress authenticity and self-determination. Attempts to incorporate these principles into an interventionist format may take different forms in which present knowledge, perceptions and beliefs are taken as the starting point for the inquiry of new concepts or strategies in work contexts. The authors caution against a strictly interventionist interpretation in this respect, which would revert to prescription and outlining that runs counter to finding authentic solutions. The cases in Part 3 show us organizations that have learned to adopt their own solutions. In other senarios, it might help to be able to fall back on ingredients that may draft solutions for particular organizational contexts.

REFERENCES

Anderson, J.R., Greeno, J.G., Reder, L.M., and Simon, H. (2000). 'Perspectives on learning, thinking and activity', *Educational Researcher*, vol. 29, no. 11–14.

Baldwin, R.G. and Austin, A.E. (1995) 'Toward greater understanding of faculty research collaboration'. *Review of Higher Education*, vol. 19, no. 2, pp 45–70.

Brooks, A.K. (1994) 'Power and the production of knowledge: collective team learning in work organizations', *HRD Quarterly* no. 5, pp 213–228.

Butler, D.L. and Winne, P.H. (1995) 'Feedback and self-regulated learning: a theoretical synthesis', *Review of Educational Research*, vol 65, no.3. pp 245–82.

Claxton, G., Atkinson, T., Osborn, M., and Wallace, M. (eds) (1996) *Liberating the Learner*, New York, Routledge.

Cobb, P. (1994) 'Where is the mind? Constructivist and sociocultural perspectives on mathematical development', *Educational Researcher*, vol. 23, no. 7, pp 13–20.

Drucker, P.F. (1993) *Post Capitalist Society*. New York, HarperCollins.

Egan, K. (1997) *The Educated Mind*. Chicago, IL, Chicago University Press.

Eraut, M. (1994) *Developing Professional Knowledge and Competence*, London, Falmer Press.

Engeström, Y. (1994) 'Teachers as collaborative thinkers', in Carlgren, I. (ed.) *Teachers' Minds and Actions*, London, Falmer Press.

Fenstermacher, G.D. (1994) 'The knower and the known: the nature of knowledge in research on teaching', in Darling-Hammond, L. (ed.) *Review of Research in Education*, no. 20, pp 3–56.

Gilroy, P. (1993) 'Reflections on Schon: an epistemological critique', in Gilroy, P. and Smith, M. (eds) *International Analysis of Teacher Education*, London, Carfax.

Huberman, M. (1995) 'Networks that alter teaching: conceptualizations, exchanges and experiments', *Teaching & Teachers*, no.1 pp 193-212.

International Encyclopedia of Research in Education (1996). Macmillan, New York.

Katzenbach, J.R. and Smith, D.G. (1993) *The Wisdom of Teams: Creating the High Performance Organization*. Boston, MA. Harvard Business School Press.

Merzel, D.G. (1993) *The Eye Never Sleeps* [in Dutch], Kluwer, Deventer.

Nonaka, I. and Takeuchi, N. (1994) 'A dynamic theory of organizational knowledge creation', *Organization Science*. vol. 5 no.1, pp 84–103.

Pintrich, P.R. Marx, R.W. and Boyle, R.A. (1993) 'Beyond cold conceptual change: the role of motivational beliefs and classroom contextual factors in the process of conceptual change', *Review of Educational Research*, vol. 63, no. 2, pp 167–200.

Probst, G. and Buchel, B. (1997) *Organizational Learning: The Competitive Advantage of the Future*. London, Prentice Hall.

Schon, D. (1983) *The Reflective Practitioner*, New York, Basic Books.

Shuell, T.J. (1990) 'Phases of meaningful learning', *Review of Educational Research*, vol. 60, pp 531–47.

Spiro, R.J. (1990) 'Cognitive flexibility and hypertext', in Nix, D. and Spiro, R. (eds) *Exploring Ideas in High Technology*, Hillsdale, Mahwah, Lawrence Erlbaum.

Taylor, C. (1991) *The Ethics of Authenticity*, Cambridge, MA., Harvard University Press.

Taylor, C. (1992) 'The politics of recognition', in Gutman, E. (ed.) *Multiculturalism and the Politics of Recognition*, Princeton, PA, Princeton University Press.

Van der Westhuizen, G.J. (1993) *Teacher Researcher Projects in South Africa: Some Trends and Issues*, Paper presented at the Annual Meeting of AERA, Atlanta, Georgia.

Wallace, M. (1995) 'When is experiential learning not experiential learning?' in Claxton, G. (ed.) *Liberating the Learner*, New York, Routledge.

Wallace, J. and Louden, W. (1994) 'Collaboration and the growth of teachers' knowledge', *Qualitative Studies in Education*, vol. 7 no. 4, pp 323–34.

Wilson, B. and Cole, P. (1992) 'A review of cognitive teaching models', *Educational Training & Development*, vol. 39, no. 4, pp 47–64.

Winslow C.D. and Bramer, W.L. (1994) *Future Work: Putting Knowledge to Work in the Knowledge Economy*, New York Macmillan.

Zimmerman, B.J. (1990) 'Self-regulated learning and academic achievement', *American Educational Research Journal*, vol. 25, pp. 3–17.

Part 4

Achieving change

9 Accomplishing change

A dialogue can be among any number of people, not just two. Even one person can have a sense of dialogue within himself, if the spirit of the dialogue is present. The picture or image that this derivation suggests is of a stream of meaning flowing among and through us and between us. This will make possible a flow of meaning in the whole group, out of which may emerge some new understanding. It's something new, that may not have been in the starting point at all. It's something creative.

Bohm, *On Dialogue* (1996:6)

Change is the only constant in the working lives of most people. It is driven forward by technology, competition and the global movement of capital. It is an inescapable feature of economic life, bringing with it uncertainties and risks that challenge all previous assumptions about the world and its future.

Aims

In this concluding chapter we shall do the following:

➤ locate the problems of change in organizations against the background of global economic change;

➤ review the dominant discourse of change analysis within contemporary management theory;

➤ set out a model of knowledge-productive change that rests on open communication and dialogue;

➤ draw together the key themes in the book to highlight that successfully accomplished change requires vision and purpose, the development of new ideas and a moral framework which treats human beings as ends in themselves and never merely as means to achieve the ends of others.

Our key proposition is that knowledge-productive change requires an explicit commitment to the values of respect for persons, fairness, freedom to think and truthfulness. All are essential conditions of creative dialogue.

The context of change

In the world of business the daily news is of movements in share prices, amalgamations, takeovers, plant closures, new business start-ups. This is a world that constantly generates a new vocabulary to describe itself. Businesses are 're-engineered', services are 'outsourced'; organizations reduce levels of staffing by 'downsizing', 'rightsizing', 'outplacing'. Managers seek everyday opportunities to rationalize the work of their organizations, to increase productivity and efficiency, to enter into partnership arrangements with overseas companies, to reach outwards to new markets and to close down older production units. There is a constant, restless search for new products, new markets, new sources of capital and new methods of production.

It is a world of fashionable ideas circulated quickly through the business press, journals, consultancy and the conference circuit. It generates and consumes the ideas that define it. Managers who 'benchmark' their organizations and work for 'total quality' in 'just-in-time' production systems requiring 'teamwork', 'flat hierarchies' and ever-increasing investment in 'human capital' through 'human resource development' strategies are using the ideas that make up the new management discourse. They seek to 'engineer' change, to 'plan for change' to implement 'strategies for change'. They have developed 'mission statements', 'measurement systems', 'aims and objectives' and 'targets' that enable them to 'evaluate' the effectiveness of what they do. Few will give a second thought to the derivation of these terms in military theory and tactics, but the roots of such thinking are clear.

Those who drive its institutions and organizations inhabit a world of uncertainty and change. It is a world with its own rituals and gurus, its own training systems in university business schools and its own travel arrangements – the business lounges of international airports. Global telecommunications enable its functionaries to transact business in real time across continents. Its business, professional and trade networks bring together a global community whose identity is increasingly 'disembedded' from particular localities and even nation states. Bauman (2000) has tried to capture this world in terms of 'liquid modernity'. Everything about it, including its personal relationships, is fluid, impermanent, transient, fast moving. The elites who make this metabolism function are responsible only to the shareholders of the companies that employ them and display no sense of obligation to the people who live in the communities where their production plants are located. The US social scientist Christoper Lasch (1995) described the new elites of the global economy as people who have abdicated any social or political responsibility for the societies in which they function. Their loyalties have no particular spatial component; they are committed only to the companies that for the moment employ them.

They are both the products of and at the same time those who create the world of change that encompasses all the communities of the globe. What they do has a direct bearing on how millions of people live and experience their lives. Those who remain well positioned in the economic arrangements of their societies benefit from the actions of these global, corporate managers. Their decisions on investment funds affect pensions, interest rates and employment prospects.

Those who are not well positioned to cope with the economic changes of information-based modernity – either as individuals, companies, communities, nation states – will surely suffer. Neither tradition nor systems of social welfare are robust enough to support the casualties of social change.

It is too easy to slide into a state of apocalyptic hopelessness in the face of such complexity. The challenge is to discover knowledge-productive ways to understand it and change the way we do things to define different futures for our societies. There are clearly limits to what can be done in this respect. The future, as we have stressed throughout this book, is unknowable. The unintended consequences of what we do may also be more telling and significant than those we have planned or tried to anticipate.

No matter. All this means is that we live with risk and uncertainty and the constant requirement to develop new ideas. History is no 'iron cage' in which we are held, powerless to act; we can act in new ways. Indeed the history of technological innovation, the growth in new markets, international networks, the growth of whole new business sectors and the constant pressures of new ideas for political change are testimony enough to the fact that humans, societies and organizations are much more geared to change than to stasis. The challenge is to understand change better and to position ourselves so that we shape its speed and direction without being overwhelmed by it.

Just as an attitude of fatalistic hopelessness is entirely unhelpful in making sense of change so, too, is a belief that change can be purposefully controlled and effectively managed. There is a 'promethean ambition' at the core of modern management ideology that organizations can be brought under rational control. It is informed by a naive trust in the intellectual resources of social sciences, for it rests on the assumption that there are tested methods of change management, systematic procedures for disguising strategies of change, of impelling and evaluating and controlling it.

The social science literature on change is extensive. To argue that it is nonetheless limited in its conceptual resources and empirical validity is not to deny that it cannot help us work our way through problems of change in knowledge-productive ways. Indeed the opposite is the case. Social science is a more or less useful toolkit of ideas that enables rational debate to take place about how problems might be solved. The premise of that debate has to be that solutions will be discovered through rational analysis and dialogue rather than be imposed by people in groups who believe that they, uniquely, know the answer. Such people are truly dangerous. Twentieth-century political history is a sordid story of misery caused by political demagogues who felt they were marching in step with history. The history of business failure is one of inept leadership which prevented new ideas and developments that would have opened new markets, products or ways of managing resources. Organizations that fail too often remain locked in ways of thinking – narratives – hark back to the tried and tested methods of the past rather than exploring new ways of driving things forward.

Our claim here is that when people in organizations are encouraged to think critically about the narratives which frame their working practices they will be in a better position to change them. More than ideas are needed, however, if change is to be allowed to happen. Organizations have to be open to new ways of thinking and their leaders willing to promote the kind of open discussion and dialogue that the generation of new ideas requires.

This proposition is, of course, based on some arguments with social science. To be explicit, the importance of dialogue in human communication is based here on the work of among others, Freire (1987), Shotter (1993), and Bohm (1996) and, from the business world, Nonaka and Horotaka (1995) who, in different ways from different traditions of theorizing, and with different emphasis, nonetheless highlight that new knowledge comes from making the tacit explicit, from people building on each other's ideas and experience and doing so under conditions when leaders and managers are willing to change in response to new information and ideas.

We offer this proposition as one to be debated, not as some kind of canonical nostrum. Indeed our point is itself an injunction to people to be critical of the social scientific ideas – including our own – that lend credibility to much contemporary management thought.

The dominant discourse of change

In contrast to the perspective underlying this book, with its stress on the creation of new meanings and new ideas as the defining characteristic of human beings working together in organizations of many different types, the dominant discourse of change management is locked in a naive mode of technical rationality. The essential premise is that change is a rational process that can be managed, planned and controlled.

This framework thinking was inspired by Fordist and Taylorian methods of production and work measurement. In the period following the Second World War, especially in the United States, management theory developed a strong functional and technical outlook. Management became the function of managing complex socio-technical systems through a range of expert-based techniques for changing human behaviour. The whole enterprise was driven forward by cold war competition – to outcompete the Soviets, to win the arms race, to put men on the moon and establish the global economic legionary of free trade and private enterprise. It was and is a framework of economic management that has been startlingly successful, though the costs of that success have not always been borne by those who have benefited from it.

It was against this background that change could be designed, engineered, prioritized, planned, evaluated, controlled, managed and coped with. A whole new human relations industry emerged to help managers cope with stress, handle conflict, manage complexity and secure business objectives. University business schools flourished, providing a practical rationale for the new managerialism, creating settings from which business gurus could pontificate to the whole business world. This diverse range of ideas and techniques is held together in a loose conceptual framework within which there is much debate and analysis about such social and psychological themes as motivation, communication, organizational development, group dynamics, inter- and intra-organizational conflict and the wider economic and political analysis of changing business environments.

The change models to be derived from these traditions of academic debate are all intended to offer managers methods of controlling complexity and uncertainty. It is to provide them with justifications for their actions that have scientific credibility and therefore certainty. It is a framework of ideas to dispel doubt. It helps managers make out a case for the reasonableness of their actions. When people inhabit the mental spaces of this discourse they become sure of what they are doing; their objectives and means to achieve them became obvious, self-evident. All thinking gets straight to the crux of the matter and decisions are based on data, evidence and reason.

Those who disagree can then be classified as Shotter suggests as 'the other' and labelled as traditionalists, people who resist change, people who live in the past, who cannot adapt. They have to be helped to think differently, to 're-frame' their understanding, perhaps to be retrained but, above all, they need to change. It is the recalcitrance and sheer stubbornness of people that explains why the high priests of change fall back on their most telling cliché: 'If you can't change the people, change the people!'

A consequence of this is that the leaders of organizations often achieve change at the expense of their employees or members. Older staff are helped to retire early; others are made redundant or are sidelined to limit their opportunities to participate in making decisions. Too often the inept management of change generates resistance, conflict and acrimony. Instead of embracing new ideas people hang on to what they believe they know to be true as the best way to do something. The underlying problem in all this is lack of clarity about the rationale for change and an unwillingness among leaders to engage creatively with new ideas or a failure to nurture others to develop them.

Change conceptualized

We have taken a liberty here to turn our account of the dominant discourse into something of a parody of it. It has enabled us, however, to highlight some key features of the conceptual ground to be debated if managers are to accomplish change successfully. Change cannot be managed before it is understood, and never successfully before agreement has been secured about the need for it and the best means to achieve it. That requires knowledge, analysis, communication, dialogue and commitment informed by values. Above all it requires an open acknowledgement that all change takes place in settings and organizations which are far more complex than the conceptual resources we have to comprehend them.

Change is a common word but a highly complex multi-dimensional phenomenon. It is ubiquitous, pervasive and unstoppable and it can take many different forms. Consider the descriptions of change in Table 9.1.

Table 9.1 Typology of Change

Negotiated	-	Imposed
Planned	-	Unplanned
Intended	-	Unintended
Incremental	-	Large scale
Simple	-	Complex
Controlled	-	Uncontrolled
Internally generated	-	Externally imposed
Supported	-	Unsupported
Short term	-	Long term
Recognized	-	Unrecognized
Sustainable	-	Unsustainable
Regular	-	Intermittent
Understood	-	Not understood
Fast	-	Slow
Piecemeal	-	Catastrophic

These dichotomies are purely conceptual and the list is not exhaustive. It is immediately clear, however, that each of these dimensions of change describes highly variable patterns of change in organizations.

It is not difficult to think of changes that were large scale, catastrophic, unintended, unplanned and rapid. The explosion at Chernobyl nuclear power station or the collapse of Barings Bank in Singapore as a result of illegal trading in derivatives are but two examples. The reform of higher education in most of the world's developed industrial society has generally been a slow, incremental, long-term, piecemeal process negotiated with byzantine complexity through the institutions of academia.

For most organizations, most of the time, change is piecemeal, incremental, continuous, negotiated and intended. The problem here, of course, is that such change may not be adequate. Faced with the essentially unpredictable pressures of a global economy, most business organizations need to change much faster than they do. Faced with the fiscal parsimony of the modern state, most public sector organizations must change profoundly to avoid the twin threats of tighter control and resource starvation. Those with responsibility for managing change need to provide inspired, prescient leadership that builds upon and at the same time serves the needs, skills and commitment of those they manage.

Three propositions of knowledge-productive change

These ideas can be crystallized into three main propositions that require extensive debate within specific organizations. Proposition one is that successfully accomplished change requires sensitive leadership and organizational development. The two are inseparable. One without the other is meaningless. The key task of leadership is to help members of an organization think about future possibilities and to co-ordinate their efforts to arrive at new solutions to operational problems. It is fashionable, but often futile, to imagine new developments come from without, from consultants or from the experience of other similar organizations, or impersonally through the blind logic of competition. They comes from within and from the experience of people working together in ways that transcend the limitations of their own knowledge base to create something new.

Proposition two is that successful strategies of change need to be formed as future developmental opportunities for organizations and the people who work in them rather than as threats, fears and anticipated resistance. Proposition three is that successful change is sensitively negotiated, owned by those who participate in it and is based on new learning to enable people to think in new ways.

These propositions depend on one another. Each term in each proposition must be carefully deconstructed and thought through in the specific circumstances of each organization. Each element has to be traced out and explored fully to assess its implications for different levels of management, for different groups of individuals and for individuals themselves.

So far the argument is little different to what could be culled from any standard management text. There are three elements to these propositions, however, that we consider to be innovative and which take the dominant discourse of change into excitingly uncharted waters.

The first is 'knowledge-productive leadership'. Knowledge-productive leadership sets a context in which people are encouraged to think. It acknowledges the fallibility and necessary uncertainty of all accounts of what the future might be. At the same time it stresses the importance of encouraging everyone to debate possible futures and draw out the implications for themselves and their organization. New ideas are crucial to this process. In practical terms this implies the development of appropriate means to invest in research and development, effective policies for staff recruitment and development and appropriate systems of rewards and recognition that enable and encourage people to use their minds. The practical side of all this is easy; the imagination needed to make it work is harder to come by.

The challenge is to live with and through the inescapable logic of super-complexity (Barnett, 2000) and to encourage a continuous stepping back from the obvious and from what has been tacitly taken for granted. It is to nurture high levels of 'meta-cognitive awareness' throughout an organization and to help people risk the freedom to think.

The second element is about openness and opportunity. People will risk thinking in new ways only if they are not criticized for doing so and when they are helped to do it. All new thinking requires new learning. People are much more likely to think in fresh ways when they see that they are valued for doing so and when they are challenged intellectually by the work they do. Under such conditions people respond to challenge with a sense of hopefulness and possibility. They feel they can engage with change, feel responsible for it, own it and work energetically to realize it.

This argument rests on a view of motivation that sees the willingness of people to work and to think as something shaped by the framework of expectations within which they live. The reasons people have for being positive about their work – their 'vocabularies of motive' or the narratives they use to explain their plans and intentions – are soundly situated. They are not the psychological properties of individuals alone but are shared – or perhaps not – in particular working contexts. The management challenge is to achieve a climate of motivation that is positive and creative. Too often, of course, management is much more successful in achieving the opposite! In a climate of increasing managerialism what is achieved is management rather than participation and development.

Thirdly, and finally, there is the link between learning, new ideas and values. The essence of our argument is this: people learn, grow and develop when they are shown respect, are valued as ends in themselves and are taken seriously by their colleagues and managers. There is therefore a dimension to knowledge-productive change that concerns values and morality and the quality of personal relationships at work. The dominant discourse of modern management is rich in people – centred around clichés such as 'people are our most important asset' or 'This organization is its people'. But if such propositions are not lived and practised in the ordinary daily round of working relationships they amount to nothing. In this context managers achieve the responses to change and associated behaviours they deserve. Indeed the gap between rhetoric and practice is what in many organizations breeds cynicism, contempt for managers and an unwillingness to contemplate or to contribute to change.

Returning to the corporate curriculum

The concept of the corporate curriculum has been a constant that runs through the narrative of this book. Our intention has been to show that it is a strong metaphor and framework for thinking about knowledge productivity in organizations. Joseph Kessels, the originator of the concept, thinks of it as a rich landscape for learning. We believe that this is an appropriate metaphor because it provides the bounded instability associated with the complex social system of the workplace from which learning, knowledge productivity and capability may be socially constructed. We therefore advocate its application as a vehicle for analysis and discussion and a framework to enable thinking about learning in specific contexts.

The alternative would be to think of it as a management tool. This would bring with it connotations of manipulation, the pragmatic manager intent on dominating the discourse for the purpose of control. To further this, in our research we could have developed the 'tool' metaphor by creating a questionnaire for people to complete in order to determine and measure their corporate curriculum. This, we believe, would be dishonest and misleading. It taps directly into the idea that the corporate curriculum is a 'thing' that can be described through a series of questions unrelated to the situation and context of practice. Consequently it could be measured and therefore controlled. This way of thinking is the 'outcome' or 'destination' approach to learning rather than the journey or travelling concept.

Instead, we conceive of the rich landscape as a vehicle for dialogue and debate and believe that as such it offers the opportunity for reflexivity in action. Consider Illustration 9.1, on the corporate curriculum.

Illustration 9.1

Studies in 82 Health Care and Welfare Organizations

In a research project carried out in 82 departments of institutions in health care and welfare in the Netherlands the dynamics of learning within a work environment were analysed.

The basic assumption behind the research is the idea that a 'rich learning landscape' affects the workers individually and collectively in such a way that they learn how to do things better, or how to change or innovate in their work. The research findings strongly support this relationship and suggest that the link between learning environments and people's abilities to deliver are in fact very significant. This implies that it is all the more valuable to discuss the 'seven elements of a corporate curriculum' widely as a way of changing the work environment into 'rich landscapes' of learning.

Based on these findings and conclusions, we present a few examples of practices that illustrate the general idea of how to add richness to a learning landscape within an organization.

A rich learning landscape

We discovered that a 'corporate curriculum' includes a number of functions which might be fulfilled or realized in practice. These include the folllowing:

- By doing their work people acquire knowledge and skill related to their particular profession or discipline and they learn how to solve professional problems 'on location'.
- When alerted to the importance of dialogue and reflection people learn how to reflect on what they are doing.
- Through practice people learn how to communicate and co-operate with others.
- Through practice in appropriate learning environments individuals learn how to regulate their own emotions, preferences and motivation in relation to other people.

Each of these areas of learning requires a certain mix of measures, partly required by the function that is to be realized, partly by contextual constraints or characteristics of the organization involved. The functions of the 'corporate curriculum' may be served and developed by enabling people in the workplace to do the following:

- network with a variety of people, internal and external to the organization;
- receive adequate feedback (particularly middle managers who tend to be ignored in times of change);
- evolve planning through an interactive process of reflection and revision; it is apparent that planning is more a 'looping' process than a linear one;
- communicate with clients, colleagues and competitors – communication and co-operation are key sources of learning;
- create a motivational climate for oneself and for others.

As argued earlier, turning a work situation into a rich learning environment is not merely to the benefit of the individual but is an investment in the quality of both the work organization and society. It impacts on people's capacity to innovate and progress.

Our research shows that the framework of a 'corporate curriculum' provides three main tangible benefits, as follows:

1 a language to enable people to discuss learning at work;
2 an instrument for analysis of the current position;
3 a plan for future development.

The corporate curriculum offers a 'rich landscape' of learning but the facilitation of learning is also a 'rich landscape'. This means that managers in a knowledge economy become facilitators of learning, mentors and coaches. Their performance is acknowledged through their ability to create a learning climate in a team whose membership may alter according to the needs of the issues under consideration.

Beyond knowledge management

Knowledge management is commonly conceived as being the explicit and systematic management of knowledge. The assumption is that knowledge is a commodity and a product of learning. It is conceived by many as the province of ITC specialists. In this context a further consideration is of the social processes of creating, collecting and organizing, disseminating and using knowledge for commercial gain or strategic progress. We believe that the notion of the exploitation of knowledge is probably akin to the exploitation of people. This places us in a world of moral questions. Perhaps the 'exploration' of knowledge has more to offer people as a concept?

A further consideration is the 'dominant narrative' or 'mindset' of management thinking. This, we have argued, is a key determinant to the creation of a knowledge-productive environment. We have argued that many, perhaps the majority, of managers' beliefs about management are rooted in an assumed rationality which suggests that people and their behaviours can be explained deterministically. This very dominant mode of thinking has been the driver of the modern industrialized world with the resultant knowledge being 'characterised by a form of rationality that disengages the mind from the body and from the world' (Apffel-Marglin and Marglin, 1996:3). While it may be argued (Apffel-Marglin and Marglin, 1996) that the dominant deterministic logic (particularly prevalent in western thinking) has been responsible for much progress in terms of industrial development it could additionally be said that it is responsible for 'social fragmentation' and 'environmental destruction' (Apeffel-Marglin, 1996:2). The positivist approach to knowledge acquisition, with its roots in Newtonian scientific methodology, is underpinned by the idea of 'rightness'. But this is breaking down 'there is no longer a right knowledge, but many coexisting conflicting pieces of knowledge' (Von Krogh *et al.*, 1994:54). And, 'Sociological positivism's strict emulation of the natural sciences has been tried and its benefits have now been exhausted' (Reed and Harvey, 1992:354) for 'Positivist canons can suffice only in the closed domain of the experimental setting' (Reed and Harvey, 1992:356).

Consequently, in the social science context, the assumption of 'predictability' or 'determinism' is now increasingly being challenged and giving way to the idea that human behaviour is based on a highly complex series of dependencies and variables which we cannot predict. Understanding people and our behaviours is about creating and developing 'meaning' (Bruner, 1990) holistically from the complex situation in question. Sense making is part of a knowledge-productive environment.

We believe that serious attempts at knowledge management in organizations must take into account people in the widest sense. An important issue is then, 'What form should it take?' We believe it needs to be in the context of a 'rich landscape' of learning as articulated throughout this book.

To go beyond knowledge management is a movement towards a more humane organization where attention needs to be paid to social processes of dialogue, openness, diversity, tolerance, uncertainty, complexity, trust, relationships, reflection, re-framing, restoration and reflexivity.

The social implications of the knowledge economy take us beyond simple codified or explicit knowledge and into a world beyond the technical or rational and into what Habermas calls a 'life-world understanding'. It is here that we develop the tacit and go beyond knowledge to reflective and reflexive knowing. We go beyond practical 'effectiveness' to practical wisdom, to concern for dialogue rather than the specification of outcomes and on into a sophisticated understanding of the process of learning rather than faith in the easy transferability of skills associated with training courses and the 'closed' curriculum.

Change is the only certain feature of the work-based organization. Change, we have argued, is inextricably bound up with learning, and learning to be knowledge-productive is fundamentally a social activity. Being knowledge-productive offers organizations an opportunity to reframe their contexts and situations and to build a strategically capable social system that is flexible and adaptive, creative and innovative and able to engage in its activities to the satisfaction of all its stakeholders. This takes us beyond knowledge management and into the realms of a new conceptualization of work. It is a both a huge challenge and an opportunity, and a journey that holds many new adventures.

Critique of the book

Olav Sorenson, *UCLA's Anderson Graduate School of Management, USA*

A view from the other side of the ocean

Empires do not suffer emptiness of purpose at the time of their creation. It is when they have become established that aims are lost and replaced by vague rituals.

Maud'dib, in *Dune Messiah* by Frank Herbert

Having journeyed this far you have probably begun to form your own thoughts about what you should do to help unleash the creativity lying dormant in an organization. To continue stimulating your thoughts, this critique seeks to leave you with a perspective on how the concepts found in the preceding chapters relate to the latest academic research on organizational learning. Here, you will find both a call for caution – to balance creativity with order – and praise for this book's focus on an issue largely ignored in the academic literature: the importance of managing people.

In its most basic formulation organizational learning involves just two processes: the generation of new knowledge and the incorporation of that knowledge into the firm's operations. Firms that wish to learn effectively must manage both of these processes successfully. Knowledge building without systematic implementation promotes inconsistency; and co-ordination without the consistent invigoration of new ideas can lead to stagnation. Together, though, these activities can form the basis of a sustainable competitive advantage.

In all fairness even the old scientific management school, so heavily criticized in modern times, had this same goal of improving the functioning of the organization through the development and implementation of knowledge. However, Fredrick Taylor and his supporters conceived of the knowledge-building process as occurring centrally – indeed adherents of this tradition frequently employed large numbers of researchers to determine precisely which processes would yield the most efficient operations. To implement it, they wrote detailed operating procedures to govern even minor aspects of the employees' daily activities. Though currently out of favour, these techniques led to tremendous improvements in productivity and the quality of life, bringing many formerly luxury goods – such as the automobile – to the homes of the masses.

So why has interest shifted from scientific management to empowering the worker? The answer lies in the power of decentralized learning in the knowledge-generation process. Much of the new and useful information needed to run a business effectively comes through trial-and-error learning. Many examples of this process appeared in the preceding chapters (Chapter 4 contains several). An employee notices something that they believe could be done better; they have an inspiration, an idea, which they act on; and then they observe whether that action improves outcomes – adopting those ideas that improve performance while discarding those that do not. In a firm with centralized learning a few designated individuals carry out this research; however, when managers empower workers, hundreds or thousands of employees can experiment with different ideas simultaneously – dramatically expanding the firm's ability to generate new and useful information.

This principle lies behind the genius of Wal-mart. The company devolves authority over marketing decisions on multiple levels: store managers control store policy; nonetheless, they cede many decisions to the heads of individual departments within the store. Those department heads in turn allocate authority over some policies to their own subordinates. Using both their creativity and their knowledge of local markets, these employees decide what products to stock, what to price them at, and how to promote them. Thus, over the expanse of Wal-mart's entire system of stores, literally thousands of marketing experiments occur every week. The entire company operates as one gigantic knowledge-building machine.

The corporate curriculum seeks to release this type of knowledge-generation power. Research and experience teach us that organizations find it increasingly difficult to learn new things as they mature. Bureaucratic rules and tradition stifle employee originality, and formal organizational structures restrict the flow of information. The advantage of the corporate curriculum appears to come from making people aware of these constraints and encouraging them to transcend them, thereby unlocking employee creativity and the organization's potential for learning.

Knowledge building by itself, however, does not lead to effective organizational learning; firms also need mechanisms for selecting and implementing the best ideas across the company. For example, at Wal-mart, regional vice-presidents visit a large number of stores each week, report back their findings and broadcast a weekly briefing to store managers on the most successful retailing innovations. Promoting the diffusion of valuable knowledge is not a trivial task. Individual-level incentives (even promotions) – which typically reward people for their performance relative to their peers – can encourage individuals to keep valuable knowledge to themselves so that they alone benefit from it. Companies that diffuse knowledge well often rely on corporate culture to inoculate against this selfishness; for example, GE and McKinsey make knowledge hoarding one of the most serious 'sins' within the firm. Other companies, such as Wal-mart and Taco Bell (a fast-food restaurant chain), solve this problem through extensive monitoring and sophisticated information technology.

An excessive emphasis on creativity can also hamper organizational learning. Learning benefits the firm by identifying more effective operating procedures. Once efficient practices have been identified you would generally prefer employees to follow those high productivity routines rather than discarding them in favour of some ill-conceived experiment. Nonetheless, experimentation entails precisely such a tradeoff. Quite simply, the difficulty of trial-and-error learning is that most trials fail! Thus, for organizations to operate effectively, creativity must usually occur within some bounds.

The ideal point for balancing creativity with order depends on the variability of the markets your firm faces. In relatively homogenous, stable markets, it pays to weight control more heavily than creativity. In these steady environments the marginal return to new knowledge declines rapidly; on average, experimentation costs more than it yields. On the other hand, when operating over a diverse set of markets or competing in an industry subject to rapid changes in technology or consumer tastes, the firm needs to learn as quickly as possible; each shift in the business environment renews the value of new knowledge. Thus firms contending with these markets should unshackle employees from their restraints and encourage creativity. Nevertheless, though the optimal mix varies from firm to firm, the need for a balance does not.

The academic literature actually identifies a variety of managerial levers that leaders can use to balance this tradeoff between learning and efficiency – something March (1991) calls the tension between exploration and exploitation. For example, product strategy offers one means of navigating this tradeoff (Sorenson, 2000). By offering more products with more variety in their attributes firms can increase their ability to gather information about consumer preferences. Conversely, by focusing their product lines, companies can exploit economies of scale and operate more efficiently. Organizational design and incentives provide additional mechanisms for balancing these competing processes. Bradach (1998) in his study of franchise organizations argues that chains must balance franchising – which stimulates experimentation – with corporate ownership and control – that advances standardization and consistent quality. More generally, incentive systems that emphasize objective outcomes, such as stock options and explicit bonus systems, promote adaptation; the option-like quality of these compensation schemes implies that their expected value increases with variance, so employees take risks. Meanwhile, subjective compensation systems encourage more consistent performance and information sharing. Similarly, functional organizational structures promote efficiency through economies of scale, while divisional forms allow for more effective learning by tying metrics of organizational performance more closely to product markets. With such a variety of managerial levers available you would do well to think about stimulating organizational renewal not only through the management of people but also through the intelligent use of other business policies.

Nonetheless academic researchers could also learn from the corporate curriculum. Business school education no longer teaches students to manage; rather, it primarily gives them a set of tools for making decisions. This emphasis follows the research traditions of economics and sociology in focusing on the importance of easily observable features, such as organizational structures and incentives. But, intangibles – such as employer expectations – also play an important role in motivating employees. Research in educational sociology provides a powerful illustration. Rosenthal and Jacobson (1968) randomly assigned 20 per cent of the students in one school a label of showing unusual promise. Without indicating the random nature of the assignment they told the children's teachers their classifications. By the middle of the year the students labelled as 'gifted' were outpacing the rest of the class. Let me make this perfectly clear: these labels had nothing to do with any tests or the students' actual abilities! No parallel line of research exists to test the importance of administrative skills, but this example clearly illustrates the importance of precisely the type of managerial intangibles that can have a tremendous effect on employee performance.

The corporate curriculum and the organizational transformation that it encourages offers a powerful mechanism for unleashing the creative potential which lies dormant in every organization; however, two notes of caution warrant consideration. First, effective organizational learning depends not only on the knowledge generation that employee creativity can enhance, but also on the effective selection and implementation across the firm of the useful, new routines that these employees discover. Thus managers must balance knowledge generation with knowledge utilization. Second empowering workers offers but one mechanism for managing this tradeoff; the most efficacious leaders will integrate the effective management of people with an intelligent selection of business policies to match the organization's flexibility to the markets they face.

References:

Bradach, J,L. (1998) *Franchise Organizations*, Boston, MA, Harvard Business School Press.

March, J.G. (1991) 'Exploration and exploitation', *Organization Science*, vol. 2, pp 71–87.

Rosenthal, R. and Jacobson, L. (1968) *Pygmalion in the Classroom: Teacher Expectations and Pupils' Intellectual Development*, New York, Rinehart & Winston.

Sorenson, O. (2000) 'Letting the market work for you: An evolutionary perspective on product strategy', *Strategic Management Journal*, vol. 21, pp 577–92.

Postscript

The manuscript of this book was completed by the summer of 2001. The dialogues and conversations, research and reading upon which we drew in order to write it took place over a long period of time. Some of these dialogues took place within organizations, some with postgraduate students in management or in lifelong learning, some were with colleagues in our own and other British universities, yet others were with an international group of colleagues. This group consists of academics, practitioners and consultants all drawn together by a common interest – knowledge productivity. The group meets once a year either in the United Kingdom or the Netherlands and we call ourselves The Vanwoodman Institute. The book represents an attempt on our part to make those conversations available to a wider audience and to encourage people to join us or to engage others in debate about the themes we have discussed.

A key theme for us is that of dialogue. It is our belief that it is through creative dialogue with one another that new ideas are formed. We were able to write the book because we ourselves are part of a network of great talkers who respond to ideas and often put new ones into practice. It is for this reason that the book incorporates comments *on* and extensions *of* our own text by others. The reader can then weigh up arguments, points and perspectives and form their own views about the value of these ideas.

After the manuscript was completed, and we were able to read the commentaries of our own work, we realized a postscript was needed. Two things compelled this conclusion. The first was that, as we shall argue, there were parts of our message that needed to be strengthened, clarified and made more explicit. Our commentators have prompted us to think again and to consider the ways in which the arguments of this book need further support.

Secondly, since completing the manuscript, there have been many occasions when we talked together about what the knowledge-productive challenge was in relation to a wide range of problems. What are the solutions to the problems of the British rail transport system? How can the foot and mouth disease that has destroyed much of the agricultural economy in Britain be overcome? Are there credible alternatives to instability in financial markets? Much nearer home is the question of how to manage universities during times of great change.

In addition, we have been astonished during this period to read of knowledge breakthroughs in different areas of scientific research, e.g. recent advances in cancer therapy, and we are determined to understand more about knowledge-productivity in the domains of science and technology. If we knew more about scientific creativity, we have speculated, we might gain greater insight into how innovation and creativity might be stimulated in the workplace.

In each of these examples there is a problem of change, of uncertainty, of the need for new knowledge, of the need to step outside conventional frameworks of thinking. Our work on knowledge-productivity – though we have never really been happy with the phrase – should help us contribute to these discussions. We felt quite encouraged both by what we had done and the work that lay ahead beyond this book.

The rationality of terror

Then, however, our whole world changed and we began to wonder whether our work had any relevance to anything that really mattered. We began to write this postscript on 21 September 2001, 10 days after the terrorist attacks on the World Trade Center in New York, the Pentagon in Washington and the plane crash in Pennsylvania that could well have hit the White House. The television images of the planes crashing into the World Trade Center will haunt the memories of all who saw them and mark out a moment for all of us against which we will think about the rest of our lives. For these events have created a new world order.

As we write, a fleet is sailing towards the Gulf, an international armed force is being assembled, political leaders throughout the world are forming an international coalition against terrorism. Millions of ordinary people, including us, look on in fear, completely mystified about the likely outcomes but certain of one thing: the future we all face is not now the one we anticipated or hoped for.

The terrorist attack on the United States was, arguably, the most successful terrorist attack ever. It was carefully planned, executed with a ruthless brilliance and successful beyond expectation or imagination. It has challenged the might of the world's most powerful military machines. It exposed weaknesses in security for which heads will have to roll and it has induced profound change in how we must understand the dynamics of global society. The old frameworks for thinking about the global order of our lives, its political fracture lines, religious and ideological diversity and its sustainability in environmental terms, are all shown to be inadequate.

The risks we all now face – of escalating war, terrorism, instability in economic life and the growing threat of racial violence wherever there are ethnic minorities – have a global, apocalyptic character. We now live in a world whose future is much more uncertain than it ever was. The uncertainties are beyond our normal risk-assessment tools to measure. The unintended consequences of everything that will be done to attack terrorism, or defend it, are inestimable. In the worst possible sense, the future of the world is now an open one.

The tragedy, we believe, is that the events of 11 September 2001 were the result of very creative thinking. Those who planned them were well organized. They have a clear value base from which to work. Their teamworking skills were of the highest order. They were able to recruit the best people for the job and they worked out a strategy that prevented their detection. They achieved their objectives in ways that changed the world and are likely to create the optimal conditions for further success. They have become martyrs in the eyes of those who share their world outlook. They have destroyed the certainties of US and western political life. They have forced world leaders to think again about the politics of the Middle East, about underdevelopment, the social roots of terrorism.

More fundamentally, they have prompted some observers to wonder whether the political values of liberalism and rationality that have been so important in western societies are robust enough to meet the challenges of a terrorism inspired by a distorted religious world view. The British political journalist, Cristina Odone, wrote in the broadsheet, liberal newspaper, *The Observer,* on 30 September 2001 that the terrorists 'killed off the optimistic mindset that intellectuals and many among the middle class have subscribed to for the past two centuries'. She is referring here to the 'enlightened principles of liberty, tolerance, equality and rationalism'. When the only rules that matter are divine and the only true life a spiritual one, liberal rationalists appear foolish and over-optimistic about human nature and the possibilities of a better society of the future. The belief that people can build a better world following the principles of reason, justice and fairness seems to her to be a doctrine that has been, as she puts it 'torched by the Taliban'.

We hope and believe she is profoundly wrong. The events of 11 September are not indicative of a human failure to live in the realm of reason. Quite the contrary. They are evidence that reason needs stronger institutional supports. Democratic societies must nurture democratic discourse and not only in the formal realm of politics. The worlds of work and of community are domains in which people share their understanding and develop new ideas. They are domains – or can be – of collaborative learning and of the development of new solutions to old problems.

The terrorists were, however, successful learners. They acted rationally. They worked collaboratively, used up-to-date technologies of communication and discovered ways to unleash their terror with lethal success. Those who seek to maintain a democratic world order need to become even more effective in stimulating the ideas skills and value commitments that will sustain democratic practice throughout all the domains of our economic and public lives. The requirement is for rationality tempered by the values of freedom, truthfulness, human rights and justice.

The nature of the world order after the collapse of communism was never very clear. Now it is even less so. The terrorists have reminded the world's military leaders that the powerful apparatus of military might is powerless in the face of ideologically inspired terrorism. The powerless have, ingeniously, discovered a way to power. They have been able to demonstrate the ironic tragedy that their success was to a large degree possible because of the way they had themselves been cultivated by the west. The social and economic conditions that have spawned terrorism, including the skills of terror itself, have been nurtured within the global arrangements and technologies of modern society. With a vengeance has the Apprentice turned Sorcerer.

The events of 11 September have highlighted debates about the future of the global, information economy – and of the success and failure of commercial organizations within it – cannot avoid debate about the kinds of values that govern economic and political life. We agree entirely with the management journalist, Simon Caulkin, when he pointed out (*The Observer*, 7 October 2001) that much business and management thinking of the past decade is based on a denial that business had any wider responsibility for its actions. What Caulkin calls 'business fundamentalism' is, after 11 September, dead. He is absolutely right, in our view, to point out that business has now to look to the long-term conditions of its own sustainability. Business needs both government and a good public infrastructure to succeed. Above all, 'the health of firms and societies depends on closing the unsustainable gulf that has grown up in the 1990s between the haves and the have nots' (p 10). This is, as Caulkin says, the real world.

It has become a political imperative to consider the values that govern economic action. It is a sociological imperative to check out the kinds of values that are being lived out in the ordinary routines of political and commercial life and which govern the conduct and attitudes of people at work and in their communities. For here lies the source of all our collective problems as well as their solution.

From the global to the local

How is this relevant to the ideas of this book? Or to points made by our colleagues who have commented on our work? First, we are human beings with families whose health and welfare depends on there being a public domain in which they can live safely, where their human rights are respected and they can contribute positively to society. The terrorists have shown that such a public domain is fragile, global and poorly understood. The global information economy supplied us all with the means to see the collapsing towers of the World Trade Center and to call up friends and colleagues in the United States. Technology alone, however, will not enable us to see into the minds of terrorists, or understand their perception of the way of life we lead or how they understand the political order of our world.

A key thread linking the arguments of our book concerns power and inequality within the global economic order. The World Trade Center did symbolize western domination of the global economy. The free trade policies promoted by western governments are hotly debated now by those who see the global economy as deeply unequal. The activities of anti-global protesters at Seattle, Davos and Genoa just cannot be ignored. There are many in the Islamic world who see western civilization as godless and violent. The political instabilities of the global economy have accelerated unmanageable patterns of migration and the collapse of communism has produced regional problems in the Balkans, the Caucasus and, of course, in the Indian subcontinent and the Gulf. Religious differences are interwoven with social and political conflicts in ways that extend well beyond the kinds of political comprehension that are part of western political life. Power is a key resource of the global economy and how it is used shapes the constraints within which nation states and all the public and commercial organizations within them function.

The global market is not just a market. If that were the case we would understand its rules. It is a much more complex political arrangement for the control and distribution of key resources. It is an impersonal mechanism that nevertheless incorporates everyone. We found it sad and ironic, though we were not surprised, that in the wake of the terrorist attack, world stock market prices fell and airline companies throughout the world began to shed staff and cut back services. The 'economy' worked in this instance independently of the political system and made all talk of mutual support, solidarity and standing firm against the external threat seem empty. But how can commercial organizations escape the ruthless logic of the market? New ways of thinking are needed, new ideas about what the global economy itself should become. Who will shape that debate? What values will guide the participants?

Two ideas discussed in this book can be built upon to answer these questions. Our account of the knowledge systems of modern society highlights that there is a complex interaction between events – and new learning – that take place at international, national, regional and local levels. Individuals and organizations are inextricably bound up with these networks of ideas and information. The challenge for them is to understand their roles within it and to keep abreast of the changes taking place in the world. At each level of organizational complexity there is an imperative to look outwards, to think about the future, to interpret the world in new ways and to check out how well an organization and its members are keeping up to date, sharing ideas, valuing each other's contributions and achieving their goals.

In our own work we shall attend more to these questions: how do people in organizations develop this capacity for reflection that Barnett (2000) has characterized as 'structural reflexivity`? How can they be helped to do it more effectively? What obstacles in the minds of senior managers or shareholders or line managers prevents them from releasing the intellectual energies of people? What cultural barriers in the workplace or the community prevent people from realizing their own *agency*, their goals, and prevent them from seeing the ways they themselves need to develop in order to do so?

Reflexivity is the key to our second proposition. We shall explore further how far members of organizations understand that their own thoughts and actions reflect back on the world to change it. This aspect of reflexivity has been discussed, as we have shown, by Soros (2000). We do change the world by acting within it. The challenge Soros has identified is to find the best ways within the uncertainties of the global economy to balance competition and competitiveness with the necessity of co-operation, to ensure that there is a framework of values to maintain high levels of stability in global markets. Further research into the values governing business practice becomes a central objective for us to understand knowledge productivity better.

Resources for a journey of discovery and hope

In Joseph Kessels' contribution, he talks of the need for a 'rich landscape' of learning and suggests that we are approaching the end of 'management' as we currently conceive of it. In this context Kessel raises an important point that is linked to morality and values. He calls his contribution 'you cannot be smart against your will'. This is the crux of the issue: people learning in a social context and agreeing, voluntarily, to participate in the process. This cannot be forced, and if managers attempt to force it they will fail. This is relevant in the wake of the sheer horror of recent world events. The terrorists were bound together by common aims and values and the new world order which is beginning to unfold following these atrocities is showing that we can hold our differences and still co-operate. The concept of diversity of religion and values is taking shape as we write.

Within the context of knowledge productivity such diversity is essential, and it is not about 'putting up' with each other but more about creating genuine tolerance of difference, living with it as normal rather than defining others as outsiders. Rogers' (in Chapter 2) core conditions for learning take on new significance indeed.

We were clear when we wrote this book that there had to be a discussion of values in relation to the theme of knowledge productivity. We have to admit, however, that we were a little worried about how our views on this might be received. We wondered whether we would be thought of as other-worldly academics. Joseph Kessels has encouraged us greatly to follow up this concern with values as something absolutely central to a better understanding of how people learn and work and how organizations might develop in the future. The events of 11 September make this a moral imperative for us all.

Harm Tillema extends the notion of values in diversity by raising the idea of authenticity. Tillema recognizes that the notion of knowledge productivity is shot through with tensions in paradox. Authenticity is a moral ideal, but without the honesty that is generated by such an ideal we become manipulators employing techniques aimed at treating people as a 'means' to an 'end' rather than 'ends' in themselves. The disregard of the sanctity of human life inherent in terrorism is the ultimate expression of treating people as 'means'.

One of the defining features of present-day political and economic life is uncertainty. Previous frameworks of understanding and managing economic and political life are no longer adequate. The imperative to think creatively, to develop ways of knowing that reach beyond existing modes of understanding, is irresistible. The danger, of course, is that we shall fall back on the old ones. What is true for governments is equally true for commercial organizations. Uncertainty corrodes the ability to plan yet requires new kinds of planning. We agree with Tillema: dialogue, negotiation and authentic conversation is the way to tolerate diversity and to become knowledge productive at the same time.

Jussi Koski adds to our contribution on creativity. The creative approach is very much needed when we are faced with uncertainty. The standard human response to uncertainty is to rationalize, to fall back on the technical, the solutions of the past. If we are truly to develop new ways we must encourage creativity. This we agree with Koski. However, we differ slightly from him in that we believe that creativity is a function of social circumstance rather than something within individuals. If this is the case, social circumstances have to be looked at and perhaps, in Koski's terms, the creativity of individuals given licence to flourish.

One development in the current world situation is the controlled response of the United States to the attack. On the evidence of the past – former President Clinton's response to earlier terror attacks in East Africa – world opinion was that something or someone would have been attacked almost immediately in response. Currently there seems a more reasoned response and a recognition that the more common reactions of the past may be wholly inappropriate in this context. Other world leaders are making a contribution to the debate and being listened to. New frameworks of international political co-operation are being built. The response to terror is being organized on several different fronts – military, diplomatic and financial – and is also being developed on longer-term timescales. There is evidence of much new, creative thinking in international affairs and military strategy.

We have argued that the need to rethink, re-frame and be creative is a central aspect of knowledge productivity. This imperative is now irresistible. We hope some of the ideas developed in this book encourage people to take seriously our injunction to think, to use their minds, to engage in debate with one another. Our own conclusions from our own enquiries are somewhat open ended. We remain uncertain about many ideas. We are certain, however, that there is much in the contemporary discourse of business management that is dangerously unhelpful to all those managers, including ourselves, who struggle with the complexity of the modern business environment. The shelves of management bookshops round the world are filled with texts promising quick fixes to business problems. The '10-minute' manager is a reality; those who believe there are clear steps to solve problems, be creative or live effectively with stress are well supplied with texts to fuel their fantasies and gurus to cloak the banality of what they preach with a semblance of academic respectability. All we offer is the encouragement to people to use their minds, to think and to build on their capacity to think imaginatively, to talk to others, to listen, to plan, to ponder the values that matter and to check constantly how well they are doing any of these things.

Olav Sorenson's contribution adds, not so much a cautionary note, but rather, a call for balance. We sense in Sorenson's contribution the response that postgraduate students and practical managers often fear: 'It all depends!' We believe that such a response to management questions is the most authentic, the most creative and the one which invites most debate. In specific contexts it is hard to generalize and individual businesses are often in such specific contexts. Sorenson tells us that the corporate curriculum is a helpful concept. Our case studies show that.

Olav also calls for more application and greater pragmatism. In many ways he is right. We wanted our book to be simultaneously theoretical and practical. This is a difficult balance to achieve. Perhaps we could have been more empirical, referenced more or been more applied? We are sure that this is valid criticism. But we hope our book has encouraged discussion, agreement and disagreement simultaneously. We hope that it has encouraged thought, for we believe that the 'thinking' manager is the successful manager. There is nothing so practical as a good theory! At the same time, theory without values is blind. Let us debate both together!

References

Adam, B. Beck, U. and Loon, T. Van (2000) *The Risk Society and Beyond: Critical Issues for Social Theory*, London, Sage.

Alred. G and Garvey, B. (2000) 'Learning to produce knowledge: the contribution of mentoring', In *Mentoring and Tutoring*, vol. 8, no. 3, pp 261–72.

Alred, G., Garvey, B. and Smith, R.D. (1996) 'First person mentoring', *Career Development International*, vol. 1, no. 5, pp 10–14.

Altbach, P.G. (1987) 'What do you know? How the west dominates the worldwide distribution of knowledge', *The Times Higher Education Supplement*, 20 February, p 16.

Apffel-Marglin, F. and Marglin, S.A. (1996) *Decolonizing Knowledge: From Development to Dialogue*, Clarendon Press, Oxford.

Argyris, C. and Schon, D.A. (1981) *Organizational Learning*, Reading, MA, Addison-Wesley.

Bauman, Z. (2000) *Liquid Modernity*, Cambridge, Polity Press.

Barrett, F.J. (1998) 'Managing and improvising: lessons from jazz', *Career Development International*, vol. 3, no. 7, pp 283–6.

Barnett, R. (1994) *The Limits of Competence*, Buckingham, SRHE and Open University Press.

Barnett, R. (2000a) *Realizing the University in an Age of Supercomplexity*, Buckingham, SRHE and Open University Press.

Barnett, R. (2000b) 'Working knowledge', in Garrick, J and Rhodes, C. (eds) *Research and Knowledge at Work*, London, Routledge, pp 15–32.

Beck, U. (1992) *The Risk Society: Towards a New Modernity*, London, Sage.

Beck, U., Giddens, A. and Lasch, C. (1994) *Reflexive Modernization: Politics, Tradition and Aesthetics in the Modern Social Order*, Cambridge, Polity Press.

Beevor, A. (1998) *Stalingrad*, Harmondsworth, Penguin.

Bernstein, B. (1971) 'On the classification and framing of educational knowledge' in Young, M.F.D. (ed.) *Knowledge and Control: New Directions for the Sociology of Education*, London, Open University, Collier-Macmillan, pp 47–69.

Bettis, R.A. and Prahalad, C.K. (1995) 'The dominant logic: retrospective and extension', *Strategic Management Journal*, vol. 16, pp 5–14.

Blakstad, M. and Cooper, A. (1995) *The Communicating Organisation*, London, Institute of Personnel and Development.

References

Boisot, M., (1995), *Information Space: A Framework for Learning in Organizations, Institutions and Culture*, London, Routledge.

Boisot, M., Lemmon, T., Griffiths, D. and Mole, V. (1996) 'Spinning a good yarn: the identification of core competencies at Courtaulds', *International Journal of Technology Management*, Special Issue on the 5th International Forum on Technology Management, vol. 11, nos 3/4, pp 425–40.

Bohm, D. (1996) *On Dialogue*, (ed.) Lee Nichol, Harmondsworth, Penguin.

Bourdieu, P. (1974) 'The school as a conservative force in Eggleston', J. (ed.) *Contemporary Research in the Sociology of Education*, London, Methuen, pp 32–47.

Broad, M.L. and Newstom, J.W. (1992) *Transfer of Training: Action-packed Strategies to Ensure High Payoff from Training Investments*, Reading, MA, Addison-Wesley.

Bruner, J. (1986) 'Vygotsky: a historical and conceptual perspective', in Wertsch, J.V. (ed.) *Culture, Communication and Cognition: Vygotskian perspectives*, Cambridge, London and New York, Cambridge University Press.

Bruner, J. (1990) *Acts of Meaning*, Cambridge, MA, Harvard University Press.

Burns, T. and Stalker G.M. (1961) *The Management of Innovation*, London, Tavistock.

Burrell, G. and Morgan. G. (1979) *Social Paradigms and Organisational Analysis*, Aldershot, Gower.

Campbell, A. and Alexander, M. (1997) 'What's wrong with strategy?' *Harvard Business Review*, Nov-Dec, pp 43–50.

Castells, M. (1996) *The Rise of the Network Society*, Oxford, Blackwell.

Castells, M. (2000) *The End of the Millenium* (2nd edn) Oxford, Blackwell.

Chomsky, N. (1992) *Deterring Democracy*, London,Vintage.

Clawson, J.G. (1996) 'Mentoring in the information age', *Leadership and Organization Development Journal*, vol. 17, no 3, pp 6–15.

Clutterbuck, D. (1992) *Everyone Needs a Mentor*. IPM reprint.

Csikszentmihalyi, M. (1997) *Living Well: The Psychology of Everyday Life*, London, Weidenfeld & Nicolson.

Daloz, L.A. (1986) *Effective Teaching and Mentoring*, San Fransico, CA, Jossey Bass.

Dore, R. (1976) *The Diploma Disease: Education, Qualification and Development*, London, Allen and Unwin.

Drucker, P. F. (1992) *Managing in a Time of Great Change*, Oxford, Butterworth-Heinemann Ltd.

Egan, G., (1993) 'The shadow side', *Management Today*, September, pp 33–8.

Engeström, Y., Virkkunen, J. Helle, M., Pihlaja J., and Poikela, R. (1996) 'The change laboratory as a tool for transforming work', *Lifelong Learning in Europe*, vol. 2, pp 10-17.

Emler, N. and Heather, N. (1980) 'Intelligence: an ideological bias of conventional psychology', in Salmon, P. (ed.) *Coming to Know*, London, Routledge and Kegan Paul, London. In Garvey. B., and Alred, G. (2001) 'Mentoring and the tolerance of complexity', *Futures*, vol. 33, no. 6, pp 519–30.

Etzkowitz, H., Schuler, (E. Jr and) Gilbrandsen M. (2000) 'The evolution of the entrepreneurial university', in Jacob, M. and Hellstrom, T. (eds) *The Future of Knowledge Production in the Academy*, Buckingham, SRHE and Open University Press, pp 40–61.

Field (2000) *Lifelong Learning and the New Educational Order*, London, Trentham Books.

Freire, P. (with Ira Shor) (1987) *A Pedagogy for Liberation: Dialogues on Transforming Education*, Basingstoke, Macmillan.

Gardner, H. (1997) *Extraordinary Minds: Portraits of Exceptional Individuals and an Examination of our Extraordinariness*, London, Weidenfeld & Nicolson.

Garrick, J. (1998) *Informal Learning in the Workplace*, London, Routledge and Kegan Paul.

Garvey, B. and Alred, G. (2001) 'Mentoring and the tolerance of complexity', *Futures*, vol. 33, no. 6, pp 519–31.

Garvey, B. (1999) 'Mentoring and the changing paradigm', *Mentoring and Tutoring*, vol. 7, no. 1, pp 41–54.

Garvey, B.(1995) 'Healthy signs for mentoring', *Education and Training*, vol. 37, no. 5, pp 12–19.

Garvey, B. (1995a) 'Let the actions match the words' pp 111–23 in Clutterbuck, D. and Magginson, D. (eds) *Mentoring in Action*, London, Kogan Page.

Giddens, A. (1989) *The Consequences of Modernity*, Stanford, CA, Stanford University Press.

Gibbons , M., Limoges, C., Nowotny, H., Schwarzman, S., Scott, P. and Trow, M. (1994) *The New Production of Knowledge: The Dynamics of Science and Research in Contemporary Societies*, London, Sage.

Gigliogi, P.P. (1972) 'Language and Social Context', Middlesex, England: Penguin Books in: Future negotiating skills: a development issue? Bright, D., Parkin, B., Welsh, S. *Futures* (2001) vol. 33, no. 6, pp 557–68.

Gold, J., Hamblett, J., Rix, M. (1998) 'Telling stories for managing change: A business–academic partnership', *Education Through Partnership*, vol. 4 no. 1, pp 36–46.

Goleman, D. (1996) *Emotional Intelligence*, London, Bloomsbury.

Habermas, J. (1989) *The Theory of Communicative Competence: The Critique of Functionalist Reason*, vol. 2, Cambridge, Polity Press.

Habermas, J. (1974), *Theory and Practice* (first published in 1971 as *Theorie und Praxis*), London, Heinemann.

Hall, R. (1994) 'A framework for identifying the intangible sources of sustainable competitive advantage' in *Competence-based Competition: The Strategic Management Society*, Chichester, Wiley.

Handy, C. (1991) *The Age of Unreason*, London, Arrow Business Books.

Handy, C. (1994) *The Empty Raincoat: Making Sense of the Future*, London, Hutchinson.

Handy, C. (1995) *Beyond Certainty: The changing worlds of organisations*, London, Hutchinson.

Harrison, R. (2000) *Employee Development*, (2nd edn), London, IPD.

Harrison, R. and Smith, R. (2001) 'Practical judgement: its implications for knowledge development and strategic capability', in Hellgren, B. and Lowstedt J. (eds) *Management in the Thought-Full Enterprise: European Ideas on Organizing*, Fagbokforlaget, Poland, OZGraf SA.

Honey, P. and Mumford, A. (1992) *The Manual of Learning Styles*, Maidenhead, Peter Honey.

Huselid, M. (1995) 'The impact of human resource management practices on turnover, productivity and corporate financial performance', *Academy of Management Journal*, no. 38 p 645.

Hutton, W. (1995) *The State We're In*, London, Vintage, Jonathan Cape.

Jacob, M. and Hellstrom T. (2000)' From networking researchers to the networked university' in *The Future of Knowledge Production in the Academy*, Buckingham, SRHE and Open University Press, pp 81–95.

Jarvis, P. (1992) *Paradoxes of Learning: On Becoming an Individual in Society*, San Francisco, CA, Jossey Bass Higher Education Series.

Kelly, D. (2000) 'Using vision to improve organisational communication', *Leadership & Organization Development Journal*, vol. 21, no. 2, pp. 92–101.

Kessels, J.W.M. (1996a) *Corporate Education: The Ambivalent Perspective of Knowledge Productivity*, Leiden University, Centre for Education and Instruction.

Kessels, J.W.M. (1996) 'Knowledge productivity and the corporate curriculum', in: *Knowledge Management: Organization, Competence and Methodology*, Proceedings of the Fourth International ISMICK Symposium, 21–2 October, Rotterdam, the Netherlands.

Kolb, D.A. (1984) *Experiental Learning*, Englewood Cliffs, NJ, Prentice Hall.

Kuhn, T., S. (1962) *The Structure of Scientific Revolutions*, Chicago, IL, University of Chicago Press.

Lasch, C. (1995) *The Revolt of the Elites and Betrayal of Democracy*, New York, Norton.

Lave, J. and Wenger, E. (1991) *Situated Learning: Legitimate Peripheral Participation*, Cambridge, Cambridge University Press.

Leadbetter, C. (2000) *Living on Thin Air: The New Economy: with a New Blueprint got the 21st Century*, Harmondsworth, Penguin.

Leydersdorff, L., van den Besselaar, P. and Allen, P. (eds) (1994) *Evolutionary Economics and Chaos Theory*, London, Pinter.

McLellan, D. (1971) *The Thought of Karl Marx: An Introduction*, Basingstoke, Macmillan.

Marsick,V.J. and Watkins, K.E. (1990) *Informal and Incidental Learning in the Work Place*, London, Routledge.

Medawar, P. (1986) *The Limits of Science*, Oxford, Oxford University Press.

Merton. R. (1958a) 'Science and democratic social structure', in *Social Theory and Social Structure*, (rev edn) Glencoe, IL, The Free Press, pp 550–62.

Merton, R. (1958b) *Bureaucratic Structure and Personality in Social Theory and Social Structure* (rev edn), Glencoe, The Free Press, pp 195–205.

Mills, Wright, C. (1959) *The Power Elite*, New York, Oxford University Press.

Misteil, S. (1997) *The Communicator's Pocket Book*, Alresford, Management Pocket Books.

Monbiot, G. (2000) *Captive State: The Corporate Takeover of Britain*, Basingstoke, Macmillan

Morgan, G. (1997) *Images of Organization*, London, Sage.

Nonaka, I. (1996) 'The knowledge-creating company', in Starkey, K. (ed.) *How Organisations Learn*, London, International Thomson Business Press.

Nonaka, I. and Horotaka, T. (1995) *The Knowledge-creating Company: How Japanese Companies Create the Dynamics of Innovation*, Oxford, University Press Oxford.

OECD (1996) *The Knowledge Based Economy*, Paris, Organization For Economic Cooperation and Development.

Patterson, G., West, M.A., Lawthorn, R. and Nickells, S. (1998) *Impact of People Practices on Business Performance*, London, IPD.

Polanyi, M. (1958) *Personal Knowledge: Towards a Post-critical Philosophy*, London, Routledge and Kegan Paul.

Popper, K. (1992) *Unended Quest: An Intellectual Autobiography*, London, Routledge.

Prahalad, C.K. (1997) 'Strategies for growth', in Gibson, R. (ed.) *Rethinking the Future*, London, Nicholas Brealey.

Pfeffer, J. (1998) *The Human Equation: Building Profits by Putting People First*, Harvard Business School Press.

Rajan, A., Lanl, E. and Cahpple, K. (1998) 'Good practices in knowledge creation and exchange', in Scarbrough, H., Swan, J. and Preston, J. (1999) *Knowledge Management: A Literature Review*, London, IPD Publications.

Rigsby, J.T., Siegal, P.H. and Spiceland, J.D. (1998) 'Mentoring among management advisory serves professionals: an adaptive mechanism to cope with rapid corporate change', *Managerial Auditing Journal*, vol. 13 no. 2, pp. 107–116.

Reed, M. and Harvey, D.L. (1992) 'The new science and the old: complexity and realism', *Social Sciences Journal of the Theory of Social Science Behaviour*, vol. 22, no. 4, pp 353–80.

Rogers, C. (1961) *A Therapist's View of Psychotherapy: On Becoming a Person*, London, Constable.

Rommetveit, R. (1986) 'Language acquistition as increasing linguistic structuring of experience and symbolic behaviour control', In Wertsch, J.V. (ed.) *Culture, Communication and Cognition: Vygotskian Perspectives*, New York, Cambridge University Press.

Scarbrough, H., Swan, J. and Preston, J. (1999) *Knowledge Management: A Literature Review*, London, IPD Publications.

Schutz, A. (1945). 'On multiple realties', *Philosophical and Phemonenological Research*, 5, 533–576, in Wertsch, J.V. (ed), *Culture, Communication and Cognition:Vygotskian Perspectives*, New York, Cambridge University Press.

Seltzer, K. and Bentley, T. (1999) *The Creative Age: Knowledge and Skills for the New Economy*, London, Demos.

Senge, P. (1990) *The Fifth Discipline: The Art and Practice of the Learning Organization*, New York, Doubleday/Currency.

Senge, P.M. (1992) *The Fifth Discipline*, Chatham, Century Business.

Sennett, R. (1998) *The Corrosion of Character: the Personal Consequences of Work in the New Capitalism*, New York, Norton.

Shotter, J. (1993) *Cultural Politics of Everyday Life*, Buckingham, Open University Press.

Shotter, J. (undated) Inside dialogic realities: from an abstract-systematic to a participatory-wholistic understanding of communication (final version) submitted to *Southern Communication Journal* from web site http://pubpages.unh.edu/~jds/ SCJ99_fin1_pap.htm

Shotter, J. (1998) *Review of: Theodore Zeldin, Conversation*, London, Harvill Press, p 103, from web site http://pubpages.unh.edu/~jds/SCJ99_fin1_pap.htm

Skyrme, D. www.ionet.net/~jburch/c9612ke.html

Skyrme, D. and Amidon, D. (1997) 'Creating the knowledge-based business', Business Intelligence, *The Observer*, 28 November.

Slim, W.J. (Field Marshal Viscount) (1986) *Defeat into Victory*, London, Pan.

Smith, F. (1994) *Understanding Reading*, 5th edn, Hove, UK, Lawerence Erlbaum Associates.

Soros, G. (2000) *Open Society: Reforming Global Capitalism*, London, Little Brown.

Space Syntax www.bartlett.ucl.ac.uk/spacesyntax/offices/offices.html

Stehr, N. (1994) *Knowledge Societies*, London, Sage.

Stacey, R.D. (1995) 'The science of complexity: an alternative perspective for strategic change processes', *Strategic Management Journal*, vol. 16, pp 477–95.

Stock,D (ed) (1993) *Kieslowski on Kieslowski*, London, Faber & Faber.

Schutz, A. (1945) 'On multiple realities', *Philosophical and Phenomenological Research*, 5, 533-576, in Wertsch. J.V. (ed.) *Culture, Communication and Cognition: Vygotskian Perspectives*, New York, Cambridge University Press.

The Commission of the European Communities (2000) *A Memorandum on Lifelong Learning*, Brussels.

The G8 Group (1999) *Cologne Memorandum on Lifelong Learning*, www.library.utoronto.ca/g7/summit/1999koln/charter.htm

Tardif, T. Z. and Sternberg, R.J. (eds) (1988) *The Nature of Creativity: Contemporary Psychological Perspectives*, Cambridge, Cambridge University Press.

Von Krogh, G., Roos, J. and Slocum, K. (1994) 'An essay on corporate epistemology', *Strategic Management Journal*, vol. 15, 53-71, Wiley.

Waldrop, M. M. (1992) *Complexity: The Emerging Science at the Edge of Order and Chaos*, London, Viking.

Williamson, B. (1998) *Lifeworlds and Learning: Essays in the Theory, Philosophy and Practice of Lifelong Learning*, Leicester, National Institute of Adult and Continuing Education (NIACE).

Williamson, B. (2001) 'Creativity, the corporate curriculum and the future: a case study', *Futures*, vol. 33, no.6, pp 541–55.

Index